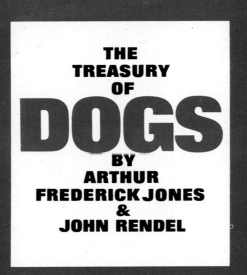

THE
TREASURY
OF
DOGS
BY
ARTHUR
FREDERICK JONES
&
JOHN RENDEL

A RIDGE PRESS BOOK
GOLDEN PRESS/NEW YORK

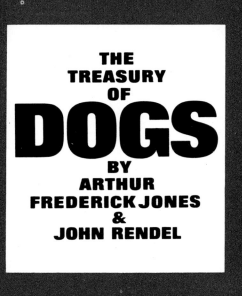

THE TREASURY OF
DOGS
BY
ARTHUR
FREDERICK JONES
&
JOHN RENDEL

PHOTOGRAPHS BY WALTER CHANDOHA

Editor in Chief: JERRY MASON

Editor: ADOLPH SUEHSDORF

Art Director: ALBERT SQUILLACE

Associate Editor: EVELYN HANNON

Art Research: PETER LACEY

Art Associate: DAVID NAMIAS

Art Production: DORIS MULLANE

■

Prepared and produced by
The Ridge Press, Inc. Printed in the
United States of America
Published by Golden Press
850 Third Avenue,
New York 22, New York.
©1964 by Golden Press
and the Ridge Press, Inc.
Library of Congress Catalog
Card Number: 64-19472

This edition prepared
for distribution by
Crown Publishers, Inc.

CONTENTS

6

WORKING DOGS 106

7

TERRIERS 142

8

NON-SPORTING DOGS 166

9

TOYS 182

SPECIAL BREEDS 204

10

CHOOSING THE FAMILY PET 214

11

KNOWING THE VETERINARIAN 224

12

TEACHING AND LEARNING 232

13

THE WORLD OF DOG SHOWS 242

INTRODUCTION

One of life's warmest and most available pleasures is the companionship of a dog. The dog

is wholehearted and almost always eager. Whatever you want to do, the dog wants to do, too.

A walk on the beach? Fine! Scale the Alps? Why not. Once around the moon? The little dog

laughs to see such sport. As for availability, there seems to have been no period in recorded

history when dogs were scarce. From time to time, certain breeds may be hard to come by,

but the dog per se, never. He is always at hand. ▪ Particularly is this true today. Dogs are

at a new peak of popularity. There is, in fact, no reliable census of the canine population

anywhere, but in the United States alone even the most conservative arithmetic arrives at

a total in the scores of millions. More dogs than ever before are being enrolled in obedience-

training courses, entered in field-trial competitions, paraded in show rings, and registered

with the American Kennel Club. ▪ And as always happens when a trend gathers momentum,

people's interest becomes both more comprehensive and sharper. The family shopping for

a pet is no longer content to take a nondescript pup from the litter down the street. More

likely, it is discovering the quite fascinating differences among a wide range of breeds and learning to insist on quality. This means a purebred dog. ▪ Without prejudice to the everyday dog of mixed or unknown ancestry—he, too, is a warm and available friend—the fact of the matter is that the purebred is almost bound to be a better dog. Because he must meet a standard, he is inevitably a handsomer dog. Because his sporting or working function requires it, he often is a sounder and more capable dog. Because he must have the personality of his breed, he is usually a more stable and reliable dog. ▪ This is a book about purebred dogs. Each of the authors has spent some forty years in the company of these excellent creatures, observing them, studying them, and absorbing the wisdom of veteran owners, breeders, handlers, and judges. A distillation of much that has been learned is in these pages. Hopefully, *The Treasury of Dogs* will be a reference work of value to the many people who already own a purebred, and a helpful guide for those about to choose their first one. ▪ This is a field in which no opinions are lightly held, and in which partisan feelings run high. But on one point all are agreed. The enthusiasm for fine dogs, once acquired, lasts a lifetime. *Arthur Frederick Jones, John Rendel.* NEW YORK, 1964.

1 HOW THE FRIENDSHIP GREW

It seems to have been in the Old Stone Age, about 25,000 or 30,000 years ago, that man and dog first struck up their abiding friendship. This is, of course, an archaeological guess, not a certainty, but it is a reasonable one. Mostly it is inferred from the recovery of doglike bone fragments and teeth from ancient burial grounds, kitchen middens, lake dwelling sites, and other rubbish and ruination which mark the presence of early man.

It is anybody's guess how the friendship developed in those dim beginnings when glaciers still advanced and retreated, creating the fresh contours of a virgin world. Perhaps initially it was a relationship based on utility. Dog always has been a good hunter and man was not then a notably efficient one. In any event, mutual liking and mutual advantage presumably were acknowledged, and thereafter Cro-Magnon man ventured forth for food with the first domestic animal trotting at his heels or snuffling a rabbit track up ahead.

So, through the centuries the two have gone together, man becoming an evermore accomplished hunter, and dog evolving with astonishing versatility into scores of breeds and acquiring many temperaments and functions. Dogs have been bred to point, flush, course, harry, unearth, and retrieve furred and feathered game. They have become specialists in bringing to bay the deer, elk, boar, otter, badger, fox, wolf, bear, antelope, lion, and—the tapestries tell us—the unicorn. They are excellent sheepherders, the scourge of rats and rabbits, and the trusty sentinel of house and home. They are movie stars, military messengers, guides for the blind, and astronauts.

And they are pets. In all the wide earth there is no other creature—including other men —with whom man has lived so peaceably and successfully, or on whom he has lavished such loyalty, affection, and respect. Possibly, this is because dogs at their best embody many of the virtues man admires most in himself: patience, courage, obedience, tolerance, enthusiasm, humor, devotion. They are gentle, companionable, and confidential with children. They are gallant with women. And not a few men are the better for having had to live up to their dog's estimation of them.

Zoologically speaking, the dog is *canis familiaris,* a member of the *canidae* group of carnivores, which makes him a cousin of the wolf, the fox, and the jackal. The many evolutionary stages through which he has passed seem to have begun some 40,000,000 to 60,000,000 years ago with a weasellike creature called Miacis, the paterfamilias from whom is descended the bear, raccoon, hyena, civet, and today's domestic cat. The most nearly doglike of the dog's ancestors probably was Cynodictus, a slender-bodied, short-legged animal about the size of a fox, that is considered to be a direct forebear of the dogs we know today.

What breed, then, was the first dog to make his way with man? No one knows, although very possibly by that time Cynodictus and his descendants had evolved into the great "parental" dogs from which so many of our contemporary purebreds have sprung. On the continent of Europe this might have been a Spitz type, the stocky, sharp-featured, bushy tailed fellow with the handsome neck ruff, who is perpetuated today in the Norwegian Elkhound, Chow Chow, Samoyed, Keeshond, Pomeranian, and Siberian Husky. In the Middle East it would very likely have been the Saluki, the probable progenitor of the Greyhound, the Afghan, and the Borzoi. In Asia it could well have been the Tibetan mastiff, a dog still in existence, whose characteristics have long since become part of our big, blunt-muzzled, foursquare dogs, such as the Boxer, Bulldog, Great Dane, Rottweiler, St. Bernard, Great Pyrenees, and Newfoundland.

Or, of course, it might have been none of these. The American Kennel Club currently recognizes 115 breeds, but there are at least that many more which are known in various countries of the world.

Usually these are herding or working dogs who have served long and honorably in the country of their origin and simply have not come to the attention, or aroused the interest, of professional breeders or breed fanciers. Many of these breeds come of an ancient lineage and could perhaps have been the prototype dog.

Finally, there are the many wild and semi-wild dogs existing around the world, such as the Australian Dingo, any of which may in fact be closer in type to the dog who chose to make friends with man than our currently domesticated breeds.

All we can be sure of, however, is that the earliest known visual representations of dogs are Sumerian carvings dating to 6000 or 5000 B.C. These are little stone figures which appear to be Salukis and undeniably help to establish this breed's claim to being the oldest one on earth. The claim, of course, is not undisputed. Greyhound fanciers are sure the ancient pictures and figurines are all of Greyhounds. And the skeleton of a Norwegian Elkhound was found in a cave in western Norway and dated between 5000 and 4000 B.C. Since such dates cannot be absolute, it is quite possible that the Elkhound is as old as the Saluki and perhaps even older.

Written and pictorial evidence of the dog survives in fair quantity, although breeds are not always identifiable. Either the scribe does not bother to report carefully or the artist renders his subject imprecisely, or they are dealing with dogs no longer known to us. Indeterminate dogs are represented on ceremonial objects dug up near the site of Thebes, in Greece, and estimated as having originated between 4400 and 4000 B.C. A lamasery in Tibet contains a manuscript which states that "dogs were used to destroy wolves and protect sheep in the remotest times." Since the manuscript itself dates to around 3000 B.C., "the remotest times" must lie in a dim past indeed.

Egypt is a particularly rich source of pictures and information concerning dogs. She enjoyed a powerful, long-lived, and sophisticated civilization, and many of her magnificently painted tombs and temples, and hieroglyphic writings and inscriptions have been preserved in her hot, dry climate. We know that as early as 3700 B.C. the Egyptians were familiar with twenty-one different breeds of dog. The Pharaohs hunted the lion and the gazelle with the aid of dogs, and pictures of their pets and hunting companions are everywhere found on their tombs. That of the Pharaoh Amten, dating from 2900 to 2751 B.C., shows a lean hunting dog that must be either a Saluki or a Greyhound. The sepulcher of Prince Ram-em-ka, of 2481 B.C., depicts a hunter and his dogs—again Greyhound types—pursuing an antelope. A bas-relief of great but uncertain age preserves an unmistakable Basenji with wrinkled brow, tightly curled tail; and a bell around his neck to augment his small voice during the chase.

Hunting was the dog's principal function. For the countryman he guarded flocks and herds—small, intelligent dogs being used to manage and maneuver them in the field, and large, powerful dogs being kept to fight off wolves, bears, and other predators. But for the aristocracy, which could afford to train and maintain him, the dog was a companion of the hunt.

There were many kinds of hunting, depending on the quarry, the terrain, and the type of dog. One of the earliest treatises on the subject is *The Master of Game,* written in England about 1405 by Edward, Duke of York. This is a painstaking, beautifully illuminated discourse on the proper conduct of hunts by one who was himself master of game for his cousin, King Henry IV. Much of it is a translation of a still earlier French work, *La Chasse,* better known as *Gaston Phoebus,* the nom de plume of a fiery nobleman, Count Gaston de la Foix. Edward's original contributions, however, indicate that the English used five kinds of hounds: 1) A running hound or "Harier," which was used on hare, roe (the Old World deer), and hart (the red deer). 2) The Greyhound, apparently the universal hunting dog; he was used to course—to run to exhaustion—boar, hare, fox, wolf, hart, and wild cat. 3) The alaunte, like the Greyhound, but with a "great and short head" and a ferocious nature. 4) A mastiff, used to close with boar and wolf or wherever the going was rough and dogs' lives were expendable. 5) A small spaniel—also called a "setting dog"—for catching rabbits.

The Duke's earnest medieval text and the gleaming colors of the little pictures combine to tell a bright and charming story of the stages of a hunt 500 years ago. The nobles astride their horses are gaily caparisoned and sound their hunting horns bravely. Accompanying them on foot are hurrying pikemen, foresters perhaps, ready to assist the kill, and dog handlers drawn on by eager hounds tugging at their leashes.

Then the dogs are unslipped and the chase is on. "It is a fair thing," the Duke exults, "to see the wit and the knowledge that God hath given to good hounds."

The hart at last is coursed, encircled by his foes, and cut down. The carcass is dressed in the field. Tidbits are flung to the dogs that first sighted the quarry. And finally, at the kennels, the sick or injured dogs are tended by the kennelmen.

For all Edward's careful and animated detail, however, he leaves us in a quandary about his dogs. Why no mention of the Foxhound, known in England since the reign of King John in the opening years of the thirteenth century? Or of the Bloodhound, a descendant of the Talbot brought from France by William the Conqueror, and a favorite of John's son, King Henry III? Or are these breeds somewhere hidden in the ill-defined terms "running hound" and "alaunte"?

Virtually every game animal man has seen fit to pursue has been memorialized in the name of a dog bred to the task of hunting it: Foxhound, Deerhound, Wolfhound, Badgerhound (Dachshund),

and so forth. Although the names are now attached to specific breeds, it is clear from the Duke's list that at least three of his five dogs could be considered deerhounds. Thus his nomenclature tells us less than it might.

"Greyhound" means the slender, tucked-up, smooth-coated racer we know today, but in that time he was a bigger, chestier dog and very likely included the rough-coated varieties designated today as the Scottish Deerhound, Irish Wolfhound, and Borzoi (or Russian Wolfhound). None but royalty could own a greyhound and killing one was punishable by death.

The alaunte evidently had the greyhound body, but not the small, narrow head. Geoffrey Chaucer, in the Knight's contribution to the *Canterbury Tales,* says of Lycurgus, King of Thrace:

About his chaar there wenten white alauntz
Twenty and mo, as grete as any steer,
To hunten at the leoun or the deer....

King of Thrace or not, Lycurgus sounds as though he would be right at home in an English forest. The chaar (chariot) is a Byzantine touch, and so is the lion, but hunting the deer with a pack of alauntes was sport such as Chaucer himself might on occasion have joined in.

The mastiff was an old breed in England even in the Duke's time. There is speculation that Phoenicians sailing boldly outside the sheltering Mediterranean may have introduced the dog on a trading expedition to Iron Age Britain. True or not, there are mastiffs depicted in the Bayeux tapestry celebrating the Norman conquest of Britain in 1066.

The running hound, or "Harier," is another case of the name describing a function, not the dog. The hound may well have been a far cry from the contemporary Harrier, but there is little doubt that this is the breed under discussion. "Hariers" were familiar hunting dogs in England 150 years before the Duke wrote.

So, too, the "Spanyel"—although it was not until the nineteenth century that any differentiation was

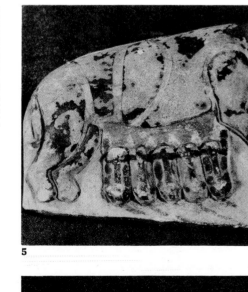

1 Egyptian dog carved in basalt (283-230 B.C.).
2 Staghunt is illumination from Master of Game.
3 Ancient Greek coin had dog Jevice. **4** Domesticated dogs hunt with early man (c. 8000 B.C.). **5** Chinese bas-relief of nursing litter. **6** Unknown Roman hound. **7** Carved ivory hound is Egyptian toy of 1355 B.C. Rod moves jaw.

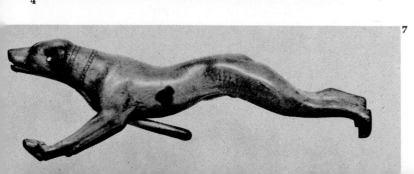

1   3
4
5
6
7

made among the various sizes and types of spaniels, so it is hard to say just what was chasing rabbits for Edward, Duke of York.

The pleasures of hunting, like most medieval pleasures, were reserved for those of gentle blood. Forest lands were the King's. The game thereon was also his, and poachers—such as Robin Hood— were severely dealt with. The earliest "Forest Laws" we know of are King Canute's, passed at a parliament at Winchester in 1016. Even the peasant's dogs were specifically enjoined from nipping at the royal deer and could be hamstrung and otherwise mutilated for violations of the law. This, plus the devastation wrought by a hunting party riding through grainfields, or the exactions of a royal entourage descending on a sparse country village, made the noble hunter less than welcome.

The story is told of James I, who, during a stag hunt in 1624, was displeased to find Fowler, a favored hound, missing at day's end. When the hunt resumed next day, however, Fowler reappeared bearing a note around his neck: "Good Mr. Fowler," it said, "we pray you speak to the King (for he hears you every day, and so doth he not us) that it will please his Majestie to go back to London, for els the country wilbe undoon; all our provision is spent already, and we are not able to intertayne him longer."

It was not clear who the petitioner might be, but James chose to regard it as a jest and remained to hunt for another two weeks.

It was also James who comforted his consort, Queen Anne, with a diamond worth £2,000 after she aimed at a deer and hit instead Jewell, the King's favorite dog.

Honey-tongued Will Shakespeare, whose plays abound with allusions to hawking and hunting and other sports of his day, creates many a bright image with references to dogs.

In *Henry VI,* Part 3, Queen Margaret urges her Lancastrian husband, the King, to ride away because his enemies, the Yorkist princes Edward and

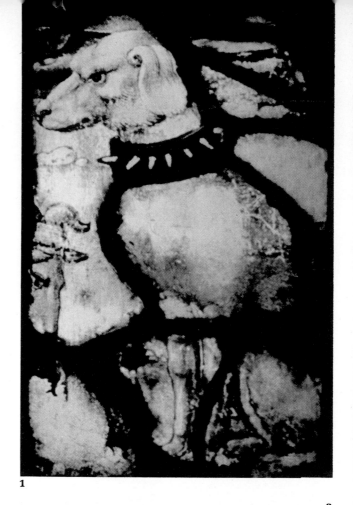

1

2

3

4

1 *Spiked collar suggests
that stained-glass dog at Cambridge
University was guard or hunter.*
2 *Oddly shaped Chinese dog
of 13th century has setter's tail.*
3 *A 16th-century sporting breed
called "Dunne Hounde."* 4 *St. Eustace
engraving by Dürer shows
recognizable 16th-century Greyhounds.*
5 *Hefty spaniel type sports with
small boy in painting by
Hendrick Goltzius, dated 1597.*

5

1

2

3

4

5

Richard, are pursuing "like a brace of greyhounds having the fearful flying hare in sight."

Iago, scheming to make Cassio drunk as part of his foul plot to enrage Othello and destroy him, says in an aside: "He'll be as full of quarrel and offence as my young mistress' dog."

Brutus scorns Cassius: "I had rather be a dog, and bay the moon, than such a Roman." Richard III—Crookback—complains that his misshapen form makes even "dogs bark at me as I halt by them." And Hamlet tells us that "...the dog will have his day."

Shakespeare also was partial to the use of "dog" as an epithet—as, indeed, is all literature. (By a curious inversion, the dog is ennobled by behaving like man, although man is rarely more base than when acting like a dog.) The forty-odd references to the dog in the Bible are nearly all derogatory. For instance, from I Samuel: Goliath to David, "Am I a dog, that thou comest to me with staves?"

Classic authors are full of comment on dogs, most of it highly complimentary. Ovid mentions the greyhound, Herodotus the mastiff. Xenophon wrote at length on the harrier in *Hunting with Dogs*. Arrian is at pains to explain, about 150 A.D., that the true sportsman does not mind if the hare escapes, as long as the course has been exciting. Pliny the Elder, in his sometimes foolish, always fascinating *Natural History,* gives a marvelous little description of a scent hound, a pointer-type whose performance in the field has changed little since Pliny observed it in the first century A.D. "It discovers and traces out the tracks of the animal," he writes, "leading by the leash the sportsman who accompanies it straight up to the prey; and soon as ever it has perceived it, how silent it is, and how secret but significant is the indication which it gives, first by the tail and afterwards by the nose! Hence it is that even when worn out with old age, blind, and feeble, they are carried by the huntsman in his arms, being still able to point out the coverts where the game is concealed, by snuffing with their muzzles at the wind."

One of the oldest and surely one of the best dog stories ever told is Homer's account of Ulysses' return from Troy after the passage of many years. No one recognizes him except his hunting hound, Argos. Now infirm and nearly blind, the old dog drags himself to his feet and seeks to lick Ulysses' hand. He is too weak. He falters and dies. Ulysses turns to his companion, Eumaeus, the swineherd, and says, "A good hound lies there. Once I think he was so swift that no beast in the deep places of the woods could flee from him."

Very early in the game, the faithful companion of the chase was rewarded with burial beside his master. Egypt mummified the Pharaoh's favorite dogs and entombed them with him. (There were cemeteries for the mummified remains of less exalted dogs.) Scandinavian warrior chiefs—as every reader or viewer of *Beau Geste* knows—were sent to the hereafter with a dog at their feet, very probably a Norwegian Elkhound. Despite what Beau told Digby and John, however, the ship was more likely to be buried with the chief, his weapons, and the dog aboard than to be sent to sea in flames.

In various places at various points in time the dog became a god. To the Egyptians he was a guardian god who warned of the seasonal overflowing of the Nile through the agency of the Dog Star, Sirius. This first-magnitude star in the constellation of Canis Major, the large dog, is one of the brightest sparklers in the heavens. Its appearance always was a signal to the Egyptians to move their livestock beyond the reach of the river.

1 *Greyhound painted by Veronese in late 16th century has heavier body and running gear than contemporary dog.* 2 *Rubens painted picture of hounds assisting 17th-century fox and wolf hunt.* 3, 4, 5 *Three 18th-century pictures of spaniels. Portrait (top) is by Drouais, sketch by Tiepolo, and painting of white toy dog by Fragonard.*

According to legend, Sirius was the dog of the great hunter, Orion. In the sky his companion is Procyon, the brightest star of the Canis Minor constellation. The rise of Sirius also traditionally marks the so-called "dog days" of July and August when dogs are supposed to go mad, but do not necessarily do so.

The Greeks believed the dog could shield them from earthly dangers. In Ethiopia at one time the dog was so revered he was made king. The Peruvian Indians worshiped him. In fact, it was probably a rare primitive or pagan society that did not at one point or another find a place for the dog in its pantheon.

Just as readily, ambivalent man also imputed dark and sinister powers to the dog. Many cultures which seem otherwise to respect and admire the dog have legends, ghost stories, superstitions, and everyday sayings that put Rover in a very bad light indeed. The Chinese, for instance, believed in dog demons. They were not horrors, but they were mischievous, and they frightened and upset people. Corollary to this was the performance of the heavenly dog, T'ien Ken, whose passage from his celestial abode to the earth always caused comets and thunder. During eclipses in China there was a huge crashing of cymbals, a thorough thumping of drums, and loud lamentations to keep T'ien Ken from swallowing the sun.

Elsewhere the dog was thought to be supernatural, a harbinger of death. In India, in Wales, across the continent of Europe—everywhere probably—people believe that when a dog howls a man is dying. Two of Hercules' twelve labors involved monster dogs: the tenth, when he had to destroy Geryon of Gades and his two-headed dog, Orthrus; and the twelfth, when he had to subdue Cerberus, the three-headed guardian of the gates of hell.

It was not only the ancients, of course, who scared themselves with improbable beasts. Who does not remember Sherlock Holmes' bizarre adventure with the Hound of the Baskervilles? The Hound proved to be half Bloodhound and half Mastiff, and "the size of a small lioness," an awesome creature, surely, although somehow less so than Cerberus.

Many legendary dogs are almost universally known. Gelert, for instance. In the familiar western version of this story, Gelert is a "rough-coated greyhound"—or, probably, a Scottish Deerhound—given to Llewellyn, a prince of Wales, by King John. This would place the story around 1200, although another version ignores John and dates the incident at 970 A.D. In any event, Gelert is the prince's most highly prized and faithful hound. One day Llewellyn goes off, leaving his baby son in the care of the dog. He returns to find Gelert covered with blood and the child nowhere in sight. Enraged at the thought that the dog should have betrayed his trust and killed his son, Llewellyn wreaks vengeance:

> Hell-hound!—by thee my child's devour'd!
>   The frantic father cried:
> And to the hilt his vengeful sword,
>   He plung'd in Gelert's side.

Gelert's dying yelp is answered by a cry from the boy. Searching frantically, Llewellyn finds his son under a bed and nearby the body of a wolf killed by Gelert in defense of the child. Grief-stricken at his murderous haste, Llewellyn erects a chapel, Bethgelert, at the foot of Mt. Snowden and buries the tragic hound there.

"Lion Dog"—Artist obviously never saw a Pekingese.

Chien Barbet

A sad and lovely story from the wild Welsh hills, it is. Swift retribution and swift remorse. How like its country and its times.

Yes, except that the story originated far to the east, perhaps in India. There is an Arabic version. And it is also to be found in a collection of legends and romances in Latin. In each instance, of course, the story is adapted to local circumstances and told as indigenous folklore.

In the famous story of the Seven Sleepers of Ephesus, curiously enough, the dog disappears from one version to the next. In the Moslem version, the faithful hound Kitmer (or Katmer, Kratim, or Kratimer) watches over the seven noble youths for 309 years without sleeping or touching food himself. This patient self-abnegation gave rise among Moslems to a popular definition of a miser as one who would not even throw a bone to the dog of the Seven Sleepers.

By the time Gibbon relates the story in his *Decline and Fall of the Roman Empire,* the sleepers have become seven Christian youths fleeing persecution by the Emperor Decius, about 250 A.D. They enter a cavern, fall into a hibernating sleep, and emerge 187 years later as fifth-century Rip Van Winkles wandering through a world they never made. There is no mention of Kitmer whatever.

Even the bloody tale of the implacable Dog of Montargis is supposed to have antecedents elsewhere. In the French version, dating to around 1371, Aubry de Montdidier is murdered by his companion, Richard de Macaire, in the forest of Montargis. Montdidier's dog observes the slaying and from that time forward becomes savage and vicious whenever he meets Macaire. Eventually, the dog leads a search party to the body of his master, whereupon King Charles V, known as "the Wise," grants an ordeal of battle. This was a medieval method of adjudicating disputes whereby the accuser and the accused, or champions acting for them, met in single combat. God was pre-sumed to strengthen the arm of the virtuous and burden the guilty with defeat and death. Might literally made right. And so it was with the Dog of Montargis. He killed Macaire in battle, thereby proving the villain's guilt and avenging his master.

The warrior dog, like his warrior master, presents a somewhat ill-favored aspect to the world. Properly trained he becomes savage, vicious, a weapon. His use in battle extended over many centuries. Egyptian and Assyrian tombs dating to 2000 B.C. bear pictures of combat animals. Cyrus of Persia employed them. So did Rome. And so did the early Britons, who sent Mastiffs against the legions that invaded the British Isles under Julius Caesar in 55 B.C. These dogs must have been impressive. Specimens were shipped back to Rome to fight other animals or condemned criminals in the spectacles at the Circus Maximus.

Attila the Hun used another strain of mastiff during his sweeping campaign of destruction through Europe, and Genghis Khan used a Tibetan mastiff in his invasion of Europe 700 years later.

War dogs could be struck down by swords and spears, but their fast reflexes often enabled them to avoid an enemy's thrust and leap for his throat. Hand to hand, a huge mastiff trained to kill could be a formidable adversary. It is also quite possible that the dogs were most effective in panicking enemy horses and in diverting the enemy soldier's attention with growls and bites while friendly troops brained him with a battleaxe.

A strange little Irish legend gives a brief picture of a dog in battle. The story concerns a fabulous Irish Wolfhound named Ailbe, who was so swift he "could run through all Leinster in one day." The fame of the dog spread and eventually envoys arrived at the home of the dog's owner, MacDatho. They came from Ailill and Medb, chiefs of Connaught, and from Conchobar, chief of Ulster. On the spot, each offered 6,000 milch cows and a chariot drawn by a span of the finest horses. MacDatho dared not choose between such powerful purchasers and at his wife's suggestion promised the dog to each, separately. He then arranged for both to come on the same day to receive the dog.

Naturally, on the appointed day, Connaught and Ulster and their retinues sought a solution to the problem by fighting. At the height of the battle, MacDatho loosed Ailbe to choose sides for himself. The hound aligned himself with Ulster and attacked the men of Connaught. Ailill and Medb turned their chariot and retreated toward Connaught. Ailbe pursued them and seized the shaft of the chariot. The charioteer leaned forward and slashed the hound with his sword, severing the head from the body. Yet even in death the strong jaws remained clenched from Ballaghmoon to Farbill. There, in Westheath, the head finally dropped into a ford, afterwards known as Ath Cind Chon, or Hound's Head Ford.

Ailbe, of course, was not a true war dog. Perhaps if he had been he would have been wearing a spiked collar and thus have warded off the charioteer's blow. War dogs often wore such collars to keep enemy dogs from snapping at their jugular vein. The body armor designed for them was unsuccessful, however. It impeded their movements and became a greater hazard than protection.

History records no victories won by war dogs. But no matter. Man always drafts his old friend for useful service, according to the times, the seasons, and his needs.

Those who have loved the dog have memorialized him in many ways, artists particularly. A large number of the great masters have been pleased to tuck a dog somewhere into their canvases. Vero-

nese, the great Venetian, put everything from Mastiffs to lap dogs in his. Van Dyck painted a Mastiff, too, in his famous portrait of King Charles I's children. Dürer was partial to the Schnauzer, as were Rembrandt and Sir Joshua Reynolds. Gainsborough's portraits of the Dukes of Buccleuch include a Dandie Dinmont and Old English Sheepdog. Titian, Velasquez, and Fragonard painted the Papillon. Botticelli did Greyhounds. Hals, Rubens, Lucas Cranach, Holbein, Watteau, Goya, Murillo, Van Eyck—the list runs on. Many of these paintings give us our best guide to the color and conformation of a breed in one country—or century—or another.

Other men used dogs other ways. From Queen Elizabeth's reign onward, on the continent as well as in England, dogs were enlisted for cruel and bloody sports for the entertainment of humankind, there was dogfighting and the baiting of bulls, bears, and badgers. There is nothing to be said in favor of any of them, at least not by contemporary standards of what constitutes legitimate sport, but they must be noted if only because of the dogs that evolved from the savage warfare of the pits.

The baiting sports did not require any particular type of dog. They were simply a matter of harassing a tethered animal to death, and any mastiff-type or mongrel could join a pack and his human friends in accomplishing the task. There was, in fact, an old style of bulldog, which originally was used to help round up and hold bulls for the butcher. He became a bullbaiter, but proved too slow and clumsy and too short in the face, for dogfighting. He could not get the jump on his opponent or apply what now is known as an unshakable bulldog grip.

About 1835, someone bred him to a white English terrier, a breed which no longer exists, and began the development of today's Bull Terrier. The animal was staunch and muscular. He weighed up to 40 pounds and was sustained by a brutal and tenacious spirit. He was a terror in the fighting pit and preferred death to surrender.

1

3

2

4

Dogfights and the like, certainly those contests held in such notorious arenas as London's Westminster pit, were urban diversions and persisted into the nineteenth century.

Country folk continued to hunt, although as time passed the sport underwent changes. Staghunting was in decline by the early eighteenth century and riding to hounds meant in pursuit of the hare. The gentry kept packs of Harriers. More humble farmers might each contribute a hound or two to make up a pack on an appointed hunting day.

Foxhunting was recognized as more genteel sport, but the hare-hunting Harriers outnumbered the Foxhound packs until well into the nineteenth century. For one thing, foxes were in short supply. Records of the time show that there was a flourishing business in importing foxes from the continent. For another thing, the hounds of the era seem not to have had the keen and discriminating scenting powers that the extensive breeding efforts of the nineteenth century eventually implanted. They evidently were quite incapable of unscrambling conflicting scents or of following a track with any speed. It has been suggested that the practice of starting hunts at dawn—"D'ye ken John Peel at the break of the day"—was in the hope of catching the fox before his night's meal was digested and, therefore, while he was too sluggish to outdistance the hounds.

In the nineteenth century such conditions were rapidly improved. Everything yielded to science, and the patient and affluent sportsmen of the time tidied up old breeds and created new ones for every conceivable sporting purpose. Herr Dobermann created his Pinscher, young Korthals his Wirehaired Pointing Griffon, and Captain John Edwardes the Sealyham. Monsieur Enaud rehabili-
lated the Brittany Spaniel and Captain G. A. Graham the Irish Wolfhound. Practically all the retrievers were children of the nineteenth century. So was the Weimaraner, the American Cocker Spaniel, and the Wirehaired Dachshund.

The first known dog show—for pointers and setters only—was held at Newcastle, England, in 1859. Paris had the first French show in 1865. England's Kennel Club was founded in 1873, the American Kennel Club in 1884. Comparative late-comers in the long history of the dog, these now-venerable institutions will have much to say about the dog's future by the standards they maintain for the breeds admitted to their studbooks.

Today the purebred dog is big business. Thousands of people are involved with him professionally. Many more enthusiastic thousands are amateurs—owners, aficionados, fans, buffs, railbirds with a rooting interest.

The dog is surviving this turn in his long-standing relationship with his human friends as he has survived all that has gone before, with equanimity, devotion, and a cheerful spirit.

We shall never be rid of him now! He has even penetrated the languages of the world. In English, certainly, some of the most familiar of the old sayings are folk wisdom concerning the dog: "It is hard to teach an old dog new tricks," "A barking dog seldom bites," "Let sleeping dogs lie." Jonathan Swift described a heavy shower as raining cats and dogs. Ancient Aesop put the dog in the manger. An Elizabethan poet, John Heywood, requests a hair of the dog that bit him as a hangover remedy. And St. Bernard, in a sermon of about 1155 A.D., said simply: "Love me, love my dog."

Whatever size, shape, or color shall henceforth be decreed for the dog, and regardless of the functions, duties, and services he may be asked to perform, there seems little doubt but that he will continue to be himself and thereby retain his unique place in the affections of mankind.

1 St. Bernards to the rescue. 2 Brussels dogcatchers net a nondescript Belgian street dog such as may have sired Brussels Griffon.
3 Visitors to early (1867) dog show admire Spitz.
4 Informal display of dogs, London, 1851.

2 A NEW LIFE IN AMERICA

The passenger list of the Pilgrim ship *Mayflower* included a Mastiff bitch and a "Spannell." The record tells us no more than this. Whose dogs they were or how they eventually fared in that bleak New England so unlike the old, we do not know. Since there was then only one variety of Mastiff, we can imagine what the bigger dog must have been like. But the "Spannell"? In 1620, spaniels were undifferentiated as to size. That canine pilgrim could have been anything from a Toy to a Springer. Both of them, not being a breeding pair, must have been pets.

They were not the first dogs to set foot on the shores of the New World—nor were their masters the first men. But scanty as the reference to them may be, it is a reasonable starting point for the history of dogs in America. For from that time forward the recurring theme is the westward migration of European breeds to re-establish themselves in the United States or to mate with local stock to start a new strain. Of the 115 breeds currently registered by the American Kennel Club, only seven are native to the United States. Fifty-two originally came from England, Ireland, Scotland, and Wales, and fifty-six from the rest of the world.

Before the Pilgrims, information about dogs in the Americas is scattered and tantalizing. Descriptions are vague. Nomenclature is imprecise. Columbus is supposed to have taken big dogs, like Bloodhounds, on his first voyage in 1492 to "intimidate the Indians." On one of the West Indian islands he noted a small hairless variety of dog.

The diary of one of Hernando de Soto's men notes that on the overland journey which ended with the discovery of the Mississippi River in 1542 the Spaniards had scent hounds to warn of Indian ambush. Hernando Cortes is supposed to have used big, keen-nosed hounds for scouting in Mexico. It might even be assumed that Leif Ericson had Norwegian Elkhounds with him when he discovered North America in about 1000 A.D.

The natives of the Americas had dogs, although what kinds they may have been is unclear. Governor William Bradford of the Plymouth Colony reported that Captain Myles Standish encountered an Indian party with dogs while on a reconnaissance of the areas surrounding the settlement.

As in most other societies, the dog had prominent roles in the religious life and folklore of the Indian tribes. The Iroquois mollified the Great Spirit by the annual sacrifice of a spotless white dog. The dog was chosen for his trustworthiness, for his reliability in consummating the covenant with the Great Spirit—and because of this he was regarded as a sacrifice of high value.

The Plains Indians believed that eating a dog would imbue them with the animal's courage. The Toltec Indians of Mexico buried dogs with their dead. They believed the new spirit had a journey to make through the dark regions of the underworld and would need a dog to serve as a guide.

For the settlers of the American colonies the dog was a sentinel, a hunting partner, and on occasion a war dog.

Accounts of early New England life report several instances in which the barking of dogs aroused a settlement in time to repel an Indian attack. By 1648 the Massachusetts Bay Colony was authorizing the towns under its jurisdiction to buy hounds to help in the "destruction of wolves." By the beginning of the eighteenth century, during Queen Anne's War, British troops were using dogs as auxiliaries to accompany small patrols sent into the woods to search for Indians.

A Massachusetts lady swept downstream while trying to cross a ford was saved by her dog. This was in 1644 and must be very close to the first of the thousands of noble-dog-to-the-rescue stories which fill the North American annals of mankind.

The noble dog also got himself into some trouble. Salem, Massachusetts, which seems to have had a punishing spirit right from the start, found it necessary to impose dog laws by 1635. There and elsewhere dogs killed sheep and pigs, bit horses and cattle, and entered meetinghouses unbidden during services.

The first dogs imported for hunting in America were a pack of English Foxhounds which came with one Robert Brooke, a friend of Lord Baltimore, to the Crown Colony of Virginia in 1650. Brooke used them to hunt—deer, however, not fox. Virginia and Maryland became the first great centers of hound breeding in America. The colonists here lived like English gentry, enjoyed riding to hounds, and soon discovered that the sport required better dogs than they had. Game was abundant in the new country, but the terrain was more rugged, more primitive, more undeveloped than England. Hunting the raccoon, the gray fox, or the red fox required dogs with good speed and tracking ability, but more than that with stamina and a driving spirit.

The red fox was himself an import. The first of them for which any record exists were brought from England in 1738 and released on the eastern shore of Maryland. They and their brethren evidently flourished, for within a very few years sportsmen were trying to breed hounds with talents to match them.

Since the country was large, the fox wily, and the sporting breeders persistent, the varieties and strains of American Foxhound that finally evolved were almost beyond counting.

Among those to realize that crossbreeding might produce a keener hound was George Washington. In 1785, after the Revolution but before his election as President, Washington asked his friend and former comrade-in-arms, the Marquis de Lafayette, to send him some French hounds that might be crossed with his standard black-and-tan Virginia hounds. Lafayette readily agreed and sent the General seven dogs—some say foxhounds, some say staghounds. They were shipped to America in the care of John Quincy Adams. The future President was then eighteen years old and serving as an assistant to his father, John Adams, the first American ambassador to the Court of St. James's. Again, it is not clear just how successful the cross was. Some accounts say that Washington was rather disappointed in the outcome.

The blunt fact is that prior to 1878, when purebreds began to be registered, the pattern and results of most breeding experiments are untraceable or unknown.

The development of today's famous Walker hounds, for instance, is a long and somewhat tangled story that begins in the 1850's when General George Washington Maupin of Kentucky was given one of the fabulous sires of all time, the almost legendary Tennessee Lead. At first "Uncle Wash" didn't know what a prize he had. The dog didn't look like much, and furthermore he had been stolen. Tom Harriss, a livestock dealer, had been traveling through eastern Tennessee on his way home to Kentucky when a pack raced across his path in pursuit of a deer. Evidently the hunters weren't yet in sight, because old Tom just grabbed himself a dog and kept going. Back home again, he gave the hound to his friend, the General.

Tennessee Lead, as he later was called, was a medium-sized black dog with a thin coat and a ratty tail; his greatness was all inside. Oddly enough, except for a superlative fox sense, his attributes were not unusual. But the combination was superb.

Sometime after acquiring Tennessee Lead, "Uncle Wash" imported a pair of English Foxhounds to breed with his local Virginia and Kentucky stock. These were Rifler and Marth, also great dogs.

This infusion of new blood established the Maupin hounds and also had its effect on the pack of John W. Walker, the General's near neighbor and friendly rival. After "Uncle Wash" died, the Walker family carried on the refinement of the Walker-Maupin hounds, and Walker descendants are still among the leading breeders today. The

Walker hound, however, is more than a family affair. He has become the most popular strain of foxhound in the United States, and it takes a number of breeders to meet the demand. Experts describe the Walker as a strong, rugged dog, with good bone and a heavy coat, not exceptionally fast, but with great stamina. He also "packs well" —does not scatter—and has a mellow voice, or what is known as "a musical mouth."

The Walker is only one among many. There also are Trigg hounds, Ogles, Birdsongs, Buckfields, Julys, and Trumbos, to name just a few. All of them hunt the fox. Many of them are named after the southern breeders most responsible for their development. (Julys, however, spring from a dog named after the month he arrived at the breeder's home.) And most of the breeds are each other's cousins. The Trigg, for ex- ample, is based on Birdsong stock with judicious crosses of July, Maupin, and Walker blood. The development of the dog by Colonel Haiden C. Trigg in the 1860's was close enough to the era of "Uncle Wash" for close relatives of Rifler, Marth, and Tennessee Lead to be introduced into the line.

The old Virginia Foxhound is also believed to be the foundation stock of today's Black & Tan Coonhound. There seems not to have been anything very scientific about the development. A bigger dog was needed to hunt bigger game, and the foxhound, which after all was not unused to deer, was bred up to the job. Judging by the contemporary Black & Tan, the Bloodhound came in strongly somewhere along the way. The Coonhound has many Bloodhound characteristics, although none as pronounced as in the parent breed. He is somewhat ponderous, has the low-hung ear, the heavy

American Indian dog (above) was painted by John Audubon in 1845. Fanciful hunt scene (above, right) purports to show George Washington waving on a pack of Virginia Foxhounds. Frederic Remington lithograph (right) shows duck hunters of 1889 with liver-colored retriever—probably an American Water Spaniel.

Wood engraving of Westminster Show in New York, 1877, first major dog exhibition in U.S.

flews (pendulous upper lips), the deep, resonant voice. He also follows his quarry's foot scent, with nose to the ground, unlike the foxhound, whose nose is in the air—"breast high"—seeking a body scent of his elusive quarry.

The Coonhound is a hardy dog and frequently has been used to track deer, mountain lion, bobcat, and bear, as well as raccoon.

Other big-game hunters, each with his admirers and adherents, are the Redbones, Blueticks, and Plott Hounds. "Redbone" was for a long time simply the generic name for almost any old red-colored, heavy-bodied, flap-eared hunting dog. In recent years, however, a serious effort has been made to refine the Redbone and bring out the more distinguished features of his heritage. He seems to trace back to the ubiquitous Mr. George F. L. Birdsong and to the remnants of T. Y. Henry's pack—

T. Y. was patriot Patrick's grandson—which Mr. Birdsong acquired. Redbones used to wear a black saddle, but this has been bred out and the dog is now a solid color. He too will track bear and lion, and "trees" instinctively. (This is the quality of barking with a particular sound to summon the hunter and of staying at the tree up which the quarry has fled.)

Blueticks are descendants of some strains of English Foxhound. The bluish color of the mixed hairs and the tan of his points make this a handsome as well as swift and very capable coonhound.

Plott Hounds originally were brought from Germany to North Carolina by Jonathan Plott in 1750. They were and still are boar-hunting dogs, but the breed has been closely controlled by the Plott family and the dog is neither numerous nor exten-

sively used outside of the Great Smoky Mountain region of Tennessee.

The fox- and coonhounds evolved as highly functional dogs. They suited the requirements of sport. They kept predators and vermin in check. And they helped bring in meat for the larder.

It is a curious point that the Fox Terrier, another old, celebrated, and functional breed, had no place in the sporting life of colonial days. Game was so plentiful that the terrier's art and skill—following the fox to ground—was not needed. If a fox went into his den, the hunt blithely swept on. Why take the time and trouble to unearth him? The hounds would scare up something else in a hurry. ("Anything from a pig to a snake," said foreign visitors who found back-country hunts in America something less than genteel.)

Hounds were not the only dogs in America.

However, they were popular on the frontier, as well as in the settled areas of the eastern seaboard, and they were among the dogs that accompanied early pioneers westward. But the migration of dogs to America went on throughout the eighteenth and nineteenth centuries and involved all breeds.

Pointers and setters, both quite different from the gun dogs known today, arrived in pre-Revolutionary War times and so, evidently, did the Collie. Beagles and Bassets, also a long way from the contemporary breeds, were present in the early nineteenth century. The Great Pyrenees came in 1824, again through the agency of the Marquis de Lafayette, now an elderly gentleman of sixty-seven. He sent a pair to his friend, J. S. Skinner, editor of *The American Agriculturist,* recommending them for "wool-growers" whose flocks were threatened by wolves or "sheep-killing dogs." Unfortunately, the pair were males and nothing came of the Marquis' good suggestion for another century, when a breeding program for Great Pyrenees finally was undertaken in the United States. In 1842 the Gordon Setter arrived. Various Toy breeds seem also to have been imported, although just which ones is not clear.

The Civil War disrupted the nation's life for some five years, but shortly thereafter the importation of fine dogs from abroad was resumed and by the 1870's most of the great sporting breeds of today were reaching or had achieved their full development.

As the nation grew more settled and more prosperous, and firearms more proficient, the shooting of wild fowl and game birds for sport came into vogue. As early as 1854 the great pseudonymous sporting writer "Frank Forester" (Henry W. Herbert) was complaining of the difficulty of getting good retrievers, by which he meant spaniels. He simply was ahead of his time. All the best water retrievers were yet to come and the best bird dogs would not appear until programmed breeding—geared to the standards and requirements of the field trial—was undertaken, and a dog register was established, in the years following 1875.

In the 1870's and 1880's, too, the market hunters were at work on the Great Plains. The last spurt of expansion after the Civil War was compressing virtually all that was left of virgin America into the plains between the Mississippi and the Rockies. Here the bison would be slaughtered by the millions to provide the nation with "buffalo robes." Here, too, the gunners stood under the great flyways, where the skies were dark with birds, and fired away to supply delicacies for gourmet diners in big-city restaurants. Much of the retrieving was done by Gordon Setters. In 1875 the newly arrived Irish Setter captivated the sportsman shooter, but the Gordon remained far and away the favorite gun dog of the commercial hunter.

Besides the American Foxhound and the Black & Tan Coonhound, three other native American dogs were developed during the nineteenth century.

Eskimo dogs could be Malamutes or Huskies.

The Chesapeake Bay Retriever started with two Newfoundland puppies that were rescued from a British ship that went down off the Maryland coast in 1807. The American Water Spaniel, whose origins are obscure, seems nevertheless to have been well-known in the Midwest before the Civil War. And the Boston Terrier was bred in Boston in the 1870's. (The Cocker, sixth of the seven breeds credited to America, had arrived from England by the 1880's, but his development to his current type was largely a twentieth-century project.)

With the year 1875 the modern era of dog history begins, and most of what has happened since in field trials, dog shows, obedience training, and breed development is the concern of the following chapters.

A few words may be said here, however, on the direction of dog breeding in the United States, for it has undergone many changes since the colonists first began to produce their own stock. In the beginning it was principally governed by a policy of mating "like to like." The houndmen used this method to perpetuate strains with the most drive and scenting power. So did Pointer men.

As far as performance is concerned, excellent results have been achieved, but for some breeds it has meant a sacrifice of working ability. Many a handsome hunter is deficient in the field.

In the late nineteenth century and the first thirty years of the twentieth, American show exhibitors also seemed to be trying to match the proficiency of European breeders by mass-production methods. Countless litters of puppies would be produced each year, with each owner hoping to find a few outstanding dogs. Sometimes the method worked, but more often the puppies whelped at a kennel would be of mediocre quality. It was not unusual to find kennels with more than a hundred dogs, most of them American-bred. The big winners—if any—were likely to be foreign imports.

World War II cut off the sources of imported show stock. And when the United States entered

"Breaking the Home Ties" meant leaving faithful, rough-coated working dog, as well as family.

the conflict in 1941, kennel help became almost impossible to find. Kennels were forced to reduce to a size that the owner and his family could manage by themselves.

This really was a blessing in disguise. Matings were planned more carefully, more scientifically. Puppies were fewer but better. And with fewer, dogs, more attention could be given to each litter.

When the war ended and the importation of foreign stock could be resumed, many breeders did not avail themselves of the opportunity. They preferred to develop their own stock, now usually limited to about a dozen closely supervised dogs. This had its rewards. To the surprise of many,

American-bred dogs began to win important show honors over imported specimens.

Among the principal innovations in twentieth-century dogdom in the United States were dog racing, the appearance of dogs in motion pictures, the training of dogs for service in the two world wars, and—most importantly—the training of dogs as guides for the blind.

Racing has meant to a great extent Greyhound racing, a sport long popular and heavily bet in England. It was taken up in the United States in 1919 with the first successful operation of an electrically propelled lure.

The standard dog track is a quarter-mile oval.

Intelligence of German Shepherd Dogs makes them ideal guides (left), better military dogs than Malamutes (right).

Races are run at distances of from three sixteenths of a mile to a half mile. A popular race is five sixteenths of a mile or 550 yards. An average Greyhound can run this in thirty-two seconds or at a rate of thirty-seven miles per hour.

Greyhound racing is very much like horse racing on a smaller scale. Eight dogs, wearing racing muzzles and numbered blankets, are usually entered in each race. They break from stalls in a starting gate, are electrically timed during the race, and photographed at the finish. Ten contests make up an evening's program. Pari-mutuel betting accompanies the action. The sport is highly popular in Massachusetts, Oregon, Florida, and wherever else it is legal.

Greyhound owners, breeders, and fans also are partial to the sport of coursing. This is a controlled version of the Greyhound's centuries-old business of running down rabbits. It is conducted in a 450-yard by 150-yard pen, and is enjoyed mostly in the Mid- and Southwest.

Where there is snow there is sled-dog racing, especially in Alaska where the highest money stakes are offered. Teams usually are made up of Siberian or Alaskan Huskies. America's seventh and last native-bred dog, the Alaskan Malamute, is still a good draft dog, but no longer used for racing. There also are crossbreeds and even such apparently out-of-place dogs as Pointers and Irish Setters. Teams are usually comprised of nine dogs, although there may be as many as fourteen and as few as five. In good condition, they can sustain a twelve- to fourteen-mile-an-hour pace.

The emergence of dogs as movie stars is perhaps no surprise considering the many other elements of man's life in which the dog has been involved. Probably the most famous of all dog performers was Rin-Tin-Tin, the German Shepherd that was found in a Boche trench during World War I. Lassie and perhaps one or two other dogs of the age of sound pictures and television may

Original Rin-Tin-Tin was silent-movie favorite.

have been seen by more people, but Rin-Tin-Tin at the peak of silent-picture stardom was almost a national craze. The tremendous upsurge in the popularity of the German Shepherd in the 1920's could be traced almost entirely to Rinty.

The cleverness of his performances also made abundantly clear what most dog lovers have always known: that the German Shepherd stands very close to the top in intelligence.

This point was demonstrated again during World War II when it was necessary for man's best friend to revert to his role of war dog. Some 10,000 dogs eventually were trained and assigned to duty as messenger dogs, scouts, sentries, and sled and pack dogs. Of all the breeds involved, including the Doberman Pinscher, the Belgian Sheepdog, the Collie, and the Giant Schnauzer, the most satisfactory on all scores was the German Shepherd.

Finally, the German Shepherd has proved himself to be one of the few breeds capable of assuming the enormous responsibility of a guide for the blind. The story of The Seeing Eye, Inc., and the several other organizations in this unique field is by now as familiar as it is remarkable. Yet it deserves a brief retelling in any book that seeks to celebrate the dog.

In 1927 a young man named Morris S. Frank, who was blind, heard of the work being done in Germany to provide guide dogs for blinded veterans of World War I. He heard of it through an article by Mrs. Dorothy H. Eustis, who was herself training dogs in Switzerland for utilitarian work with the Swiss army and police. Frank wrote to Mrs. Eustis and she invited him to Switzerland. She said she would train a guide dog for him, but that he must learn to use it. He did.

In 1928 he returned home with Buddy, a German Shepherd and the first "seeing-eye" dog in the United States. Frank's success covering thousands of miles in a variety of situations with Buddy as his sole guide encouraged Mrs. Eustis to return to the United States, too, and to establish the seeing-eye organization at Morristown, New Jersey.

Since then other fine groups have entered the field, all of them operating in basically the same way. They undertake to train dogs for their enormously important task. And they train blind people how to work with their dogs—and how to care for them.

The dogs are mostly German Shepherds, although some Boxers, some Labrador Retrievers, and some Golden Retrievers also have proved successful. Dogs usually are a year to fourteen months old before training begins. With the faithful assistance of these dogs, their masters have been able to move freely through a hazardous world and to find themselves over a hundred different occupations.

The guide dog is as fine a capstone as one could wish for the story of man's friendship with dogs. If man has at times used his friend senselessly or cruelly, he has yet been repaid with fidelity. He has been given service without servility and devotion without thought of reward.

3 THE NATURE OF THE DOG

The dog's noble nature has been eulogized many times and with fervor. Yet perhaps none has said it more grandiloquently than Senator George C. Vest, of Missouri, while addressing a jury on behalf of a farmer whose foxhound had been shot by a neighbor. Speaking in 1870, a period that liked curlicues on everything, the distinguished Senator noted that although friends and relatives may turn against you, "the one absolutely unselfish friend that man can have in this selfish world, the one that never deserts him, the one that never proves ungrateful or treacherous, is his dog."

"Gentlemen of the jury, a man's dog stands by him in prosperity and in poverty, in health and in sickness. He will sleep on the cold ground, where the wintry winds blow and the snow drives fiercely, if only he may be near his master's side. He will kiss the hand that has no food to offer; he will lick the wounds and sores that come in encounter with the roughness of the world. He guards the sleep of his pauper master as if he were a prince. When all other friends desert, he remains.

When riches take wing and reputation falls to pieces he is as constant in his love as the sun in its journey through the heavens. If fortune drives the master out, an outcast in the world, friendless and homeless, the faithful dog asks no higher privilege than that of accompanying him to guard against danger, to fight against his enemies, and when the last scene of all comes, and death takes the master in its embrace and his body is laid upon the cold ground, no matter if all other friends pursue their way, there by his graveside will the noble dog be found, his head between his paws, his eyes sad but open in alert watchfulness, faithful and true, even to death."

(Sob!)

The jury awarded the farmer $500 for the loss of his foxhound. As he had sued for only $200, we have a fair measure of the degree to which the jury was stirred by the Senator's oratory.

It is, of course, one of the endearing characteristics of dogs that they are steadfast, loyal, and true. Their friendship for man is admirably direct, wholehearted, and unquestioning. Where the per-

Motley farm dog helps drive livestock for family "Moving Farther Westward" (1888).

suasive Senator departs from logic, however, is in implying that a dog is capable of moral judgments, that he somehow understands the failings of his disreputable, dead-beat master, but is charitably disposed to overlook them. This he does not and cannot do. For the dog is not a paragon, and he cannot distinguish abstract good from evil, or so runs expert opinion today.

Charles Darwin, interestingly enough, was not so sure and neither was Louis Agassiz, the Harvard naturalist. These two giants of nineteenth-century science, who agreed on little else, thought that "dogs possess something very like a conscience." Yet if conscience is the faculty for telling right from wrong, it hardly seems fair for the dog to be naturally endowed with this subtle power of discrimination when philosophers must struggle so to achieve it.

Perhaps the point is that the dog has a rough sense of good and bad as they apply directly to him, but cannot project it to evaluate the actions of others. For it is certain that a dog can tell kindness from cruelty in the treatment he receives, and

he comes to know what is regarded as acceptable and unacceptable in his own behavior. (Guilt is rarely more graphic than in the hangdog expression and slumping posture of a delinquent canine.) But he has no observable ethical standards he applies to people or expects them to measure up to. By and large, he is prepared to like people who like him, and he will give as much loyalty to the embezzler as to the bank president or to Senator Vest's fallen hero. "The dog knows his master," goes an old saying, "but not his master's master."

To say it, however, changes nothing. Mankind has always enjoyed attributing human characteristics and motivations to his animal friends and probably is not about to stop.

Somewhat in this vein is one of the most famous and heartfelt tributes ever offered a dog—Lord Byron's epitaph for his Newfoundland, Boatswain. The poet was deeply attached to the dog. It was a present from his father, whom he seldom saw, and was given to him as a puppy when he was thirteen and in his first year at Harrow. When the dog died fourteen years later, Byron had the following lines inscribed on its headstone:

Near this spot
Are deposited the remains of one
Who possessed beauty without vanity,
Strength without insolence,
Courage without ferocity,
And all the virtues of man without his vices.
This praise, which would be unmeaning flattery
If inscribed over human ashes,
Is but a just tribute to the memory of
Boatswain, a dog.

Obviously, this was an exemplary dog, although Byron probably was anthropomorphizing when he said Boatswain had man's virtuousness without his viciousness.

As a matter of fact, one of history's more fascinating anecdotes about dogs has its point and poignancy in the faithlessness of a royal hound. This is the story in Froissart's *Chronicles* of a

1

3

2

1,2 *Studies of dogs, probably hunters, by 17th-century artists.* **3** *Thomas Gainsborough's 18th-century Pomeranians show Spitz inheritance, are otherwise radically different.* **4** *"Fisherman's Dog"—a Landseer Newfie.*

4

meeting between Richard II and Henry Boling-broke, Duke of Lancaster, who will soon depose him and become King Henry IV. It is a melancholy time for Richard, a weak and friendless king whose reign and whose life will end together.

It is 1399. King and King-to-be are talking in the court of Flint Castle. As Froissart tells it, "King Richard had a greyhound called Mathe, who always waited upon the king, and would know no man else. For whensoever the king did ride, he that kept the greyhound did let him loose, and he would straight run to the king and fawn upon him, and leap with his forefeet upon the king's shoulders. And as the king and the Duke of Lancaster talked together in the court, the greyhound, who was wont to leap upon the king, left the king and came to the Duke of Lancaster and made to him the same friendly countenance and cheer as he was wont to do to the king. The Duke, who knew not the greyhound, demanded of the king what the greyhound would do. 'Cousin,' quoth the king, 'it is a great good token to you, and an evil sign to me.' 'Sir, how know you that?' quoth the Duke. 'I know it well,' quoth the king. 'The greyhound maketh you cheer this day as king of England, as ye shall be, and I shall be deposed. The greyhound hath this knowledge naturally; therefore, take him to you. He will follow you and forsake me.' The

Duke understood well those words and cherished the greyhound, who would never after follow King Richard but followed the Duke of Lancaster."

What now shall we say of the nature of the dog? First that he is neither so noble as the Senator would have us believe, nor so fickle and false as the chronicler tells us. The dog has a community of interest with his human friends and enjoys a closer relationship with them than any other domesticated animal. He is generally intelligent, he likes to work and be useful, and he thrives on appreciation and praise. But his nature is canine, his concerns are doggy. His comprehension of the world is conditioned by his needs and bounded by the range and capacity of his senses.

His needs are simple and immediate: food, shelter from weather and from enemies, a congenial family environment, sex, and physical activity, whether at play or work.

This is a fairly prosaic list of requirements, but none of them should be taken for granted. The congeniality of the family atmosphere, for instance, has been found to be of crucial importance in shaping the personality of the puppy and in encouraging the development of a sociable nature.

In England it has long been established practice for kennels to place an expectant dam "out at walk"—with a human family—so that she would be able to whelp her pups and raise them among people. Many of the breeding kennels were on big estates and the farm hands and grooms welcomed the opportunity to make a little something extra by taking care of the bitch and her new litter. Breeders preferred homes in which there were children. They found that pups whose first weeks were spent in the warm, comfortable, and friendly atmosphere of a home grew up with much more personality than those confined to kennel pens.

The keen perceptions of the English breeders have been confirmed in recent years at the Roscoe B. Jackson Memorial Laboratory in Maine. Tests set up to determine the critical periods in a puppy's life have shown that the first three weeks are a period of development. At this time the pup has no learning ability. The big awakening comes in the fourth week. Now he learns to play and to know and accept people. And this is when he most needs the security of the puppy nest.

By the end of the fourth week he should be well adjusted to his surroundings, and in the fifth and sixth weeks he can be weaned and housebroken. He should not, however, be given to a new owner until these stages have been reached. The best time for changing the environment and moving a pup to a new home is from the seventh to the twelfth weeks. The young dog by then will have had all the parental care he needs, plus a normal and natural introduction to humankind which will stand him in good stead throughout his life.

A most practical application of these lessons was made by Guide Dogs for the Blind, one of the leading organizations in this field, which maintains its training headquarters at San Rafael, California. It had been breeding the dogs it trained for the blind, but felt that a disproportionately high percentage was proving unsuitable for training. In search of an answer, Clarence J. Pfaffenberger, a director of Guide Dogs, visited the Jackson laboratory. As a result, all pups intended to be guides now are raised by young 4-H Club members. The early and healthy association with people has produced a far greater number of stable and successfully oriented dogs as possible candidates for the training course.

A dog registers the world around him chiefly by his senses of smell and hearing. A good nose is

Whatever or whoever is lost, Bloodhounds can find.

Long-eared, high-domed Bloodhound reclines at ease.

most particularly an attribute of the sporting dogs and hounds, but even the least well-endowed breeds have equipment superior to man's. Specifically, the area of mucous membrane containing the nerve cells that respond to olfactory stimulation is much larger in dogs than in man. The structure of the dog's head also permits him to get the message more emphatically than man because a greater and more direct flow of scent-laden air strikes the membrane. Altogether the dog has a high degree of sensitivity that enables him to identify people unerringly, unscramble a confusing muddle of trails in pursuit of game, and to detect scents incredibly faint or diluted.

Pointing dogs sniff the air for traces of body scent. Tracking and trailing dogs, including those employed by the police, sniff the ground for evidence of foot scent. Odor intensifies as the dog approaches the source; he, therefore, follows the strengthening stimulus.

The dog's hearing is also more acute than man's. He can hear higher tones, as any dog owner who has ever used a "silent whistle" knows. This device emits a sound beyond the human range of audibility, but well within the dog's, for he responds to it readily. He also can detect fainter sounds, and he can locate the source of a sound more accurately. He can, for instance, tell better than a man whether a sound has emanated from the higher or lower of two sources, or from which of two sources situated side by side.

In discriminating among tones, however, his hearing is grosser than man's. Notes must be a whole tone apart, or more, before he can discern a difference. And he is less able than man to tell which of two sounds is farther away.

On the other hand, he often can interpret his master's meaning from the tone of his voice, without understanding any of the words being spoken.

Whatever he hears, he seems to hear with great precision. It often is puzzling how dogs are able to recognize the sound of an automobile they have

English Setter and Pointer are favorite hunting dogs.

never ridden in, or perhaps have never even seen. In one such case, the dog barked every time the car came near the house, although he could not see it, and as far as anyone could tell, had never seen his master get into it. There was only one possible explanation: He had heard his master's footsteps walking toward the car and then had heard the motor start, thereby associating the two. The master, incidentally, lived on a busy city street. Hundreds of automobiles passed the house in the course of a day, many of the same make as the master's. Yet not once did the dog ever confuse another car with the one that belonged at his house.

The most deficient of all the dog's senses is sight. His vision is quite limited and considerably less keen than man's. He sees objects less clearly and has difficulty identifying and interpreting them. Because of the placement of the eyes in the head, many breeds have a larger field of vision than man. They can see to the side, to the rear, or overhead—to some extent at any rate—without moving. This also means, however, that most of them have a smaller binocular field, a smaller area that can be seen by both eyes at once. Since two viewpoints are what make three-dimensional, stereoscopic vision possible, the dog automatically has less depth perception and less ability to focus on fine detail.

The dog also is color blind. He does not know it, of course, so he has no conception of what he is missing. As someone has said, he sees the world as a black-and-white movie.

With all his limitations, the dog can differentiate varying degrees of brightness as well as man, and he is acutely aware of movement. He pays little or no attention to the inert objects in his environment, but his eye is immediately caught by motion. This, of course, explains the success of

sight hounds, like the Afghan, which can spot a rabbit's twitch at eighty yards.

Very sensibly, the dog compensates for his relatively weak eyesight with his superior nose and sharp hearing. The combination gets him through life quite adequately and only occasionally can he be fooled. In such a case a friend, perhaps, approaches at dusk and his moving form is seen before his footfall is heard or his scent has been caught. The dog barks furiously—and then wriggles with embarrassment when the familiar voice speaks reassuringly or the familiar scent is noted. This is merely a hasty reaction to the dim impression received by the eye, before the stronger senses can confirm it.

What about intelligence? How bright are dogs? Generally, quite bright. Not all dogs, not all breeds, and not under all circumstances, but if one recognizes that a satisfactory definition of intelligence is quite elusive and that dogs in the aggregate are no easier to categorize than people, then a few generalizations may be attempted.

"We can divide animals into people with intelligence and people with talent," says an epigram. "The dog and the elephant are people with intelligence; the nightingale and the silkworm, people of talent." The implication, of course, is that the dog is not innately an artist but has the wit to learn, which is certainly one component of intelligence.

That dogs can learn, every dispassionate observer must agree. Even quite stupid little dogs have been known to master the knack of opening a door or carrying a package, while the feats of really smart dogs can be phenomenal.

Many of the everyday achievements that spring readily to mind are the result of long and patient training, which means that there has been willingness as well as ability. Think, for instance, of obedience training, hunting and retrieving skills in the field, vaudeville tricks, police work, military service, motion-picture acting, sheepherding, and guiding the blind. Few, if any, of these could be performed by an unintelligent dog.

In some instances, of course—in herding sheep or pursuing game—instinct enters in. Most dogs have some tendency to point and retrieve. Purebred bird-dog puppies will point long before their field training has begun. But instinct does not teach the dog not to flinch at the sound of a gun, or to hold firm until ordered to retrieve, or to return the quarry uneaten.

To be sure, there are limitations on the dog's intelligence. The awesome Dr. Sam Johnson observed to James Boswell that dogs, in his estimation, lacked the power of comparing. "A dog will take a small piece of meat as readily as a large," he rumbled, "when both are before him." Perhaps so, but can we be sure that the dog understands the choice presented to him? Does he know that seizing one piece will mean loss of the other? Perhaps his actions would be different if he did.

Consider, too, the educated dog of Edinburgh. As told to us by the Scots naturalist, William Smellie—ah, there's a name to entrance a dog!—the story relates how a pieman hawking his wares in the street one day was moved to give a pie to a

It is the nature of the dog to work willingly and play wholeheartedly with his human friends. From left: Modern, all-black Newfie, Beagle, hound-type mongrel, Saluki.

particularly appealing dog. Next day, same time, same place, the dog is on hand for his pie, to the amusement of his master and the master's friends conversing on a doorstep nearby. So the pieman shows the dog a penny and motions toward the master. Smart dog! He runs to the master, tail wagging, and begs. Master puts a penny in his mouth. Dog returns to pieman and gets his pie.

Unless the dog had noted the exchange of pennies for pies in the past, his quick association that a coin was the intermediate step between wanting and getting a pie was nothing short of extraordinary.

The trouble with many evaluations of the dog's intelligence is that they have been based on situations a dog had no good, doggy reason to solve (for instance, tests requiring man-type physical actions). Or which he solved illogically by human standards ("He was so impatient for a biscuit he spilled the whole box on the floor!"). Or which he failed to solve for reasons completely beyond him (as would have been true had the master's coin been counterfeit). By his own criteria, it is possible that the dog is even brighter than his partisans think he is.

The dog lives very much in the present. He has a poor memory of things past and he has no concept whatever of the future. He neither thinks nor plans ahead. He does not wonder what he'll be when he grows up. He is not concerned with tonight's meal, tomorrow's weather, or next week's fox or pheasant. He ponders not on death.

The dog is not thereby a shiftless or a heedless sort. He has a well-defined range of emotions which he expresses vigorously and openly. He leaps and wags for joy, raises his hackles and curls his lip in rage, and droops perceptibly when sad. And he can be a jealous one, too. Funny as it may sound, one of the difficult times in a dog's life comes when a baby arrives at the home of the childless couple for whom he has been the center of attention. Finding himself displaced in his peo-

ple's affections can make a dog sulky, snappish, and unreliable. Wise owners will see that the dog continues to be treated as part of the family and is given an even more important role as playmate and protector of the new baby.

This, perhaps, goes to the heart of the dog's motivation. Thousands of years of close association have made him man's creature, and in this fact lies his principal incentive and his hope of happiness. "The great pleasure of a dog," wrote the English novelist Samuel Butler, "is that you may make a fool of yourself with him and not only will he not scold you, but he will make a fool of himself, too."

Here, if ever there was, is the agreeable and obliging companion, a jolly fellow, a Falstaffian dog, more lively and more fun than Senator Vest's long-faced, obsequious wretch. His desire to learn is in large part a desire to please. It seems to be well-established that the dog takes no pride in his own cleverness, and surely he does not do handstands or wear a sunbonnet for his own amusement. It is the approval of his oldest friend on earth that he wishes with all his heart to win. For this is the nature of the dog.

Two fox dogs by Thomas Gainsborough.

THE BREEDS

4 SPORTING DOGS

These are the gun dogs. Several of them—pointing and setting breeds, the "Spanyells,"

the Vizsla—are of ancient lineage and stem from ancestors that were indispensible

companions of the medieval hunt. But most are creations of the nineteenth century and

bred to the requirements of wing shooting. Each brings unique talents to bear on the

problems of finding and/or retrieving the quarry, but all of them perform wholeheartedly,

with wit, energy, fidelity, and style. To describe this, there has developed a special

vocabulary of excellence. Sporting dogs, it is said, must be staunch and full of hunt.

Mark well the fall of bird or duck. Have a good nose, a tender mouth, and a merry tail.

CHESAPEAKE BAY RETRIEVER

He may be no beauty, but he is a thoroughly admirable and proficient dog, and his champions believe he is the best of all the retrievers. He can swim a mile, has been known to retrieve more than 200 ducks in a day, and rarely errs in making a recovery. He is so intelligent he even has been trained as a guide dog for the blind. ■ Everything about him contributes to the efficiency of his performance. His dense, oily coat makes him impervious to the iciest water. His great strength makes him both tireless and aggressive. He has the large, webbed feet of the enthusiastic swimmer and a keen nose put to the service of a capacious memory. ■ The genealogy of the Chesapeake is uncertain, although most authorities agree he began with two puppies from Newfoundland who were rescued with the crew of an English brig wrecked off the coast of Maryland in 1807. The Britishers were taken aboard the American ship *Canton* and disembarked at Chesapeake Bay, where a number of their rescuers had their homes. ■ In gratitude for the hospitality that was shown them, the English-

men gave the pups to their benefactors. One of the pair was a dingy red male named Sailor, the other a black female called Canton. There is no record that the two ever were mated, but at maturity both were bred to other hunting dogs of the bay area. ■ By 1885 the Chesapeake breed was standardized and had become approximately what it is today. It seems likely that Flat-Coated and Curly-Coated Retrievers participated in the evolution and that somewhere along the way a Coonhound contributed the Chesapeake's distinctive yellow eye. The Standard of Perfection calls for a color that will blend with surroundings; this means anything from dark brown to the faded tan called "dead grass." The minimum height for a female is 21 inches at the shoulder, the maximum for the male is 26. The average adult dog weighs 65 to 70 pounds. ■ Despite the Chesapeake's affection for the water—his joyous, full-bodied plunge is characteristic—and his high reputation as a ducking dog, he also is a creditable retriever of game birds on land.

GOLDEN RETRIEVER

This excellent retriever—second only to the Labrador in current popularity—is another of the many triumphs of the English dog breeders of the nineteenth century. For many years it was believed that he had descended from the Russian Tracker, a big guard dog used to herd sheep in the Caucasus. According to this colorful but entirely fanciful account, a troupe of trackers performing in a circus at Brighton was seen, admired, and bought by Sir Dudley Marjoribanks to become the foundation stock of the breed. ▪ In fact, the Golden stems from a male dog named Nous, the only yellow pup in an otherwise black litter of Flat-Coated Retrievers. Marjoribanks—now Lord Tweedmouth—purchased Nous from a Brighton cobbler who had been given the dog as settlement of a debt. In 1868, Nous was mated to a Tweed Water Spaniel, a breed now extinct, and the resulting litter was the starting point of today's Goldens. The dog was classified as a Flat- (or Wavy-) Coated Retriever until the Kennel Club (England) recognized the breed in 1913.

The Golden is a noble dog. His strongest character traits are admirable ones. For all his strength, he is a gentle fellow. He is loyal, earnest, and willing. His intelligence makes him easy to train; he scores consistently well in obedience trials. Some Goldens are guide dogs for the blind. ■ Perhaps most endearing is his enthusiasm. He loves his work. Waterfowl retrieving is his forte. He is a powerful swimmer; his dense, lustrous coat is virtually waterproof, and he has the stamina to take the roughest going. He has a tender mouth and a good nose. He can wind his quarry from fifty yards. He also is well regarded as a retriever of upland game birds. His sweet nature and attractive appearance are making him enormously popular as a companion dog, as well. A.K.C. registrations of Goldens have increased greatly in recent years, currently number over 3,000. ■ The Golden is a substantial dog, the Standard specifying a shoulder height maximum of 22½ inches for females, 24 inches for males. Weights range from around 55 to 60 pounds for females to 60 to 75 for males.

CURLY-COATED RETRIEVER

For this fine dog, virtue has been its own reward. Although one of the oldest of the retrieving breeds, and a handsome and capable performer to boot, he has never achieved great popularity and is today among the least known, least numerous gun dogs in the field or on the bench. This is unfortunate, for a steadier, more sweet-tempered, harder-working dog is hard to find. ▪ His coat is his most distinctive feature. From the crown of his head to the tip of his tail he is a mass of tight, black or liver-colored curls. These shed water superbly and, together with his great aptitude for swimming, make him a fine wild-fowl retriever. He has a good memory, locates quickly, and dives willingly for cripples. He is also employed in upland retrieving, although here his thick curls are a disadvantage. They attract burrs and twigs, and require extra grooming. ▪ The Curly Retriever is one of the several breeds that traces its origin to the St. John's-type Newfoundland. The first one of these reached England in 1835 aboard a sailing vessel carrying a cargo of salt cod. The crew's water-front boasts of the dog's swimming ability reached the ears of British breeders and aroused their interest. Other Newfoundlands were imported and various experimental crosses were begun. One of the first was with the now-extinct English Water Spaniel. Another, soon after, was with a retrieving setter. Most authorities now agree that a subsequent crossing with an Irish Water Spaniel contributed both the curly coat and the liver color. By 1855, the Curly-Coated Retriever was a true strain and a very close approximation of the dog we know today. (In the 1880's there was a cross with the Poodle to tighten the curl of the coat.) ▪ The Standard does not specify size or weight, but the usual Curly Retriever stands about 24 inches at the shoulder. Because of longer, lighter-boned legs, he appears to be a bit rangier than other retrievers. He is fond of people and has proved himself to be both a faithful companion and an excellent guard dog.

FLAT-COATED RETRIEVER

This is another Englishman and another descendant of the famous St. John's Newfoundland. His development was the result of many crossings, however, particularly with the Labrador, who was involved in the first crossing and whom he most resembles. Gordon and Irish Setters also are prominent in his background; these evidently were introduced to improve his "bird sense." But generally, under his somewhat heavier coat, he has the conformation of the Lab. Early breeders of the Flat Coat in England tried to limit the coat color to black, but the Standard of Perfection currently accepts both black and liver. ▪ The breed was established by 1860, when the Flat Coat—or Wavy Coat, as it then was called—was first exhibited at a Birmingham dog show. The specimen on display was described as larger than a Labrador, which means that there has been some reduction in size (Flat Coats and Labs are now the same size and weight), but otherwise the dog of a century ago was the one we know today. In England he often is called the "gamekeeper's dog" because of his wide use on the hunting preserves and the moors. ▪ Despite the venerable age of the breed, the Flat-Coated Retriever is still a rare dog in the United States and one whose capabilities are little known to hunters. Nonetheless, he does the traditional work of the retriever very well. He is a natural water dog and an exceptional swimmer, as his heritage would suggest. He marks game well and wastes no time bringing it to the gunner. Like other retrievers, he has proved proficient in upland game work as well, and has even had some success with the difficult pheasant. ▪ Aside from his ability in the field, he has a friendly disposition that makes him a welcome house pet. He needs no more care than a Labrador; while the coat is longer, it does not require an excessive amount of brushing. And, of course, it sheds water easily. He is a sturdy and pleasant dog (60 to 70 pounds, 24½ inches maximum height at the shoulder for males).

LABRADOR RETRIEVER

The Labrador is the most popular of all retrievers, and furthermore he comes from Newfoundland. His name is a mystery, for it is well and widely known that he first came to the attention of English dog breeders in the early nineteenth century when commercial fishermen brought home specimens of the breed from Newfoundland. One of the Earls of Malmesbury, who were pioneer breeders of the dog, refers to his "Labradors" in a letter of 1887, but it is also clear that he knows the breed's true place of origin, and there is no indication why or when the Labrador name had been appropriated. ■ In any event, the breed is related to the big, rough-coated Newfoundland, although it is smaller and has an unknown ancestor—possibly a flat-coated retriever—who contributed his short coat. The Lab loves water. Puppies bound gaily into the ocean and move about, aided by a webbing that extends to the outer joint of the toes, almost as freely as if they were on land. A mature dog can thrust through the water so powerfully that most of his body rides above the surface of the water. Even winter-cold water does not bother him. His coat, though short, is wonderfully dense and oily. ■ A distinctive feature is his "otter" tail, which is very thick at the base, tapers toward the tip, and is covered with the same short, dense hair as the coat. ■ There is no more intelligent dog than the Labrador, but he is not one to take directions without reason. He can be stubborn and he prefers to work out retrieving problems by himself. Once trained, he makes a flawless aid to the hunter and will retrieve pheasant in upland shooting as well as ducks in marshland. Labradors have deep love for their masters, but there is nothing slavish about it. They tend to treat their human friends as equals and expect to be one of the family. ■ Labradors stand 21½ to 24½ inches at the shoulder and weigh from 55 to 75 pounds. Three colors are permitted in the show ring: solid black, yellow (from light cream to fox red), and chocolate.

Sussex Spaniel (top) is short-legged and heavy set, has good nose and rich coat. He is steady worker, but too slow for American hunting conditions. Field Spaniel (bottom) is taller and heavier than Sussex. His skills are about the same.

SUSSEX & FIELD SPANIELS

The early history of the spaniel family is confused and uncertain. Its members became popular as hunting dogs in England in the late fourteenth century, but breeding was not yet a proper science and there was a wide variety of sizes, colors, and conformations within the boundaries of each breed. Many evolving types were considered to be "mutations" of Cocker Spaniels. ■ The Sussex and the Field Spaniel are separate and distinct spaniel types, related to each other and known since the sixteenth century, but rarely seen in the United States. The Sussex is notable primarily for his rich, golden-liver coat and for his excellent nose. Otherwise, he is short-legged and heavy set, a determined worker, but far too slow for American hunting conditions. His forte is the steady pursuit of game through very heavy cover; he is inclined to sing out when he picks up a scent. And if he has been properly trained he can be a highly satisfactory retriever. His top height is 16 inches, top weight 45 pounds.

■ The Field Spaniel is taller than his friend and somewhat heftier. He stands 18 inches at the withers and may scale 55 pounds, or as much as the larger Springer. His skills as a hunter are about the same: slow and steady through heavy cover, a style more appreciated in England than the United States. ■ The dog we have today began as a cross between the Sussex (who was being asked to contribute his nose) and the Welsh Springer. The resulting type was bred to the largest of the Cockers (already known as the Field Spaniel) in hopes of combining the best qualities of all three breeds. This produced the contemporary Field Spaniel. Originally, Field Spaniels were all black, the prevailing Cocker color. But today they may be black, liver, golden liver, mahogany red, or roan, which is a mixture of white and colored hairs. ■ This is an honest, intelligent dog who perseveres and endures. He is teachable and, because of his even disposition, a fine companion in the home, as well as a helper in the field.

BRITTANY SPANIEL

The Brittany is an unusual combination of talents. He resembles a setter and behaves like one. He is the only spaniel that points game. And he is a good retriever. ▪ His kinship with the setter is a matter of induction rather than fact, but if it is true it helps to explain his curious cross-channel isolation from the rest of the staunch, British-bred spaniel types. For it is known that Irish marauders beset Gaul in the fifth century A.D., and that early Irishmen favored a red-and-white hunting dog who was a forebear of today's golden-red setter. Now, if the Irish raiders took such a dog along on their adventure in Gaul, it becomes clear how an orange- (or liver-) and-white, setter-type spaniel grew up in France. ▪ In fact, the Brittany is rather smaller than a setter (17½ to 20½ inches v. 24 to 25). His hunting range is somewhat narrower than the setter's or the Pointer's, although he is the widest ranging of all the spaniels, including the well-loved Springer. He also lacks the setter's plumed tail. Many Brittanys are born tailless, the others are docked to the 4-inch stub specified by the Standard of Perfection. ▪ The present-day Brittany is largely the creation of a French sportsman named Arthur Enaud, who became interested in the breed around the turn of the century. The breed had deteriorated, but Monsieur Enaud liked its performance in the field and decided to tidy up its appearance. The tradition of taillessness already had been established; Enaud's goals were to preserve this, preserve the Brittany's fine nose, and intensify the orange-and-white color scheme. ▪ As is true of so many breeds, the procedure that achieved the result is not precisely known, but Monsieur did infuse new blood into the line with two Pointer types that had both the desired color and the nose: the Italian Bracco and the French Braque de Bourbonnais. The Braque also had a short tail! By 1907, the Brittany had been rehabilitated. ▪ Like many spaniels, the Brittany responds best to the light hand and the gentle voice.

CLUMBER SPANIEL

In his native England, the Clumber is described as "the retired gentleman's shooting dog." He is a short-legged, heavy-set fellow, a slow-moving and deliberate worker, the Basset Hound of the spaniel family. As such he has proved ideal for a great many retired army officers and civil servants who want their sport at a sedate pace in the limited hunting grounds of the suburban areas where they live. ▪ The Clumber's origin is in dispute. For a long time it was believed he had developed from a cross between the Basset and an Alpine Spaniel, which is related to the St. Bernard. This would account for the long, heavy body propped on short legs and for the heavy head, pendulous lips, and drooping eyelids— a characteristic called "haw." Yet there have been many heavy-boned varieties of spaniel, including Cockers with heavy heads and haw. The first Clumbers also were supposed to have come from France. The story went that the first ones in England were a group of the Basset-Alpine crosses which had been presented to

Henry Clinton, Duke of Newcastle, about 1760 by the Duc de Noailles. Newcastle thereafter made the dogs his special interest and bred them at his estate, Clumber Park, the name later attaching to the breed. ▪ British authorities now contend that there may have been Clumbers at Clumber Park, but they didn't come from France. For in spite of the legendary generosity of Monsieur le Duc, there just is no other evidence of dogs of this type in France in the eighteenth century. ▪ Whatever his lineage, the Clumber is a willing and thorough worker at flushing many types of small game. He learns easily and never forgets his lessons. He is intelligent, loyal, and a good watchdog, who will not make friends when he shouldn't. ▪ Clumbers have the typical spaniel coat: silky and straight. The color is white, with attractive lemon or orange markings on head, ears, and legs. The dog stands 18 inches at the shoulder and weighs 55 to 65 pounds—as much as the big Irish Water Spaniel.

ENGLISH & WELSH SPRINGER SPANIELS

Springers are named for the exuberant manner in which they leap and bound in pursuit of game. It is a cheerful and amusing sight. Springers are lively, fast-moving dogs. They quarter their ground eagerly, the merry stub tail wagging enthusiastically. But when on the track of a rabbit, a running pheasant, or a fallen bird, the nose comes up and the trotting gait is accelerated to running strides and arcing leaps that make the long ears flap wildly. ▪ Everyone who has Springers is convinced the dog does his work well because he enjoys it and because it pleases him to please his master. In any event, he is amenable to training. He flushes grouse, woodcock, anything with wings. He drops to ground promptly after sending his quarry into the air. He holds steady after the gun has fired, marks well the

fall of the bird, and fetches only when given the word. Webbed feet make him as able in swamp as in briar patch, and although he is not equipped for icy water, he is a creditable retriever of ducks. ▪ The English Springer is one of the larger spaniels, standing 18 to 20 inches at the shoulder and weighing 40 to 55 pounds. ▪ Although spaniels have played a conspicuous role in hunting history, it has been only in the relatively recent past that they have been differentiated. In the nineteenth century, they were designated by weight, everything being considered a Cocker unless it weighed enough (over 28 pounds) to be called a Springer, a Field Spaniel, or whatever. It was not until 1902 that the Springer was set apart from the other spaniels and was given his own place in the studbook. ▪ His cousin,

the Welsh Springer Spaniel, is a much more stolid fellow. He is faithful and hard working, has a fine nose, and performs well in water, but seems generally to have a more sober personality. He is a hardy fellow who can adapt without difficulty to any kind of cover and in all manner of weather. ■ Aside from the fact that both are spaniels, the Welsh and English Springers are not particularly close. The Welsh was developed in Wales for possibly a century or more before he came to the attention of British sportsmen. Selective breeding rather than crosses make him what he is. He is always red and white, although the English may be black and white, liver and white, or white with liver, black, or tan markings. The Welsh is smaller than the English, standing 17 inches and weighing 35 to 45 pounds.

Which is the Welsh Springer?
He stands at left. The other three are English
Springers, a slightly larger breed but
otherwise a close match.

AMERICAN WATER SPANIEL

The American Water Spaniel was developed in the midwestern United States by men more interested in sport than in dog shows. It is not known exactly when this effort was begun, but the curly-coated little dog was breeding true shortly after the end of the Civil War. He probably stems from the now-extinct English Water Spaniel, with a strong infusion of Curly-Coated Retriever, and a dash of Irish Water Spaniel. The presence of the Irish cousin is usually inferred from the curly, liver-colored coat, although this could have been the contribution of the Curly Retriever. And there is an even stronger possibility that coat color, the spaniel head, and over-all size (15 to 18 inches at the shoulder) trace back to the Sussex Spaniel. ■ The result is an extremely efficient little hunter who can flush and retrieve almost any kind of small feathered or furred game. He can work thickets, covert, or rough ground, as well as water, and is used on rabbits, prairie chicken, grouse, quail, woodcock, pheasant, and ducks. He is an excellent swimmer and has a very retentive memory. He can watch a hunter drop four or five birds and, when sent out to retrieve, will bring back every one. He has the cheerful and affectionate spaniel disposition. He undertakes his tasks with high spirits and a merry tail; when well trained there is no more thorough and enthusiastic worker. ■ His coat is solid liver or dark chocolate in color. It is closely curled, even gives the appearance of marcel waves. The legs have a short feathering. The eyes usually are hazel, brown, or some dark hue that harmonizes with the coat. Dogs range in weight between 28 and 45 pounds (bitches 25 to 40). ■ The breed was not recognized by the American Kennel Club until 1940. It is, of course, primarily a gun dog, but as one of the few purely American developments it has been attracting interest in the show ring and registrations have increased in recent years. It is more popular than the Irish Water Spaniel. People who have kept him as a pet find him a good watchdog.

IRISH WATER SPANIEL

Since the Irish are an imaginative people, the research-er on Erin's dogs encounters at least as much legend as fact. It is said, for instance, that St. Patrick is re-sponsible for the Irish Water Spaniel's most distinc-tive features: his topknot and his "rat tail." In ages past, the topknot grew on the tail. It attracted fish as the dog swam by, but when they bit they were out of reach of the dog's jaws. So, with an assist from St. Patrick, the lure was transferred to the spaniel's head, where he could catch any fish that drew near. Since then, however, the dog has had a rather skimpily dressed tail. ■ In fact, the topknot is an array of long, loose curls which grow in a peak between the dog's eyes; the tail is thick at the base, with tight curls for two or three inches, then tapering to a point and for most of this length covered only by short hairs. They are features of a dog developed in the south of Ireland, although probably springing originally from the now-extinct English Water Spaniel and perhaps the Poodle

and the Portuguese Water Dog. ■ The Irish Spaniel was one of the first retrievers brought to the United States and was quickly accepted, particularly in the Midwest, where he was a favored dog of the market hunters through the 1870's and 1880's. He proved to be hard working and reliable. He marked well and seldom missed a cripple. He also has been used in upland shooting, particularly on pheasant, but his extremely curly coat becomes hopelessly tangled. ■ He is the larg-est of all the spaniels, standing 21 to 24 inches at the shoulder and weighing 45 to 65 pounds. The only ac-ceptable color is liver. ■ The Irish Water Spaniel is something of a clown—not foolish, but humorous and playful. Partly this is due to a slow maturation: It will be two years before a dog is full grown and he often retains much of his puppy playfulness. He is an affec-tionate dog, eager and able to learn, and easy to handle, although capable of thinking for himself. Those who have once had one will have no other breed.

COCKER SPANIEL

This is one of the most popular dogs in the world. In the United States in recent years the Poodle has exceeded him, but no breed has ever come even close to the Cocker's astonishing record of seventeen straight years (1936 through 1952) as the No. 1 dog. He also is close to the top in every country where dogs are registered. ▪ The Cocker in America traces back to the 1880's when the first breeding stock was imported from England. American breeders, however, began a series of selective-breeding experiments to make changes they believed would produce a dog better suited to field conditions in the United States. By 1935 the differences between the parent English type and the American offspring were so marked that the American Kennel Club registered the two as separate breeds. ▪ The American breeding pattern had produced a beauty. He was four to six pounds lighter than his British cousin, shorter in the leg and broader in the chest. The head was domed, the eyes were large and somewhat more prominent, and the stop—the step up from nose to forehead—was more pronounced. Three color varieties were recognized: solid black, any solid color other than black, which may include anything from pure white to dark red, and parti-colored, which is black, tan, red, or other markings on a white background. When properly groomed, the full coat and feathered ears and legs have a lustrous quality that gives the breed a most attractive appearance. The moderate popularity the Cocker had hitherto enjoyed suddenly boomed. And in this he was given something of a boost by the success of the stage and screen production of *The Barretts of Wimpole Street,* in which the role of Elizabeth Barrett's pet Cocker, Flush, was played by a succession of handsome, modern American Cockers. ▪ His eminence as pet and show dog has rather obscured the Cocker as a hunter, although when properly trained, he is an exceptional bird dog and also scores consistently well in obedience and field trials. He locates birds by sniffing the air for traces of body scent, retrieves and carries well, and has a plucky spirit that urges him through water, briars, or fences in the execution of his task. ▪ He stands 14 to 15½ inches at the withers and weighs from 22 to 28 pounds. He has a merry disposition that has made him a popular house pet.

ENGLISH COCKER SPANIEL

Until he was overshadowed by the American model, this fellow was the Cocker Spaniel. He is one of the oldest land spaniels known, originating in Spain—hence, "Spanyell"—and receiving his earliest known mention in an English sporting book in 1386. A record of the Pilgrim ship *Mayflower* noted that it carried a spaniel and a Mastiff on its voyage to the New World in 1620. Unfortunately, the spaniel was not described, so we do not know what type it was. (We can guess well enough about the Mastiff; there was only one of him and he hasn't changed much since.) ▪ In those days—in fact, until the 1890's—size was the only differentiation among spaniels. The smaller puppies in a litter were trained to hunt the woodcock and thus eventually became Cocker Spaniels. The larger ones—what we now call Springers and Field Spaniels—were used for springing game and larger birds. ▪ Once he achieved separate status, the Cocker also achieved great popularity. From the late 1920's to the early 1940's, he was the most popular breed in England and in many other parts of the world. ▪ The English Cocker is a slightly larger dog than his American counterpart. He stands a maximum of 17 inches at the shoulder. The female's minimum size limit of 15 inches is the maximum for an American male Cocker. English Cockers weigh 26 to 34 pounds. They are longer in the back, the legs, and the jaw, which makes them somewhat more capable and successful performers in field trials. They are able to cover the ground more quickly and carry downed game more easily. Not invariably, however. Some exceptionally active little American Cockers have on occasion won in spectacular fashion despite the handicap of size. ▪ The English Cocker's color schemes are the same as the American's, although dogs with white and colored hairs intermixed are somewhat more frequently encountered. ▪ Like all Cockers, he is cheerful, intelligent, unswervingly loyal to his master, and sweet-tempered with children. He takes obedience training well.

ENGLISH & IRISH SETTERS

The first person to make the comparison "as friendly as a pup" must have been thinking of a setter. For a dog with a more gracious, affectionate, playful, and genuinely happy temperament is hard to find. He—meaning either the English or Irish versions—is also a great field dog, who approaches his task with speed, spirit, and intelligence. ▪ Both setters had the same starting point as an offshoot of the old "Setting Spaniel" and the Pointer. The parent dog was known in England in the early 1500's. He was trained to locate birds, then drop to ground—or "set"—so that the hunters could creep forward with a net to drop over the quarry. Later he was trained to stand and point game. ▪ The breakaway of the Irish Setter as a distinct breed began in the early eighteenth century, and by about 1800 the all-red dog known today had been established. ▪ The major development of the English Setter was begun about 1825, when an English breeder named Edward Laverack took a strain that had had no outside

crosses for thirty-five years and bred it selectively. His efforts resulted in the strikingly handsome show dog seen today. Shortly thereafter, a Welsh sportsman named R. L. Purcell-Llewellin, who was dissatisfied with the slow pace of his setters in the field, sought to improve their hunting capabilities. He began with some Laverack setters, tested them afield, and mated only those showing proficiency in finding game and holding points. Performance was his only criterion, not size or appearance. He was eminently successful. The so-called Llewellin setter is everywhere highly regarded as one of the world's fine gun dogs. ▪ The Laverack-type English Setters stands 24 to 25 inches at the shoulder. The Llewellin is somewhat smaller. Colors range from pure white to mostly black. Usually the dog is basically white with markings of black and tan, red, orange, lemon, or liver; there also are orange and blue Beltons, which is white with markings of mixed colored and white hairs. ▪ The spectacular beauty of the

Irish Setter at right wears traditional coat of mahogany red. Spotted and splotched white coats are English Setter attire. Irishman is a fine field dog, the Englishman superb—but less often seen at shows.

Irish Setter has been at once his greatest asset and his greatest handicap. He is so popular as a show dog that he has fallen a step behind the English Setter and the Pointer as the choice dog in the field. Not that he lacks ability. When he first came to the United States shortly after the Civil War, the Irish Setter was successfully trained to point ruffed grouse, quail, and other game totally unfamiliar to him. And there are still dogs today who can hold their own in field or obedience trials. ■ But it is in the show ring that the dog is best known and loved. The sight of a beautiful Irishman in stride, with his head lifted into the breeze, his luxurious mahogany red coat glinting under the arena's lights, and his well-feathered tail swishing jauntily, never fails to rouse a show audience to thunderous applause. ■ The Irish Setter is a mite leaner than the English and usually higher at the shoulder. He runs 25 to 27 inches, and 50 to 70 pounds. The only permissible color for the Irishman is red. Although early, indigenous setters of Ireland were red and white, the all-red dog is now the standard. A small white star or blaze is barely allowed, but no black. ■ Both setters are sensitive. They are not hard to handle, but they respond best to patience and kindness. They cannot be scolded or coerced. Treat them as close friends and they will return a full measure of loyal service and regard. Both make fine house companions, but should live in an area that offers sufficient running room to keep them in condition.

GORDON SETTER

Time was when the Gordon had no equal as a field-trial dog. But that was long ago. Today the English and Irish Setters are judged to have more spirit, more drive, and more all-around ability in the field. ▪ The Gordon still has his advantages, of course. A leisurely hunter can have a very pleasant day's shooting with a well-trained Gordon as his partner and companion. The breed has a splendid nose, excellent bird sense, and seldom makes a false point on quail, ruffed grouse, or woodcock. He is a thorough dog who works fairly close to the gun. He retrieves well, in water as well as on land. And once trained, Gordon fanciers claim, he never needs retraining. ▪ He is a bit of a slowpoke, however, and his range is restricted—both very real handicaps in field trials. It is often said that his lovely black coat is difficult to see in heavy cover, but sportsmen who have hunted with him discount this. ▪ The Gordon, like other setters, has the spaniel as a common ancestor. He was known as a definite breed as early as 1620, but was not called the Gordon Setter until the late eighteenth century, when Scotland's fourth Duke of Gordon became the leading breeder. From then on, the Gordon was kept clear of crossings with other setters or spaniels. ▪ The first pair of Gordons to reach the United States was imported in 1842 by the great statesman, Daniel Webster, and his friend, George Blunt, a leading hydrographer. The breed soon became popular, particularly with the commercial hunters who bagged game birds for the big-city restaurants. A few years after the Civil War, however, the sport of running dogs at field trials began. Interest was stimulated in a variety of breeds and sportsmen began to experiment with other gun dogs. From that point on, the Gordon began to lose ground. ▪ His coloring is distinctive: a silky black with tan or mahogany-red markings on muzzle, legs, and under the tail. He ranges from 24 to 27 inches at the shoulder, weighs 55 to 75 pounds. (Females are one inch and ten pounds less.)

POINTER

The Pointer combines the best qualities of several fore-bears. From the English Foxhound came balance and staying power, from the Greyhound speed. The Blood-hound gave a measure of his incomparable scenting ability, and the "setting spaniel" his tractability and game sense. ▪ It used to be said that the Spanish Pointer was father of the breed, but now it is believed that he was in fact a different breed and that pointing dogs came into use generally throughout Europe at about the same time. In England, the first Pointers of record appear about 1650. Curiously, they were not used to locate game birds, but to find rabbits. The Pointers stood and pointed at the rabbits, and Greyhounds were brought into play to course them. By the early eight-eenth century, however, firearms had developed to a degree that made wing shooting the new sport, and the Pointer became forevermore a gun dog. About this time, the Spanish Pointer appeared in England and was crossed with his British cousin. The Spaniard was heavy and slow, but presumably he had pointing in-

stinct in abundance, and this he strengthened in the Englishman. Henceforward, no story of the Pointer's pointing ability was too fantastic to be believed. Perhaps the best—a real shaggy-dog story—was the one about the Pointer that was lost in the course of a day's hunting on the moors. A year later his owner found him—a skeleton dog still pointing a skeleton bird! Almost more incredible because they are true are the many recorded instances of dogs that held their point—nose and tail extended and one foreleg lifted—for more than an hour by the clock while waiting for their hunters to come up to them. ■ The Pointer that has evolved today is a magnificent gun dog. He is lithe and muscular, powerful yet graceful. He must have all the hunting virtues of speed, endurance, courage, and drive. But more than that, he must bespeak his function from inside out. Size, color—everything is unimportant, except that he should look and act like a hunting dog. "A good Pointer cannot be a bad color," says the Standard. But if he has balance and symmetry, if he is "smooth all

Pointer in field is all business. Physically and temperamentally, he is a magnificent hunter.

over," as the saying is, and if he has an easy gait and a rhythmic, sidewise-moving tail, and if, above all, he is full of "hunt," then he is on his way to being all that a Pointer should be. ▪ His coat is short and dense and should have a sheen. The usual colors are white with liver, lemon, orange, or black markings. Sometimes, but not frequently, dogs of this breed are solid black. ▪ The Pointers seen in the show ring and in the field are the same type. They measure 24 to 27 inches at the shoulder and weigh 50 to 60 pounds. Some field-trial trainers consider this too much bulk to carry for the thirty-five or forty-five miles a big event may demand, and they have developed a considerably smaller and faster dog. ▪ The Pointer is an even-tempered fellow, but does not have the warm and affectionate nature of the setters. He is loyal to his master, but not a one-man dog. His eagerness to hunt makes him responsive to almost any sportsman with a gun. When raised as a home dog rather than as a kennel inmate, however, he can make a fine pet.

Field-trial competitions for Pointers and Setters are major sports events across the nation.

GERMAN SHORTHAIRED & WIREHAIRED POINTERS

In Germany in the nineteenth century, when hunting became a popular pastime rather than an upper-class privilege, the crying need was for an all-purpose sporting dog. Men who did not hunt regularly or whose means did not permit them to maintain several dogs wanted a faithful companion who also was adaptable to whatever conditions were encountered in the field. German breeders obliged by developing not one but five varieties to meet the demand. All are interrelated, but only the Shorthaired and Wirehaired Pointers are known and recognized in the United States. (The others: German Griffon, Stichelhaar, and Pudelpointer.) ▪ The Shorthair is a truly versatile dog with a hound's nose for ground game, a Pointer's certainty in

locating game birds, and a retriever's fortitude in icy water and weather. He has even been used to trail and point deer. He is not fast, but he is steady, workmanlike, strong, and enduring. And he has a mild and pleasant disposition. ▪ Lack of speed has been a prime deficiency throughout his history. He began, way back, as a cross between the so-called Spanish Pointer and the Bloodhound, which blessed him with a great nose but made him run like an alderman. An infusion of English Foxhound speeded him up a bit and resulted in what was for years the classic German Pointer. A final cross —with the English Pointer—produced today's Shorthaired Pointer. ▪ The Shorthair coat is smooth, with short, thick hairs that feel tough and hard. The only

German Shorthaired Pointer (above and below) is handsome and versatile dog. Opposite: Wirehaired variety is heavily armored.

permitted colors are solid liver, liver and white, and liver roan (mixed white and liver). ▪ The Wirehaired Pointer, known in Germany as the Deutsch-Drahthaar, is a dog well armored for work in the heaviest underbrush and the coldest water. He has a distinctively heavy growth of hair on the brow that protects his eyes. His color, like the Shorthair's, is liver, liver white, or liver roan. He is a keen-nosed and energetic dog, and a loyal one-man or one-family pet. ▪ His genealogy is mixed. He has something of all the other all-purpose German hunters in him, which means all the breeds in the Shorthair's background plus Poodle and the so-called Polish Water Dog. He is still a comparatively rare breed in the United States today.

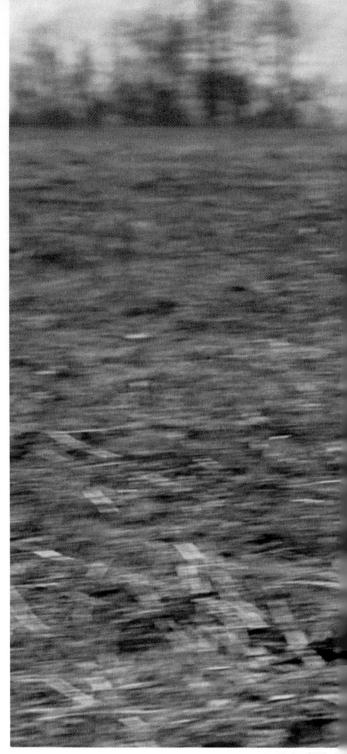

WEIMARANER

This is the "Gray Ghost," an attractive and accomplished hunter that was developed about 1815 by the nobles of the Court of Weimar, in Germany. There is little he cannot do. Originally, he was used to trail deer, boar, and bear in the Thuringian game preserves, but as the big game was killed off he became a bird dog. He is a stylish pointer, a fine retriever, and an intelligent trailer. He can work in all kinds of cover, in all kinds of weather. And he is a loyal and friendly house dog. He performs skillfully in field trials. Altogether

he is almost as good as his partisans claim he is. ■ The Weimaraner's principal ancestor was a red-tan Schweisshund (Swiss dog), an offshoot of the Bloodhound. He also has some English and Spanish Pointer in him, like his cousin, the German Shorthaired Pointer. ■ For many years the dog was the exclusive property of the Thuringian nobles. They formed a breed club whose members were not allowed to sell dogs to outsiders. Breed wardens inspected all new litters and had the power to order the destruction of any pups that did

not measure up to the Standard of Perfection. It is estimated that at no time were there more than 1,500 Weimaraners in all of Germany. ▪ The first specimens were brought to the United States in 1929 by an American sportsman who was permitted to acquire a pair only after he had been accepted as a member of the German Weimaraner Club. Restrictions have since eased a bit and other breeding stock has been imported. Today the Weimaraner is among the first twenty purebreds in popularity. ▪ He is one of the larger gun dogs, ranging from 25 to 27 inches high at the withers (females: 23 to 25) and weighing 68 to 85 pounds (females: 55 to 75). For all his size, he is graceful and well proportioned. His coloring is distinctive: silver gray to dark silver taupe for his short, sleek coat, and blue gray, gray, or light amber for his eyes. His tail is docked. It measures about 6 inches at maturity and should be carried, says the Standard, "in a manner expressing confidence and sound temperament." Both of which all Weimaraners have in abundance.

VIZSLA

The Vizsla, or Hungarian Pointer, is one of the ancient sporting breeds. He was the hunting companion of the Magyars who swept into Hungary early in the tenth century, and he seems to have bred remarkably true, with little change, in the centuries since. Recognizable portraits of him survive in primitive stone carvings of the tenth century and in an illuminated fourteenth century work on falconry. ∎ He is a sturdy, well-made dog with a lithe and graceful gait and an aristocratic air. He looks a bit like the Weimaraner, although smaller, and has a short, rusty gold coat. He ranges from 21 to 24 inches at the shoulder, and from 40 to 60 pounds. ∎ The Vizsla is a gifted hunter. He has a superior nose and moves quickly, although with caution, for he is used to working over sparsely covered terrain where mere dash may flush the quarry out of range. He also is an adept retriever, not only of upland game but of waterfowl as well. The Vizsla has lively but gentle manners and is affectionate. ∎ The Vizsla is a recent addition to the A.K.C. studbook, but is already highly popular.

WIREHAIRED POINTING GRIFFON

Stiff, wiry hairs of Griffon's coat have been likened to boar's bristles. Dog is staunch but slow.

The shaggy, bristly coated Griffon is the end point of another nineteenth century effort to combine all sporting virtues in one friendly, willing dog. He is the creation of a young Dutch sportsman named E. K. Korthals, who began his breeding experiments in 1874 with a gray-brown Griffon bitch named Mouche. ■ Korthals wanted a rugged dog with a keen nose, the pointing instinct, and the ability to trail game. His crosses were complicated and at various times involved setters, spaniels, Dutch and German Pointers, and the Otterhound, from whom the resulting Griffon inherited a talent for swimming. Korthals also bred for a stiff, harsh coat and eventually achieved hairs as bristly as a wild boar's. ■ The dog he got has proved to have everything but speed. He is intelligent and trainable, an excellent pointer, and a retriever on water or land, where his coat is ample protection against weather or thorny thicket. He cannot run, however, with most pointing dogs in the United States. ■ In size he stands between the Springer Spaniel and the English Setter (19½ to 23½ inches at the shoulder).

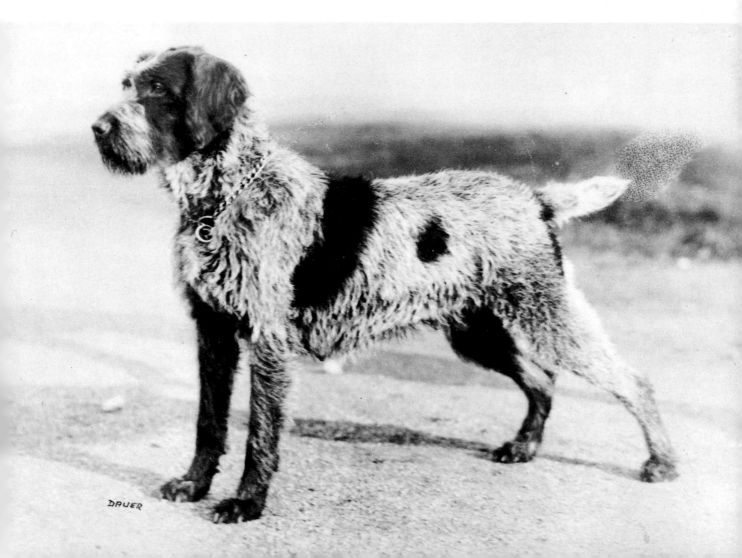

Hounds are the dogs of antiquity. Their forms grace the walls of pre-Christian temples, the faces of Grecian coins, the tombs of Pharaohs and forgotten kings. They have been carved in stone, cast in metal, woven into tapestries, and portrayed on canvas. Possession of them frequently was the exclusive privilege of the nobility. They were valued almost beyond price. They could be given, but never sold. Stealing one was punishable by death. Many have taken their names from the creature they were taught to hunt, bring to bay, and destroy. Many did their job too well and are unemployed today for want of wolves, boar, and badger to course and harry. Only the gay and ardent pursuers of fox and 'coon still play their age-old game. The rest are pets — or racers chasing Rusty at the track.

BEAGLE

Few breeds have the universal appeal of the Beagle. He scares up squirrels for young country boys with .22's. He is the adult hunter's favorite dog for rabbits. Here and there he still runs in a pack. Almost everywhere he can be found running singly in field trials. And in thousands of homes he is a cheerful and affectionate pet. ▪ His origin is obscure, but it has been suggested that he sprang from an all-white hound that was a favorite of Pwyll, a Prince of Wales in the sixth century A.D. There is no record of the breeding that developed him to his present state, but he is believed to have been separate and distinct from his cousins, the Harrier and the English Foxhound, before King John signed the Magna Carta. He always has been a small dog. In the time of England's King Henry VIII and Queen Elizabeth, he apparently was carried to the field in saddle panniers, small cases which could not contain a dog much larger than 12 inches at the shoulder. ▪ The modern Beagle is a creation of the nineteenth century. He was imported to the United States in the 1870's and used in packs to hunt rabbit and hare. He is not fast enough to be an ideal hunter of fox, but in the century since his arrival in the States, he has proved himself adept at everything else. Today he is a specialist in the cottontail, although some hunters have used him successfully on pheasant. ▪ Beagle field trials have become tremendously popular. Here (and in dog shows) the dog competes in two size divisions: 13 inches and under, and over 13 but not over 15. Smaller Beagles may be only 10 inches. (In England, the dog may run as tall as 16 inches.) The weight ranges from 20 to 40 pounds. The short coat may be "any true hound color," which usually is a black, tan, and white combination. ▪ Following World War II, the Beagle suddenly became extremely popular as a household pet, especially in cities where previously it had hardly ever been seen. As a consequence, the breed led all others in A.K.C. registrations for eight straight years.

BASSET HOUND

This is the second-best nose in dogdom. No breed but the Bloodhound, to whom the Basset is closely related, can claim greater scenting powers. In centuries past, he was a royal dog, raised to trail deer, hare, and rabbit. Today, in the United States, where he is a great favorite, he hunts fox, rabbit, and sometimes grouse. He can be taught to tree raccoon, opossum, and squirrel. And he is particularly skilled in trailing and flushing the tricky pheasant. ■ He is a low-slung, slow-moving fellow, but steady and accurate. He is a great tracker in heavy cover, either on his own or, as they did in the olden days, on the liam (leash). When he is on the scent and giving tongue, no other hound can match the bell-like tones of his deep, resounding voice. ■ The Basset is an ancient breed, known on the continent chiefly in France and Belgium, and descended from an old French Bloodhound and the St. Hubert Hound. He is described as having Foxhound coloring, the Bloodhound head, and the Dachshund running gear, which is true, al-

though none of these dogs can be said to be responsible for these features. In particular, his short, heavy-boned, outturned forelegs appear to be the result of intensive selective breeding. He stands a mere 10 to 15 inches at the shoulder and weighs 25 to 40 pounds. In show condition he may weigh ten or a dozen pounds more, but will carry it well; much of his heft is in his heavy bone. The American Basset is, nonetheless, a bulkier dog than his French cousin, but lighter and more compact than his English forebears. His coloring is that of many hounds: black, tan, and white. He has long, heavy leathered ears, and his heavily wrinkled forehead gives him an amusingly doleful expression. Actually, he is a cheerful dog that enjoys a romp and an affectionate one that is friendly and reliable with children. He is docile, intelligent, and easy to control if well treated. ■ Aside from being a fine hunter and companion dog, the Basset Hound has made a good record in field trials, obedience trials, and in the show ring.

HARRIER

The Harrier is slightly larger than the Beagle, a bit smaller than the English Foxhound, and very much like both as to type. As with most ancient breeds, no one knows exactly where the Harrier began. The famous treatise of the Greek historian, Xenophon, dating from 400 B.C., is a minute description of dogs harrying hares, and his list of ideal hound qualities could serve as a standard today, but it is certain that the contemporary Harrier was unknown to him. It is more likely that the dog developed somewhat haphazardly from crosses between various medieval hounds, and from selective breeding after the basic type was established. One theory has him an offshoot of a cross between the Beagle and the St. Hubert's Hound, but it probably was more complicated than that. The problem of tracing his derivation is also confused by the fact that until the middle of the eighteenth century "harier" meant all hounds, not just the Harrier. ■ The first recorded Harrier pack in England was the Penistone, which was founded in

1260 and continued for more than five centuries. The early Harriers were considerably smaller than the dog we know today and were followed by hunters on foot. Currently, he stands 19 to 21 inches at the shoulder, and when in the field, is followed on horseback. ■ He has been known in America since colonial times, when he was used on fox as well as hare. Today, because he is somewhat slower paced than the Foxhound, he is favored for drag hunts. Here he need have only a good nose to hold to the line of the scent bag, and running gear good enough to stay ahead of the horses. ■ The Standard of Perfection for the Harrier is the same as that for the English Foxhound, except in size. He has a smooth coat. Any hound colors are permitted; usually he is the familiar hound tricolor of black, tan, and white. ■ Because of his specialized hunting qualifications, he is seldom bred for show and very few specimens are registered with the A.K.C. He is also not well-known as a pet, although he is a friendly fellow.

BLACK & TAN COONHOUND

The "Cooner" is an American development. The exact date of his emergence as a distinct breed is unknown, but he is of ancient lineage. He traces to the Talbot hound of William the Conqueror in the eleventh century, through the Bloodhound (to whom he still has a family resemblance), to the black-and-tan Virginia Foxhound, his immediate forebear. ▪ The hunting of raccoon is a specialized sport pursued at night. The hound follows the foot scent of his quarry. The coon when pressed invariably seeks safety in the branches of a tree. This point may not be reached for several hours, but the Coonhound seldom if ever gives tongue until he is standing against the trunk of the tree where the game has taken refuge. The rich, roaring tones of the dog's "tree bark" are then a dependable signal to the hunters to move in for the kill. They know that the hound will never bark up the wrong tree. ▪ In doing his job, the Coonhound shows great keenness, drive, and determination. He works with his nose to the ground, and al-

though a bit slow—he is somewhere between the Bloodhound and the Foxhound—he is quite fast enough for the game he specializes in. ▪ The Black & Tan is a big hound, ranging from a minimum of 23 inches at the withers for the female to a maximum of 27 inches for the male. There is no specification for weight; the dog simply should have a pleasing conformation, a reasonable size for his height. He should look neither "leggy" nor "close to the ground." His entire build is lighter than that of the Bloodhound and his wrinkles fewer. He does have the Bloodhound's ear leather and coloring, however. He must be coal black, with tan marks over the eyes, on the side of the muzzle, on the chest, legs, and inside the thighs. The coat is short but dense, enabling the dog to work in extremes of heat and cold. ▪ The Black & Tan is rugged enough for bigger game than coon and has been used to hunt deer, mountain lion, bear, and bobcat. He is kept almost solely as a hunting dog. His role as a companion dog is negligible.

AMERICAN & ENGLISH FOXHOUNDS

"Next to an old Greek statue," an English poet once wrote, "there are few such combinations of grace and strength as in a fine foxhound." Anyone who has hunted the fox knows the strenuous demands of the sport and how admirably the design of the Foxhound enables him to fulfill his function. He must have good running gear and great stamina. (It is said that in a good day's hunting an English Foxhound pack may lead the horses on a chase of seventy-five miles.) He must have strong bone, well-developed knuckles, and deep pads on round, catlike feet. He must not be a "babbler," but should know when to give tongue, so that the other hounds and the hunters will know when he is on the trail. ■ The English Foxhound achieved his present form early in the eighteenth century. He is a dog of great symmetry, standing 23 to 25 inches at the withers and weighing about 85 pounds. His colors are the hound's usual black, white, and tan. ■ He is a smaller, better-balanced version of a staghound used in the sixteenth century by such avid hunters as King Henry VIII. Foxhunting was unknown at the time. Only after Oliver Cromwell destroyed the great English deer parks did Reynard become acceptable quarry for a pack of hounds. At the height of the foxhunting era in England, in the nineteenth century, there were some 200 registered packs. ■ In America the Foxhound was developed as a leggier type than his English cousin, but is about the same height and weight. He has a fine nose, endurance, speed, drive, and a musical voice. (By contrast, the French hounds Lafayette sent to General Washington to mix with his Anglo-American stock—see Chapter Two—were said to have voices "like the bells of Moscow.") ■ Today there are two major divisions of interest in hunting with American Foxhounds. One is the hunt-club meet in which members wearing club livery follow the pack on horseback, either in pursuit of a real fox or on the trail made by a bag of fox scent that has been dragged across the fields beforehand. The other is the nocturnal hunt, popular in the hill sections of many states, in which individually owned hounds seek the fox. There also are Foxhound field trials. ■ Foxhounds are utilitarian dogs and usually kept in kennels. They are rarely shown or kept as pets.

IRISH WOLFHOUND

This is the tallest dog in the world. When he stands on his hind legs, he often is more than 7 feet tall. Show-ring standards require that the breed should measure a minimum of 34 inches at the shoulder (30 inches for females). The tallest hound on record in the United States was a tremendous 39 inches. At such heights, dogs will weigh from 105 to 160 pounds. ▪ The earliest reference to the Irish Wolfhound is found in the writings of Arrian, the Greek historian, who tells how the Celts came to Greece in 273 B.C. and sacked Delphi with the aid of huge, swift hounds. The dogs were fearsome foes. They dodged the shafts hurled by the Greek spearmen and then charged so ferociously that the Greeks turned and fled. Another historical footnote is contained in a letter from a Roman consul, Quintus Aurelius Symmachus, to his brother Flavianus, stationed in Britain. The letter, written in 391 A.D., thanks Flavianus for the gift of seven Irish Wolfhounds to appear in a show at the Circus Maximus. ▪ By 1571, a Jesuit priest, Edmund Campion, is writing of the dog's role as a principal hunter of the wolf: "They [the Irish] are not without wolves and greyhound to hunt them,

bigger of bone than a colt. The Irish Wolfhound is similar in shape to a greyhound, bigger than a mastiff, and tractable as a spaniel." Like many of the reporters of an earlier time, Campion is something less than precise in his observations. The Wolfhound does not really resemble the Greyhound as much as he does a big terrier, say, like the Airedale. He has the terrier's wiry coat, a very large head, and speed for his size, but nothing like the Greyhound's. He also lacks the Greyhound's "tuck-up"—the extremely shallow body at the loin. ▪ The breed diminished with the disappearance of the wolf and elk in Europe, but has now been restored as show dog and pet. In the western United States he is occasionally used to hunt the timber wolf. ▪ In temperament he is one of the gentlest of all dogs. (Campion's observation was completely correct here.) He not only loves people, but other dogs, as well. He seems to have a great sense of justice, for there are many stories of Wolfhounds dealing severely with big dogs who are molesting smaller ones. ▪ Recognized colors are black, white, gray, brindle, red, fawn, or any color acceptable for the Deerhound.

SCOTTISH DEERHOUND

In the Middle Ages, no one below the rank of earl was permitted to own a Scottish Deerhound. The gift of a brace of them was considered a mark of great esteem; it is even said that a man condemned to die could ransom his life with a pair. Despite their size, they were companion, not kennel, dogs and the laird's favorites were likely to sleep in his chamber at night. Sir Walter Scott was a Deerhound enthusiast. He had one named Maida, whom he described as "the most perfect creature of Heaven," and he made countless references to the breed in his works. ▪ The Deerhound's origin is lost in a far past and confusingly intermingled with that of the Irish Wolfhound. Early references to a staghound, Highland deerhound, or wolfdog could mean either breed, or a single one which was later differentiated into the two breeds known today. Dr. Johannes Caius (John Kay or Key?), a Cambridge scholar who wrote a famous treatise on "Englisshe Dogges" in 1576, made a typically obscure comment when he classified what presumably was the Deerhound as a curly-coated Greyhound. ▪ The Deerhound has a good nose, is a tireless tracker, and a courageous hunter. For deer he was hunted singly or in pairs. In time, coursing as a hunting technique was supplanted by stalking and shooting. Once that occurred other breeds of dogs were in greater demand. In America, where he always has been a rare dog, the Deerhound has been used only for wolves, coyote, and rabbits. ▪ He has, meanwhile, become a show dog, beginning in Birmingham, England, in 1860. He is an impressive dog, one of the giants of the canine world. A mature Deerhound stands from 28 to 32 inches at the shoulder and may weigh from 75 to 110 pounds. His coat is harsh and wiry; dark blue gray is the preferred color, then the darker and lighter grays and brindles. Like many large dogs he is gentle, quiet, and friendly in a dignified way. He has a distinctively keen, faraway look in his eye when aroused. He needs exercise and should be given plenty of running room.

NORWEGIAN ELKHOUND

This is one of the two oldest breeds in the world. Nearly complete skeletons dating back between 4000 and 5000 B.C. have been found in western Norway, which would make the breed at least as old as the Saluki. ▪ The Elkhound was the all-purpose dog of Norway—a herder of flocks, guardian against wolves, war dog, hearthside companion, and hunter. He accompanied the Vikings on their voyages of discovery and may well have been the first European dog to set foot in North America. ▪ In the field, Elkhounds worked in pairs. They were supposed to be able to wind an elk from two miles or more and were accomplished stalkers. When they had a giant elk at bay, they harried him by darting between his sharp hooves and just out of range of his scythelike antlers, barking to summon the hunters. Because of his courage the Elkhound has also been pitted against bear and mountain lion. He has been used against lynx, otter, raccoon, and fox. He has even been employed as a gun dog and retriever of upland game. ▪ The Elkhound is a medium-sized dog, ranging in size from 18 inches at the withers for females to 20½ inches for males. He is stocky, compact, and short-backed, which means that he does not have great speed, although, of course, he has strength, great endurance, and a bold nature. Judging by the skeletal remains, he has changed very little in 7,000 years. His coat is thick, but close-lying, and is made up of gray hairs with black tips. He shades off somewhat lighter on the chest, stomach, and legs. The outer hairs are somewhat harsh, although not bristly. Beneath them there is a dense, woolly undercoat that protects him in any kind of weather. His tail is curled and carried over his back. He has a neck ruff, like the Chow Chow, the Pomeranian, and other Spitz-type breeds to which he very likely is related. ▪ The Elkhound did not become a show dog until after his appearance in a Norwegian Hunter's Association exhibition in 1877, which brought him to other breeders' attention. A Standard was written and a studbook published, and the dog soon became popular. ▪ Temperamentally, the Elkhound is a comradely, energetic, reliable dog. He is a quick learner—and for all his fiery nature in combat, he is a gentle family dog.

BLOODHOUND

There is no gentler dog than the Bloodhound. Despite the ferocious sound of his name and his relentless pursuit of Eliza in countless road-company performances of "Uncle Tom's Cabin," he has a sweet disposition and wouldn't hurt a fly. The Bloodhound tugging against the deputy sheriff's leash as he eagerly follows the trail of the escaped convict or the lost child is not being restrained from attacking his quarry, but from smothering him with affection. Observers believe it is a matter of pride: The Bloodhound is so delighted at having followed a track successfully that he wants to kiss the person he has found. ■ Whatever his motivation, the Bloodhound has no peer as a tracker. Of all known breeds of dogs, he has the best nose. He is the only dog whose matching of the scent of a man and a track is accepted as evidence in court. In many cases, Bloodhounds have been able to pick up the scent of a trail cold for many hours—in one case, 105 hours. And they have followed trails successfully as far as 138 miles! ■ The breed is an ancient one. It is believed to have been known in the Mediterranean countries before the Christian era, in Europe before the Crusades. It is not likely that the same dog has bred true throughout the centuries, but the pre-eminent scenting ability undoubtedly has been preserved through a family line. In Europe the line is supposed to have begun with two strains—the so-called St. Hubert's Hounds, which were black, and the Southern Hounds, which were white. It was a descendant of the old St. Hubert's, known as the Talbot Hound, that was brought to England, some say at the time of the Norman Conquest, some say earlier. And it is he who has been part of the breeding of many subsequent hounds. ■ The contemporary Bloodhound has long been an American favorite. For something more than a century his abilities as a "sleuthhound" have been refined, originally, perhaps to recover the runaway slave, but latterly for all phases of modern police work. ■ The Bloodhound is a distinctive-looking dog, his sadly solemn appearance accentuated by wrinkles in the loose skin of his head and neck. His smooth coat is usually tan with black or red. He stands 23 to 27 inches, weighs 80 to 110 pounds.

RHODESIAN RIDGEBACK

The Ridgeback gets his name from the "wrong-way" hair which grows along his spine. The hair simply grows forward, as though someone had combed him "against the grain" or contrary to the pattern of his coat. It is a curious and distinctive characteristic, but not unique. An indigenous Vietnamese dog called the Phu Quoc is also a ridgeback. ∎ The Rhodesian is a blend of a number of European breeds brought to Africa by Dutch, German, and French settlers in the early eighteenth century. There is Great Dane, Mastiff, Greyhound, Bloodhound, Airedale, and several other kinds of terrier in him. Yet it is from a half-wild hunting dog of the Hottentots that the ridge was acquired. ∎ Little of his European heritage is visible in the Ridgeback, except for a light, wheaten coat color much like that of the Mastiff or the fawn-colored Great Dane. He has exceptionally good scenting powers, but no other Bloodhound characteristics. His head slightly resembles the Greyhound's. But although classified as a hound, the Ridgeback appears to have less hound blood in him than any other dog in the group. He achieved his present form sometime prior to 1877, when he was first seen by European visitors. He ranges from 24 to 27 inches at the shoulder and weighs 65 to 75 pounds. ∎ He was a strong and fearless hunter, and was known as the Lion Dog for his willingness to engage the big cats. He was, of course, no match, but working in a pack he could chivy a lion out into the open under the sights of his master's rifle. It was this skill that interested visitors most, although the Rhodesian had many other talents and never had been intended as a hunting dog exclusively. He was the all-around farm dog of the African veldt. He herded livestock and poultry, served as a guard dog, and even flushed a few pheasant on occasion. ∎ He was not registered in the United States until 1950 and has grown in popularity at a surprisingly fast rate since. He is a clean dog and an even-tempered one, eager to please his master and a good companion.

BASENJI

Of all the world's hundreds of breeds, the little Basenji from Africa is the only dog that cannot bark. He is not mute; in a happy mood he can produce a sound somewhere on the scale between a chortle and a yodel. But he is barkless. ▪ The Basenji is a scent hound, with a nose so keen he can pick up a trail at eighty yards. This talent, plus his silence and light-footed, high-stepping gait, made him especially valuable in the Congo jungle, where he seems to have originated and where stealth in stalking is prized. The Basenji's performance is, in fact, so quiet that his native masters often tied around his neck a small gourd containing a few pebbles, so that the rattle would enable them to keep track of the tracker. ▪ The Basenji was known in antiquity. There are no written records, but early Egyptian tombs, such as those that have preserved evidence of the Saluki's existence, have bas-reliefs of dogs that are indisputably Basenjis. They show the gourd, or a bell, hanging from his collar, and even more precisely they show three notable Basenji characteristics: a wrinkled brow, erect ears, and a sporty, tightly curled tail carried over the back. European explorers first encountered the dog in Central Africa in 1895, but the breed did not take hold in England until 1936, in the United States until 1941. There are now more than 1,200 specimens registered. ▪ The Basenji is built more like a terrier than a hound. That is, he is almost square: His height at the shoulder is the same as his length from the chest to the root of the tail. A male Basenji stands about 17 inches, a female an inch less. He weighs 22 to 24 pounds. His coat is short and lustrous, and may be chestnut red, pure black, or black and tan. Feet and chest usually are white—like the tail tip. ▪ The Basenji is a highly intelligent and trainable dog. As a hunter he can point and retrieve birds or small game. He is also sprightly and playful, and makes a fine family companion. A fastidious dog, the Basenji cleans himself like a cat and has no doggy odor. He is an excellent pet for city dwellers.

DACHSHUND

This is the most popular dog in the Hound Group and one of the half dozen most popular purebreds in the world. He has charm, humor, a strong sense of loyalty, and a marvelous shape which has led to his being described as "a dog and a half long, and a half a dog high." ∎ He originated in Germany. There is no concrete evidence of the crossings that went into his development, although his low stature, outturned feet, and keen nose would seem to suggest a common ancestry with the Basset Hound. No other hound goes to earth, however, which would indicate that somewhere along the line the Dachshund received a strong infusion of terrier. ∎ His name means "badger dog" and it appears that there were many dogs that fulfilled the function without meeting the description as early as the Middle Ages. By the early seventeenth century the name definitely designated the both smooth- and long-haired Dachshund varieties known today. A Standard for the breed was written in 1879. The wire-haired variety has been recognized since 1890. There also are miniature sizes in each coat variety. Standard-sized specimens range from 7 to 10 inches at the shoulder and weigh from 12 to 22 pounds. Miniatures are measured by chest girth and should not exceed 13.8 inches in circum-

*Opposite: Increasingly
popular long-haired Dachs crouches
next to standard smooth-hair.
At left are wrinkle-browed
pups. Below is basic,
dog-and-a-half Dachshund.*

ference. The weight range is 7.7 to 8.8 pounds. ▪ The dogs that fought badgers were considerably larger than the Dachshunds we know today. They ran 30 or 35 pounds, as was necessary if they were to meet the 45-pound badger on even terms. The Dachshund entered the badger's lair. His low-slung body eased his way through the narrow tunnel. His feet are built for digging, for widening the passageway. And although his chest is deep and muscular, his body tapers to narrow flanks which enable him to push earth behind him as he tunnels. A terrific battle often took place deep in the badger's burrow and the little hound was necessarily

a fellow of high courage. Dachshunds in the 16- to 22-pound range were used against foxes and wounded deer. Twelve-pounders were used to start the hare and ermine. ▪ The Dachshund has an extrovert personality. Within the family circle he is a tireless comedian who loves to play tricks such as hiding personal articles. He watches the fruitless search for a short while, then runs off and returns with it in triumph. ▪ He is a hardy and vigorous dog. His dark, short coat is sleek and odorless, comes in tan, and black and tan. No longer a hunter, he is still a lively pet and a faithful watchdog with keen interest in all that goes on around him.

GREYHOUND

"A greyhounde shulde be heded like a Snake and necked like a Drake. Foted like a Kat. Tayled like a Rat." So says *The Boke of St. Albans,* fancifully but not inaccurately, of the appearance of the Greyhound in 1496. The *Boke* is an English sporting classic, but even in its own time it was not news. The Greyhound had been the hunting companion of Saxon chieftains in the ninth century. His skill in coursing had been keenly observed by the Greek poet Ovid in the first century. And his picture had appeared on Egyptian tombs 3,000 years before that. ▪ There is great confusion about the breed's name. What does "Grey" mean? Great? The Greyhound always was a dog of the nobility, the great people. Grech or greg? These were old English words for dog. Gaze or graze? Because he is a sight hound. Or does it, after all, simply mean the color, because so many Greyhounds are grey? ▪ He is a hunter no more. Once it was the pleasure of kings to watch him run down a hare after Pointers or spaniels had

started it. Now his coursing is confined to race tracks, where he chases—but never catches—"Rusty," the electric rabbit, as the $2 betters roar. In England, coursing has been formalized into competition for the famous Waterloo Cup, an event that has been run since 1836. ▪ Racing Greyhounds are specialists and seldom well-known outside their field. But many other Greyhounds are kept solely for show-ring competition. They are more beautiful in repose than the racing dog, although not likely to be able to keep up with him in the pursuit of "Rusty." Both dogs are smooth-coated, well-knit bundles of muscle with hardly an ounce of excess weight. A wire-haired variety has long been known in Russia, and a silky-haired type in Turkey, Iran, and Egypt. ▪ The Greyhound is a tall dog, ranging from 26 to 30 inches in height at the shoulder and weighing 60 to 70 pounds. He can cover nearly 18 feet per running stride. ▪ He is rarely kept as a house pet, although he has a gracious and even disposition.

WHIPPET

In the factory towns of England, the Whippet is called "the poor man's race horse," and many a quid has changed hands on the outcome of a race among these little speedsters. Over the standard course of 200 yards, the Whippet has attained a speed of thirty-five miles per hour, making him swiftest of all domestic animals for his weight. ▪ Unlike the Greyhound, whose history goes far back into ancient times, the Whippet was not developed until the 1830's, when bullbaiting and pit-fighting by dogs finally were banned by Parliament. Although both of these gory sports continued in a clandestine manner for some years, the workingmen who wanted action on their days off looked for a substitute that would keep them within the law. The Greyhound had long been known as a racer, but events such as the famous Waterloo Cup coursing meet were too costly and required too much space. So the astute dog breeders of the day crossed smaller specimens of the Greyhound with various terriers and produced a dog that could be used on a restricted course. ▪ The Whippet was introduced to the United States late in the nineteenth century by English workers in the New England textile mills. It was here, too, around Lowell and Lawrence, that American Whippet racing began. The sport is fairly widespread today, but on an amateur basis. ▪ Today's Whippet is essentially a small Greyhound. There is very little terrier left in him, although there may be some Italian Greyhound. He stands 18 to 22 inches at the shoulder, and ranges in weight from 10 to 28 pounds. He has the Greyhound's smooth coat; any color is permissible. ▪ In the past, he was known as a superior ratter and rabbit courser. Today he is a racer, a show dog, or a pet. He has a charming and affectionate nature. He is dignified, intelligent, and a good watch dog, although without the barkiness of a terrier. He is easy to care for, easy to groom, and easy to handle. Many novice handlers have been successful with him in the show ring.

AFGHAN HOUND

The Afghan is a patrician. He is stylish, exotic, a valiant hunter, and a breed of great antiquity. The hunting guides of his native Afghanistan call him "the dog of Noah's ark" and, indeed, he is pictured on Egyptian tombs dating as far back as 4000 B.C. Only the Saluki and the Norwegian Elkhound appear to be any older than this. The Afghan was unknown to the western world, however, until after World War I, when British army officers brought specimens with them on their return to England. The United States did not become acquainted with the breed until the mid-1920's. ▪ Throughout his long history, the Afghan has been a bold and skillful hunter of the leopard and a swift courser of the gazelle. He is a sight hound, who locates his quarry with extraordinarily keen eyes, rather than a keen nose. This gives him a piercing "look of eagles," as if he were searching a distant horizon for the flash of movement to betray the presence of his quarry. He also is extremely agile. He can leap to a height of ten feet, and in the mountains of Afghanistan he has been seen to spring fearlessly across a chasm and land surefootedly on a narrow ledge. He can negotiate a cross-country course with relative ease, bounding over obstacles, up hills, and across uneven terrain. In this he is aided by his uniquely constructed hipbones, which are set higher and wider apart than in any other breed. ▪ The Afghan's appearance is marked by several distinctive features: his "monkey face," his thick, silky coat, and his curved tail. "Monkey Face," a nickname several thousand years old, is found on many an Egyptian papyrus. It refers to the long muzzle which somewhat resembles that of the baboon. The coat is of a very fine texture; the long ears and all four legs are thickly feathered. And the dog sports a topknot. The thin, comparatively hairless tail curves over the back, almost in a circle. The dog is shown "as is," without trimming or cutting to any particular pattern. All coat colors are permissible, although white markings, particularly on the head, are undesirable. ▪ Afghans are sizable dogs. Their shoulder height ranges from 25 to 27 inches. They weigh from 50 to 60 pounds. Temperamentally, they may at first be aloof, but they are gay and amusing companions after they have gotten to know their friends well.

SALUKI

This beautiful sight hound shares with the Norwegian Elkhound the distinction of being the oldest of all the breeds we know today. Egyptian tombs dating back as far as 4000 or 5000 B.C. bear pictures of Salukis that show them to be virtually unchanged from that time to this. Some people claim even greater antiquity for the breed on the basis of some carved Sumerian dog figures of 6000 to 7000 B.C. which resemble Salukis. ▪ The purity of the Saluki's breeding has been preserved through the centuries by the Arab sheiks of the Middle East whose treasured companion he has been. He is, in fact, so highly prized that no Saluki is ever sold. He may only be exchanged, or given as a gift of great value. The Saluki is the only dog permitted to sleep in the tent of the sheik. From Egypt to Iran, he is known as the "noble one," *el Hor.* ▪ The Saluki is traditionally a hunter of the gazelle. He undergoes an intensive two-year training, for he must be taught to co-operate with his partner, a falcon. The raptor is released first and sweeps the sky until it locates a gazelle. It then circles the quarry, which is a signal to the hunter to release his dogs. The Salukis take their direction from the hawk until they can see the gazelle for themselves. They course the animal until the hunter is able to complete the kill. They also are swift and agile enough to course hares. ▪ It is said that the first Salukis were brought to Europe by the Crusaders, which, of course, is entirely possible, but the first definite record of one is in England in 1840. For some years the breed was merely a curiosity. A kennel was established in 1895, however, and soon thereafter specimens began competing at the dog shows. The American Kennel Club recognized the breed in 1927. ▪ Salukis range in height from 23 to 28 inches at the shoulder and weigh from 50 to 60 pounds. Almost any color is permissible; white, cream, fawn, red, tricolor, black and tan are common for the breed. Soft feathering hairs are found on his long ears, curved tail, and muscular legs. He also has hairs between his toes, which help him when running on desert sand or over rough terrain. The feathered Saluki is the "shami" variety. There is also a smooth-coated dog—the "nejdi"—which is sometimes confused with the Greyhound. Salukis have a bright, brisk temperament and are good companions.

Afghans (above) are extraordinarily
agile dogs. They have keen sight, distinctive
head with topknot, silky coat.
Salukis (below) are perhaps most ancient
canine breed on earth. They are
swift enough to overtake gazelle.

OTTERHOUND

Everyone has tried to determine the Otterhound's lineage; no two experts agree. His domed skull, his long, leathered ears, and his keen nose suggest the Bloodhound. His webbed feet and love of water should seem to trace to some variety of water spaniel. But many fanciers feel he is more like his descendant, the Airedale Terrier, except larger. Trim the Otterhound or let the Airedale grow shaggy and they would be look alikes. In nature, too, they are similar. Both are lively and aggressive hunting dogs, and both are close to—and protective of—their human families. They are great playmates for children. ▪ Perhaps there is something of all of these dogs in him—and of the old French Vendee Hound, as well. A classic fourteenth-century description of the Otterhound makes him sound like a brother of the Vendee. ▪ Otter hunting is virtually unheard of in the United States. The creature itself is relatively rare, and in any case would be rather more likely to be trapped than pursued for sport. In England, however, the sport was known for centuries. It was not wildly popular, but it seems to have been the only hunting available between April and September. It was conducted with packs of Otterhounds, whose thick outer coat and oily undercoat made them able to withstand any amount of cold water encountered. ▪ King Henry II (1133-1189) was a Master of Otterhounds, although only a record of the title, not the dog, survives. (About the earliest description is the one linking him with the Vendee Hound.) Otter hunting also was in vogue in the last half of the nineteenth century, when some twenty packs were in action and hundreds of otters were killed. The first Otterhounds in the United States arrived about 1900, but the breed has been slow to catch on and is still among the least known. ▪ The Otterhound is large, standing 24 to 26 inches at the withers and weighing up to 65 pounds. His unruly coat is generally grizzle or sandy, but often has the black-and-tan pattern of the Airedale. Show specimens are exhibited with a full coat; it occasionally has been suggested that the breed might benefit from the introduction of an attractive pattern of trimming. Otterhounds have a loud and heavy bay, suitable to their impressive size.

BORZOI

BORZOI

The elegant and graceful Borzoi, formerly known in the United States as the Russian Wolfhound, is a dog of great courage, great power, and great speed. He was bred in the early seventeenth century at the kennels of a Russian duke who evidently crossed imported Arabian Greyhounds with a heavy-coated sheep dog. The Arabians, used to coursing the gazelle in desert country, had proved unable to survive the deep cold of the Russian winters, but the native shepherd dog, which rather resembled a long-legged Collie, gave them a warm coat. By selective breeding the dog was refined. In time it became known throughout Russia as an outstanding wolf hunter. Borzois hunted in pairs. When a wolf was sighted, the mounted handler would slip both dogs at once. They would bracket the wolf and attack simultaneously. ▪ Further experiments with the type very nearly ruined the breed entirely. Greater speed was achieved in some cases, but at the expense of fundamental strength and of the dog's majestic appearance. By the late nineteenth century, the type had generally been lost except at the Perchina Kennels of the Grand Duke Nicholas and the Woronzova Kennels of one Artem Balderoff. Both kennels were located far from the centers where the breed was deteriorating. Both raised a pure strain. ▪ In 1903, an American sportsman, the late Joseph B. Thomas, went to Russia and was able to bring home specimens from both kennels. For twenty-five years afterward, his Valley Farm Kennels were a prime source of the breed in the United States, and show dogs from Thomas strains are still winning blue ribbons. ▪ Today the Borzoi occasionally is used in the western states against coyote, and he courses hare for sport, although not so well as the faster Greyhound. His principal role is as a show dog and as a companion, particularly on country estates where there is room for him to stretch his legs. ▪ The male Borzoi usually stands 28 to 31 inches at the withers and weighs 75 to 105 pounds. Females are about two inches shorter, 15 to 20 pounds lighter. The coat is long, silky, and rather curly. White is the predominant color, although there may be markings of lemon, tan, gray, black, or brindle.

6 WORKING DOGS

Strength, intelligence, and devotion characterize the Working dogs. From time immemorial, they have been the guardians of men's flocks and herds, rounding up strays with tireless skill or charging into combat with the marauding wolf or bear. As drovers they have led livestock to market. They have pulled carts and sleds, fetched and carried, served with valor as sentries, messengers, and dogs of war. Yet perhaps most remarkable of all is the vast number of people whose lives they have preserved. For centuries the good sense and good will of Working dogs have saved men, women, and children from Alpine avalanches, deep water, bullet-swept battlefields, burning houses, and other dangers and catastrophes. From their ranks are chosen the guide dogs for the blind. They are faithful servants all.

COLLIE

The Collie came to prominence in the early 1860's when Queen Victoria, making her first visit to Balmoral, Scotland, took an instant liking to him. She expressed her pleasure publicly, and Collie has been a prime favorite ever since. It was a Rough Collie that the Queen saw—the Highland shepherd's hard-working companion, the "Scot's Colley Dog." The Smooth Collie, the drover's dog of Northumberland, has never enjoyed the same popularity. ■ The origin of the Collie simply is not known. Although sheep dogs have been known for centuries, the Collie in his present form cannot be traced back farther than the late eighteenth century. Collie historians believe sheep dogs accompanied the Romans when they invaded Britain and bred with local dogs, but that a definite type probably did not evolve until sheep and cattle growing became important in the sixteenth century. ■ The Highland "Colley Dog" grew a long and luxuriant coat to protect himself from the harsh weather, and was mostly black in color. From the color he may have taken his name, for "colley" meant "black" in Anglo-Saxon and was also the name of the black-legged sheep he guarded. (Other early de-

scriptions call them "coally dogs.") The Smooth Collie is to all intents and purposes the same dog, except for the short, close-lying coat. The two varieties undoubtedly had common ancestors, and even today a Smooth Collie is obtained by breeding Rough to Smooth. Notable woodcuts of the two breeds were made in 1800 by Thomas Bewick (pronounced "Buick," like the car), the famous English artist of sporting subjects. The early shepherd's dog had a shorter muzzle and a broader head than contemporary specimens. This seems to have been the kind of Collie the colonists brought to America and the ancestor of the short-nosed "farm Collie" of today. This also was a smaller dog over-all. He measured 14 inches at the withers, as compared with today's Collie, which ranges between 22 and 26 inches. It is often said that the Collie achieved his large size and long, slim muzzle from crosses with Gordon Setters and the Newfoundland, but most experts discount this. Whatever Collie characteristics have been changed or refined have been achieved by selective breeding. ■ The "Scotch Sheep Dog" first appeared as a show class at the Birmingham Dog Society exhibition in 1860. The Queen's approbation followed in a few years. And by the 1870's, he was one of the important dogs. Breeders already were lengthening the muzzle and the head and achieving a better shape and placement of the eye. By 1875, a prize Collie had sold in England for £1,500, or about $7,500. In 1878, America saw its first exhibition Collies—a royal pair of Victoria's—at the Westminster show. The elder J. P. Morgan was among the early fanciers of the Collie. Albert Payson Terhune, of course, gave the breed a tremendous boost in the 1920's with his well-loved stories of Wolf and Lad and the other Sunnybank Collies. More recently, there have been attractive Collie stars of movies and television. ■ The Rough Collie's crowning glory is his coat, which should be abundant everywhere but on head and legs. The outer coat must be harsh, the undercoat furry. There are four colors: tricolor, which is black, tan, and white; sable and white, the sable ranging from light gold to deep mahogany; blue merle, a "marbled" blue-gray and black with white markings; and white—predominantly so, but with sable or tricolor markings. He is a handsome and delightful pet.

SMOOTH COLLIE (BELOW) AND ROUGH COLLIE.

SHETLAND SHEEPDOG

It is often thought that the Shetland Sheepdog is a miniaturized Collie—that by assiduous effort the breeders have managed to shrink the 26-inch Collie to a 13- to 16-inch Sheltie. Not so. The Sheltie always has been small, like the ponies, sheep, and cattle of his native Shetland Islands in the windswept sea north of Scotland. It is the Collie that has been enlarged. At the beginning of the nineteenth century, he was about the size of the Shetland today. ▪ Both breeds probably had a common ancestor, perhaps an earlier type of Collie, perhaps the Border Collie. Actually, there is no record of the Sheltie's origin. There are many theories as to how he got to the islands and what happened after he did. It has been proposed that he evolved from crosses of Collie-type island dogs with various fishermen's dogs from Scandinavia, Holland, Greenland, and Scotland, all of whose fishing fleets put into the islands in the summer. Perhaps, but the strongest influences visible today would seem to be Rough Collie for conformation and spaniel for disposition. ▪ The Sheltie is an extremely fine working dog. He is a swift and graceful runner (his beautiful gait has no waste motion and is worth five points on the judging scale), an agile leaper of obstacles, and a clever manipulator of his little Shetland sheep. He is rarely given much opportunity to work sheep in the United States, although on occasion he has been tried in Montana, Colorado, Idaho, and other sheep-raising states and found to be completely competent. Generally, however, he is much more actively engaged as a show dog. Recognition of the breed came late. The Kennel Club (England) did not classify it separately until 1910, and not until 1914 was it designated as the Shetland Sheepdog, rather than the Shetland Collie. The dog was introduced to the United States in 1911. ▪ The Sheltie weighs about 20 pounds. He has a heavy, Collie-type double coat, harsh on top and soft, furry, and dense underneath. The mane and the frill on the chest should be particularly abundant. His colors are black, blue merle, and sable, with varying amounts of white and/or tan. He is a bright, intelligent dog, easy to teach and quick to learn. He is a docile, sweet-natured dog and an affectionate family pet.

OLD ENGLISH SHEEPDOG

This is the shaggiest dog around. The Komondor and the Puli are pretty good, too, but the Old English Sheepdog is by all accounts even less kempt than they are. The coat is profuse, but must have quality and texture as well. The outer hairs should be long, straight, and of a hard texture. The undercoat should be soft, waterproof pile. Face and forehead hair should cover the eyes. The color should be gray, grizzle (a bluish gray), blue, or blue merle. Usually there are white markings. ▪ To keep the dog in show condition, the coat cannot be permitted to mat and must be brushed daily and combed several times a week. Even the house pet needs fairly constant attention—say, fifteen minutes of brushing a day. Particularly enthusiastic owners save the combings from their dog's coat, spin it into yarn, and make warm, durable gloves, jackets, or whatever. ▪ The Old English is not very old. His known history goes back only to 1835, and a portrait by Gainsborough purporting to furnish evidence of an earlier origin has been disputed. The painting, done in 1771, shows the Duke of Buccleuch with an arm around a dog that looks very much like an Old English Sheepdog, although a number of authorities contend that he is merely an untrimmed terrier. It is just barely possible, considering that Gainsborough painted the dog somewhat smaller than a contemporary Old English would be. ▪ There is no dispute about a painting done in 1835 by Sidney Cooper; *that* is an Old English without doubt. On the other hand, it has been pointed out that if the breed did not exist when Gainsborough was portraying the Duke, the first quarter of the nineteenth century was a strange time to start creating him. For by 1829 the steam locomotive had arrived, and within a few years there was no need for drovers' dogs to move the flocks and herds to market. Some say the Old English is a descendant of the Bearded Collie of Scotland. Others say the Russian Owtschar. Either could be true. When his great coat is clipped to the skin, he has the square build of an Airedale—his height at shoulder is the same as his length from shoulder to tail. That is, 22 or more inches. His tail customarily is docked, which results in the nickname "Bobtail."

PULI

The Puli, meaning "driver," has been a sheepherder in Hungary for ten centuries. He is one of several varieties of sheep dogs the Magyars brought with them to Europe from Asia (see also Komondor, page 125, and Kuvasz, page 137), and is believed to be descended from the Tibetan Terrier. ▪ The outstanding feature of the Puli is his coat. He has a dense, woolly undercoat and a long, profuse outer coat. In the adult dog the two layers tangle to form long cords and to contribute to a matted, unkempt appearance, somewhat like the Komondor's. Black—an unusual dull, rusty black—is the Puli's standard color, although gray or white also are permitted as long as the color is solid. Black always has been favored by the shepherds because it is easier to see a dark dog against white sheep, especially when he is in action keeping the flock on the move. ▪ The Puli —plural: Pulik—seems to come by his sheepherding skills naturally. In Hungary they grow up in proximity to the herds. The pups see the old dogs working the sheep and, as a consequence, seem never to need training or instruction by the shepherd. It is curious, too, that Pulik raised in kennels, far from their customary environment, have proved to be able herd dogs when put to work around livestock. ▪ The dog handles sheep in a confident manner. He seems to know what he is doing at all times, but particularly when one sheep tries to bolt the flock. Sometimes, when his way is blocked by the massed bodies of the sheep, he will race over their backs to get to the point where the disturbance is. ▪ The Puli was brought to the United States in the 1930's, about the same time as the Komondor and the Kuvasz, under the sponsorship of the Department of Agriculture. It was hoped that he might be of use to the woolgrowers, but by far the greater proportion of Pulik are show dogs or family pets. ▪ The Puli is a medium-sized dog, running 16 to 19 inches high at the withers and weighing about 30 pounds. He moves with a springy, bouncy gait, and is alert and easily trained. He is a devoted home dog with an affectionate nature, but on his guard with strangers. Since he is a highly active dog, it is advisable to give him space in which to run. The Standard for the breed was accepted by the A.K.C. in 1936, but he is still among the rarer breeds as far as registrations are concerned.

BOXER

The Boxer is a German dog with relatives in many parts of Europe. In type he is very much like the English Bulldog of the mid-nineteenth century. In size he is like the staghounds on sixteenth- and seventeenth-century Flemish tapestries. In fearlessness he resembles the ancient boarhounds. Probably the Mastiff is his progenitor. Probably the Great Dane and an undetermined terrier were the cross that produced the dog known everywhere—and so favorably—today. ■ The Boxer has a square build, stands 21 to 24 inches high at the shoulder, and is the same distance from the front of the chest to the rearmost point of the upper thigh. He has a short muzzle, an undershot jaw, and a terrier body, although with greater substance than any terrier. He is powerfully muscled and gives an impression of tremendous energy, strength, and stamina. The Boxer coat is short and smooth; the Standard describes it as "tight fitting." Two colors are permitted: fawn and brindle. Fawn ranges from light yellow to dark "deer red." Brindle must have clearly defined black stripes on the fawn background. White markings are permitted. A black mask is an absolute must, and the weight should range between 60 and 70 pounds. ■ The Boxer was first registered in the United States in 1904 and won his first championship in 1915. The champion was a dog owned by the late Governor Herbert H. Lehman of New York, one of the early partisans of the breed. Nonetheless, for nearly twenty years the Boxer attracted little interest or attention. Then an outstanding specimen, Ch. Check von Hunnenstein, a German import, won Best-in-Show at one of the largest exhibitions in the East, and suddenly the Boxer was in business. Fortunately, a sufficient number of good specimens of the leading German strains had been imported before World War II cut off traffic with Europe, for during the 1940's the Boxer not only took a prominent place at shows, but became tremendously popular with the pet-owning public. As frequently happens, however, "puppy factories" met the demand for Boxers with many animals of poor quality and, worse, with bad dispositions. Interest slacked off, although the breed has managed to remain high on the A.K.C. registration list. ■ A good Boxer is an affectionate dog with a great love for people. Pups are very spirited. Adult dogs become more sedate.

STANDARD & GIANT SCHNAUZER

The Standard Schnauzer is an ancient breed, probably well-established and well known even before Albrecht Dürer placed him in a painting in 1492. He had his origin in either Bavaria or Württemberg, regions devoted to farming and livestock in southern Germany, and was both a cattle drover and a ratter. He also was a watch dog; a statue at Stuttgart dated 1620 shows a night watchman making his rounds with a Schnauzer. He is the result of crosses among the black German Poodle, the gray Wolf-Spitz dog, and a wire-haired Pinscher, or terrier. The Poodle gave him his soft undercoat, the other two his harsh, wiry outer coat and his pepper-and-salt color. The hair on his muzzle and lower jaw gave rise to his name—Schnauzer—which means "bearded." He ranges in height from 17 to 20 inches and has the square terrier build. Some of the early imports from Germany were quite "sharp," and better suited for guard-dog duty than for the home. Specimens bred in the United States have a gentler nature, although basically the Standard Schnauzer is a one-family dog and cool to strangers. ■ Close kin to the Standard breed is the Miniature Schnauzer, which,

STANDARD SCHNAUZER (LEFT) AND GIANT SCHNAUZER.

however, is classified as a Terrier in the United States and will be found among this group on page 161. ▪ The Giant Schnauzer—*Riesenschnauzer* in Germany—has the same South German background as the other Schnauzers, but is the result of many more combinations. It is believed that the medium-sized Schnauzer caught the eye of Bavarian cattlemen some hundreds of years ago and that he was bred to some of the big, smooth-coated drover dogs of the area to increase his size. Great Danes also were introduced, and when these crosses altered the Schnauzer coat texture, rough-haired shepherd dogs were added to the mix to restore the wiry quality. It may well be that the Bouvier des Flandres was crossed into the line at some point. When dogs were no longer needed for cattle driving, the Giant Schnauzer became a guard dog at Munich breweries and stockyards and was for many years known as the Münchener Dog. He was virtually unknown outside Bavaria until World War I and has always been something of a rarity in the United States. He stands 21½ to 25½ inches at the shoulder and is an intensely loyal one-man or one-family dog.

GERMAN SHEPHERD DOG

The German Shepherd must be ranked among the three or four most intelligent purebred dogs in the world. (The Poodle would also have to be included, and one or two others whose selection must be left to the impartial judgment of dog fanciers everywhere.) As everyone knows, he has a remarkable record as the principal guide dog for blind persons. He is, after experience in two world wars, the only breed accepted for military service by the U.S. Armed Forces, and he has performed outstandingly in obedience competition. ■ The German Shepherd began to assume his present form toward the end of the nineteenth century. Like many other breeds, he has ancestors that go back thousands of years. Probably some of the first dogs that tended flocks could be fitted into his family tree. But breeders today are inclined to discount his early inheritance, other than to acknowledge that it gave him the beginnings of his formidable intelligence. Breeds that are supposed to have contributed features of today's dog are a Thuringian shepherd dog (wolf-gray coloration and erect ears), a Swabian working dog (size and gait), and a Württemberg dog (tail carriage). In any event, the contemporary German Shepherd is a medium-sized dog standing 27 inches at the shoulder and weighing 75 to 85 pounds. (The female is two inches and fifteen pounds less.) The back measures slightly longer than the shoulder height, which enhances the dog's matchless trotting gait. Shepherd colors range from light gray to jet black; also brindle, iron gray, black and tan, and gray with sable markings. ■ The breed first came to the United States about 1909, but did not become really popular until after World War I, when doughboys brought specimens home from Europe. The most famous of these dogs was the pup born in a German trench near Metz, which became the silent-movie star, Rin-Tin-Tin. By 1926 more than a third of all dogs registered with A.K.C. were German Shepherds. Enthusiasm for the breed was quickly dampened, however, when unscrupulous suppliers poured inferior animals into the market and a number of biting and mauling incidents occurred. ■ Careful breeding for the most desirable qualities have now brought the German Shepherd back to prominence. They are fine companion dogs, but prefer to have an active job to do.

BELGIAN SHEEPDOG

Europe always has had a large variety of shepherd dogs. *Chien de Berger*—farmer's dog—was the loose term that covered them all, regardless of size, color, or type. The confusion among them, of course, arose from the fact that few sheepherders cared what their dogs looked like as long as they did their job, and also from local pride in perpetuating a superior dog that happened to emerge from the random inbreeding of the village pack. In Belgium toward the end of the nineteenth century this meant there were seven different local varieties of sheep dog. The breed now known in the United States as the Belgian Sheepdog is one of these seven, specifically the Groenendael, which is named for the village where it developed about 1885. The dog is largely the work of a Monsieur Rose, who was interested in the long-haired, black shepherd variety and in 1885 finally got a black pair to mate. The resulting Groenendael is a solid black dog; his coat is long and straight haired. The male stands 24 to 26 inches at the withers, the female 22 to 24. The Standard of Perfection emphasizes that the bone structure should be moderately heavy in proportion to the height of the animal, but the general impression is nevertheless one of solidity without bulkiness, one even of delicacy. This is a stylish dog that moves with great spirit. There is pride in his carriage, alertness, vigor, strength. ■ He also is a highly intelligent dog and easy to train. Many American exhibitors have made it a point to enter their Belgian Sheepdogs in obedience competitions, and a number of dogs have won these trials as well as conformation championships. He is an eager and reliable worker, both as the guardian of his flocks and as a watchdog protecting the person and property of his master. In Europe, he was extensively used as a sentry dog and messenger during World War I. ■ The breed first came to the United States in 1907. Later imports proved successful in police work, and between the two world wars the breed became well-established. Actually, until 1959 all varieties of Belgian Sheepdog could be registered with the A.K.C. under that name. Subsequent to that date, however, only the Groenendael has been eligible for the designation. ■ Like the German Shepherd, the Belgian Sheepdog is companionable, but prefers to work.

Similarity of coat, conformation, and expression can be seen in these pictures of Groenendael (opposite) and Tervuren (left). Until 1959, two varieties were classed together.

BELGIAN TERVUREN & MALINOIS

These are two of the seven Belgian sheep-dog varieties, which now are registered under their own regional names. Tervuren is a village, Malines a town near Brussels. The Tervuren dog is virtually the same as the Groenendael, except for color. His coat runs from "rich fawn to russet mahogany" and with each hair having a black tip. This gives a curious sooty effect that is quite attractive. The black is especially heavy on the shoulders, back, and ribs; there is a black mask across the face and black ears. The hair is long and straight. ■ The Tervuren was developed about the same time as the Groenendael and in large part by the efforts of a single breeder. This was Monsieur Danhieux, who bred a female with a black-tipped fawn coat to one of the sires of the Groenendael to establish the beginning of the Tervuren line. The first Tervurens in the United States arrived in the early 1940's, the first registered dog in 1954. They are still quite rare, although out of the first litter whelped in America came both a champion and the winner of an obedience degree. ■ The longest name attached to any purebred dog is *Chien de Berger Belge Malinoix à poil court fauve charbonné*, or Belgian farmer's dog from Malines with a short, tawny, charcoal coat. All of which he is. He has the coloration of the Tervuren, but a conformation closer to that of the German Shepherd than to his Belgian brothers, and is consequently often confused with the Shepherd. Some contend that the Malinois has at least one crossing with the German Shepherd in his background, which is quite possible although not a certainty. ■ The Malinois is a superb sheep dog—swift, agile, tireless, and with both aptitude for and devotion to his job. Like other sheep dogs he is intelligent and teachable. He scores well in obedience trials and has been used successfully for guard work. ■ Originally he competed in shows with the Groenendael, but registrations have been so few that since 1959 he has been permitted to enter only the Miscellaneous class. (Here a dog may win first- to fourth-place ribbons, but not championship points.) ■ The Tervuren and Malinois stand 24 to 26 inches at the shoulder (22 to 24 for females), like the Groenendael, and their Standards are also couched in similar language. Those who have had experience with them say they are fine companion dogs.

BRIARD

The Briard is a French shepherd dog of great antiquity. His name derives from the department of Brie, whence also comes fine cheese, and twelfth-century documents refer to Sheep Dogs of Brie, or *Bergers de Brie*, bred by Charlemagne in the ninth. His principal duty was to guard the flocks from wolves, and when the European wolf was no longer a menace, he learned the techniques of herding and became a watchdog on farms and estates. ▪ In size, conformation, and coat, the Briard resembles the Old English Sheepdog, the Russian Owtschar, the Bearded Collie, and the three shepherd dogs of Hungary—the Komondor, Kuvasz, and Puli. A shaggy adult Puli looks almost exactly like a Briard puppy, and they have been mistaken for each other on the few occasions when these quite rare breeds have met. The most notable features of the Briard are his heavy coat and bushy eyebrows. His hard, stiff, wavy hairs often are called a "goat's coat." They shed water quickly. The eyebrows are a protection when the Briard must plunge through dense underbrush in search of a sheep, but the Standard notes that the hair of the head should not be so profuse as to prevent the dog from seeing well. In France the ears are cropped and stand erect; American-born dogs, which may not be cropped, present a different profile. There are two color classes— black and colored, which includes various shades of gray, tawny, and a combination of the two (as long as the dog does not appear to be spotted). While not a giant, the Briard is a sturdy and powerful dog standing 22 to 27 inches at the withers and weighing proportionately. He is built squarely; it is said that a Kerry Blue whose coat is shaggy and unclipped looks like a small Briard. ▪ The Briard's virtues are many. He is a somewhat slow learner, but anything learned is retained forever. He has a phenomenally acute sense of hearing. He is quiet, even stolid for anyone who is used to terriers, and has a kindly disposition and a strong sense of loyalty to his family. He is still a relatively rare dog in the United States; most Briards are show specimens. He has an unusually deep bark.

BOUVIER DES FLANDRES

This is the cattle-driving dog of Flanders. He is a big fellow with a rough coat and a rough appearance. He stands up to 27½ inches at the shoulder (22¾ inches is maximum for females) and has a thick body of considerable muscular power. His coat is tousled and unkempt. It is double thick, the undercoat fine and soft, the guard hairs rough, wiry, and so densely interwoven that it is almost impossible to see the dog's skin when the hair is parted. His color may range from fawn to black, including a variety of grays, pepper and salt, and brindle. A white star on the chest is permissible. ■ Bouvier means "cowherd" and that has been the dog's function. Like most of the working dogs of the farming and livestock-raising areas of Europe, he was bred first for performance and incidentally, if at all, for looks or uniformity of type. In the vicinity of the Franco-Belgian border that was his home grounds, he was known by a variety of names—*Vuilbaard, chien de vacher, toucheur de boeuf,* or dirty beard, cowherd's dog, cattle driver. His background is uncertain. Again, like other dogs of his time and place, he is probably a combination of various regional types. ■ The first acknowledgement of the breed by a dog-fanciers' association occurred in 1910 at an international show at Brussels. A Standard of Perfection was written and adopted in 1912. World War I, however, nearly destroyed the breed. Flanders was devastated. People were forced to flee. Dogs were lost, abandoned, or killed. Fortunately, a few first-rate dogs did manage to survive, and on these the Bouviers of the future were founded. The breed made its first appearance in the United States in the 1930's, but did not attract much attention until the late 1950's when a specimen was imported that was so outstanding it scored immediate triumphs in the variety-group competition at A.K.C. shows. Since then there has been strong and increasing interest in the breed. ■ The Bouvier is a highly adaptable dog and has managed, despite his size, to live comfortably in city apartments. He is a worker, however, and should have running room.

SAMOYED

This beautiful dog was found among—and named after —a small and exotic tribe of nomads called the Samoyed, which lives in northern Siberia, above the Arctic Circle. Legend says that he is one of the ancient dogs of the world, but there are no written records, nor has anyone discovered skeletal remains under the ice and snow. Only the tribal folklore, passed on from generation to generation, testifies to the breed's antiquity. ■ He came to the attention of the outside world when Arctic explorers of the late nineteenth century, who used them as sledge dogs, returned from their expeditions. Dog fanciers immediately were taken by the Samoyed's handsome appearance and sweet expression, and impressed by his hardiness and strength. As a draft dog he can pull one and a half times his own weight, which runs from 35 to 65 pounds, and averages 45. ■ The Samoyed stands 21 to 23½ inches high at the withers (females are 19 to 21) and wears a luxurious double coat. The undercoat is soft, thick, and woolly. The outer hairs are longer and harsher, and should stand off from the body. Male dogs in particular should have a thick ruff around the neck and shoulders. The only acceptable colors are white, white and biscuit, cream, and all biscuit. The dazzling purity of the coat is accentuated by a lustrous silver sheen. By contrast, the lips, nose, and rims of the eyelids should be black. And the eyes should be dark and almond-shaped. Altogether, he makes a striking figure. Two other distinctive features are the "Samoyed smile"—a slight curve of the lips at the corners—and the "Samoyed expression"—a look of lively interest conveyed by bright, alert eyes, erect ears, and a taut attentiveness in the stance. ■ Handsome is as handsome does. The Samoyed is doubly blessed with a pleasant, gentle disposition. His life in the North would not seem to be conducive to placid behavior, but the fact is he is not aggressive and fights only when provoked. Kindly, companionable, loyal, friendly, and highly resourceful—these are the terms one constantly encounters in descriptions of the remarkable Samoyed.

KOMONDOR

The huge Komondor has been king of the Hungarian shepherd dogs for more than 1,000 years. He arrived in Europe on the wave of a tenth century Magyar invasion, or possibly as early as the incursions of Attila the Hun. He was a descendant of the Tibetan Mastiff by way of the Aftscharka dog, a big, long-legged, heavy-coated sheepherder encountered by the Huns on the steppes of Russia. In Hungary the Aftscharka was crossed with native breeds; the result was the Komondor, the scourge of wolves on the *puszta,* or plains, of Hungary. ▪ The extraordinarily heavy and wildly unkempt white coat of the Komondor is his most notable feature. Length and raggedness, especially on head and hindquarters, are qualities to be sought. Yet when carefully reared and properly groomed, he is one of the handsomest of dogs. The coat is long, soft, dense, woolly, and never anything but white. ▪ The Komondor does not round up cattle or sheep; this is the job of smaller dogs. He is primarily a guard dog, called into action only when predators are menacing the livestock and must be driven off or killed. The Germans also have used him for police and guard work. ▪ The need for a powerful dog has permitted an unlimited size. Says the Standard of Perfection: "the bigger the better." The minimum height for a female is specified as 23½ inches at the withers, for a male 31½. No weight is indicated, but it is always in excess of 100 pounds. ▪ A creature of this size is hardly appropriate for a small apartment, and it is advisable, if not essential, to administer a daily grooming. These factors have deterred many people from considering him as a companion dog, yet his personality is an admirable one. The Standard describes him as "an earnest, courageous, and very faithful dog....He is much devoted to his master and will defend him against attack by any stranger." ▪ The Komondor first reached the United States about 1933, but the breed has grown very slowly in popularity and very few specimens are registered with the A.K.C. in any given year. ▪ The plural of Komondor is Komondorok.

ST. BERNARD

Probably the best-known fact about St. Bernards is that they do not carry small casks of brandy around their necks as a pick-me-up for the spent traveler. The mistaken, but very nearly imperishable impression that they do was started by the English artist, Sir Edwin Landseer, whose paintings of noble dogs in dramatic situations delighted the nineteenth century. The actual technique of a St. Bernard patrol was to locate a person buried under snow and then summon rescuers, or to dig its way to the person and lie beside him to warm him with the heat of their big bodies. These days the need for the dogs of St. Bernard has lessened, but many rescues still are made each year. Often the victims are skiers who have failed to read the signs of an avalanche —for which the dogs traditionally have an uncannily sure instinct. ▪ It is generally believed that the St. Bernard began with a mastiff type brought from Asia by the Romans. Talhunds, the descendants of these dogs, presumably were established in the Alpine valleys by the time St. Bernard de Menthon founded his hospice in 980 A.D. and probably were the first dogs acquired by the monks, although just when is unknown. The records of the hospice were destroyed by fire in the sixteenth century, and the earliest surviving reference to dogs is dated 1707. By then, however, the mention was so casual as to suggest that the work of the dogs was well-known everywhere. ▪ The most famous dog in the history of the hospice was the first Barry, who saved forty-one lives in the decade between 1800 and 1810. Ever since his time, an especially fine St. Bernard at the hospice is always named Barry. ▪ About 1830, the dogs of the hospice had been weakened by inbreeding and depleted by distemper and a devastating avalanche. A cross with the long-coated Newfoundland was made. The new blood revived the breed and, incidentally, changed the St. Bernard's smooth coat to the rough one it now enjoys. ▪ The St. Bernard is a giant. The Standard pegs the minimum heights at 25½ and 27½ inches, although individual dogs may grow inches taller. In good condition, a St. Bernard will weigh about 175 pounds. His color is usually various shades of red with white. His disposition is a placid one.

NEWFOUNDLAND

The Newfoundland is without question the champion swimmer of the dog world. No other breed has his phenomenal endurance, no other breed has been credited with so many stirring rescues. In the days of sail he was often taken on as ship's dog, for if ever a sailor were swept overboard in a storm there was a chance that the Newfie's amazing strength in the water could help bring about a rescue. The big dog would leap after him, make his way through the turbulent seas, and drag his man to safety—even as he dragged hundreds of foundering children to shore from millponds, canals, lakes, and streams. And more than one crew was saved because a Newfoundland was able to carry a line from ship to shore, or shore to ship, after their vessel had run onto the rocks. ■ The Newfoundland's lineage is not exactly known, but it is generally accepted that he is a cross between the black St. John's Newfoundland and the big white Great Pyrenees. This would have taken place sometime in the seventeenth century, for Great Pyrenees are known to have accompanied the Basque fishermen who established the fishing station at Rougnoust in Newfoundland in 1662. Many of the earliest Newfoundlands taken to England in trading ships were black and white, which lends some slight support to the idea of a cross between the two breeds. They also are remarkably alike in head, body, and gait. ■ The Newfie is among the giant breeds. The Standard of Perfection cites 26 to 28 inches as "a fair average height," although there is no limit on size and many specimens are much larger. Male dogs average 140 to 150 pounds, females 110 to 120. The Newfie's feet are big and well webbed for swimming. His flat, dense coat is oily and sheds water superbly. The predominant color is black, although black and whites—known as Landseers—are also shown. These are named after Sir Edwin Landseer, whose painting of just such a Newfie made the dog the rage in nineteenth-century England. ■ The Newfoundland is a fine guard dog. He is intelligent, loyal, and sweet-natured and gentle with his family. He is not unfriendly with strangers, but believes they should be introduced. He is quiet and mannerly, but because of his huge size needs room for exercise.

GREAT PYRENEES

Although the Great Pyrenees takes his name from the mountains of the Basque country on the border between France and Spain, he traces his origin to Central Asia or Siberia and to that great progenitor of the large breeds, the Tibetan Mastiff. When the Great Pyrenees arrived in Europe is not known, but skeletal remains dating between 1800 and 1000 B.C. have been found in caves and old camp sites. ▪ In the mountains he became a shepherd dog. Because of his impressive size and courage he was able to protect the flocks from wolves and bear, and by 1407 there are references to him as a sentry dog and guardian at many of the great chateaux of France. By 1675 he had been dubbed the Royal Dog of France by the Dauphin, soon to be Louis XIV, and court nobles were clamoring to have him as a pet. ▪ But mostly he was the dog of humbler folk. Some specimens found their way down to the shores of the Bay of Biscay, where they became the companions of fishermen. One theory holds that today's Newfoundland dog resulted from a cross between the St. John's Newfoundland, the ancestral dog of the retrievers, and Great Pyrenees brought to the Newfoundland fishing banks by Basque fishermen. *Le Grand Chien des Montagnes,* as the French called him, also was an accomplished smuggler. For several centuries he crossed and recrossed the French-Spanish border carrying contraband for gangs of smugglers. The goods were strapped to his back and then he made his way over trails too dangerous or little known for customs agents or border guards to follow. Good dog! ▪ The breed first came to America in 1824, when the Marquis de Lafayette, the Revolutionary War hero, brought a pair from France. ▪ The Great Pyrenees is a large dog. He measures from 25 to 32 inches at the shoulder and weighs from 90 to 125 pounds. These are ideal show-ring figures. Companion dogs may weigh much more. He has a dense double coat, white over-all. The Great Pyrenees makes a splendid companion for anyone with lots of room.

BERNESE MOUNTAIN DOG

Ancestors of the Bernese Mountain Dog came over the Alpine passes with the Roman legions that invaded Helvetia 2,000 years ago. They were used as pack animals, and because food was scarce they were released as soon as the supplies they carried were consumed. These dogs developed into four breeds that still exist today. Known generally as Swiss Mountain Dogs, they are the Entlebuch, the Appenzell, the Large Mountain Dog, and the Bernese Mountain Dog. All of them have shiny black coats, with white, tan, and brown markings, and all are excellent guard dogs. ▪ The Bernese became a draft dog, pulling carts loaded with baskets made by the weavers of the Canton of Bern. By the late nineteenth century, however, the breed was dying out and might well have disappeared but for the efforts of Franz Schertenleib. A resident of Bern and a fancier of the breed, he carefully assembled specimens to serve as breeding stock in 1892. By 1907 the breed had been reestablished and a specialty club formed. ▪ The first

Bernese Mountain Dogs came to the United States in the 1930's and for a time seemed about to become one of the popular show breeds and companion dogs. Before enough specimens could be imported to establish the breed, however, World War II began, and the few that were here had died or aged by the time the war ended. Currently the Bernese is an all-too-rare dog. ▪ He ranges in height from 21 to 27½ inches. His black coat is handsomely accented by a white chest, a striking white blaze on the muzzle, white feet, and a white tip on his black tail. He has brown on his legs and over each eye. His coat is long, soft, and wavy, but not curly. It needs relatively little grooming to keep it looking well. The breed's ears are V shaped, rather short, and hang close to the head. Some descriptions compare the Bernese to the Collie, but he more closely resembles the sturdier St. Bernard, to which he is distantly related. He is a hardy dog that thrives in all weather. And he is a good family dog, not too friendly with strangers.

GREAT DANE

No one knows what connection the Great Dane is supposed to have with Denmark. It is in Germany that he was developed, and from Germany that most of the finest specimens still come. In the course of his history he has been known as the German boarhound, the German Mastiff, the *dogue Allemand,* and the *Deutsche dogge.* There even was a solemn convocation of European show-ring judges in 1880 at which it was agreed the breed should be called the *Deutsche dogge,* and that all other names, most particularly Great Dane, should be stricken from the rolls. And so it is that everywhere outside of Germany the dog is known by the irrelevant name of Great Dane. ■ Essentially, the breed seems to have stemmed from the Mastiff, with a crossing of Irish Wolfhound that contributed the Dane's great height and speed. Like most dogs derived from the Mastiff, there are traces of him in all times and places, some as early as 2200 B.C. in Egypt, others in Greco-Roman times, still others in Britain before the Norman conquest. Some authorities believe the indeterminate Alaunt of medieval times to have been a Dane. In any event, the breed has been known in its present form since the early sixteenth century, and his name was already well-established in 1800. ■ In

Europe, the Dane was bred to hunt the fierce wild boar and was himself a creature of great ferocity. With the disappearance of the boar, however, he found himself without a purpose, for his huge size made him an unsuitable hunter for smaller game. Breeders eventually gentled his disposition and curbed his terrible temper, which permitted him to become a companion dog. Today he is seen mostly in shows and obedience trials, occasionally as a guard dog, and, of course, as a pet. He is intelligent, extremely good natured, and absolutely obedient. This is fortunate because the Dane has all the strength he needs to go his own way if he is so minded. ▪ The Great Dane ranges in size from 28 inches at the shoulder for females to between 32 and 36 inches for males. He may weigh as much as 160 pounds. His coat is short, close-lying, and easy to groom. The customary colors are fawn, brindle, steel blue, black, or harlequin (a white base on which there are torn patches of black). In Germany the Dane's ears always have been cropped so they stand erect and are pointed at the tip. ▪ Despite his size, the Great Dane seems to think of himself as a house pet, and he likes to be with the family at all times. He has even been known to adjust himself to apartment living.

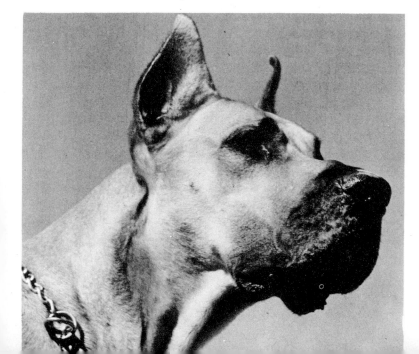

For all his size, the Great Dane is a gentle, amiable dog and a completely successful house pet. Pups above are a handsome and uncommon shade of blue. Their ears are floppy, having not yet been cropped like those of adults (left, opposite).

MASTIFF & BULLMASTIFF

The original mastiff came from Tibet and is one of the oldest dogs in the world, as well as the progenitor of many of the large breeds existing today. There is some confusion about his own line of descent, however, because for so many centuries the word "mastiff" meant any big, mongrel dog. From the evidence of ancient bas-reliefs, it appears possible that the mastiff type has reproduced itself consistently since as early as 2200 B.C. There was supposedly a purebred strain in England at the time of the Battle of Agincourt (1415). And certainly by the eighteenth century, a huge dog which would be completely recognizable today was established. ■ There is no limit on the Mastiff's size. The minimum height at the shoulder is 30 inches for males, 27½ for females. His appearance is awesome: He has a tremendously broad head, a wrinkled brow, and a black mask. His bone is heavy, and when he sets his big feet he is as immovable as granite. A stern looking fellow, he is actually quiet and friendly. His moderately short double coat is light colored—usually apricot, silver fawn, or dark brindle fawn, which is a fawn background completely covered with dark stripes. Muzzle, ears, and nose should be as dark as possible. ■ The Bullmastiff is a relatively new breed, dating to 1860 and resulting, as his name suggests, from a cross between a Bulldog and a Mastiff. His prime function was as the "Gamekeeper's Night Dog," a partner in combating poachers on the great estates of England. He was trained to knock the poacher down and keep knocking him down until help arrived. It was a good tactic since the first fall usually sent the poacher's gun flying and thereby reduced the likelihood of another gamekeeper being shot. ■ The Bulldog of those days had only recently been retired as a fighter of bulls and other dogs. He was a rangier, longer-legged dog than the modern type and far too vicious to be the gamekeeper's helper. What was wanted was a dog that could prevent a poacher from escaping but would not maim him. A Bulldog cross with the slow, heavy, better-natured Mastiff was the answer. The Bullmastiff is from 24 to 27 inches high and weighs up to 130 pounds. These days he has a tractable nature and is a fine companion.

132

DOBERMAN PINSCHER

In the Thuringian village of Apolda, Louis Dobermann was regarded as knowing more about dogs than almost any man in Europe. It was a well-deserved reputation. He was a lifelong student of dogs; of all the many civic offices he had held, the one he enjoyed most was that of dogcatcher, which gave him the freedom to observe a variety of dogs and analyze the crosses that had produced each one. ▪ About 1875, he began breeding dogs to achieve an ideal of his own. He wanted a dog that combined the mobility of the terrier, the size and strength of a working dog, and the elegance of a Toy—specifically that of the Reh Pinscher, or Roe Terrier, whose graceful prancing action made it resemble a tiny deer. By 1890, his work was nearly done, although the Doberman Pinscher he had developed was still far short of the finely tuned athlete we know today. ▪ Herr Dobermann never released a record of the crosses he used to achieve his dog, but a principal ancestor is known to be the Rottweiler. From this sturdy dog the Doberman derives much of his power and his strong instinct as a guard dog. And his black-and-tan color scheme. It also is likely that Dobermann used the old, smooth-coated German Terrier and one or more of the herding dogs that gave rise to today's German Shepherd. At a later period, after Dobermann's death, Otto Goeller of Apolda and others continued the work of refining the dog. There were crosses with the Manchester Terrier and the Greyhound. ▪ Today's Dobe is considered a masterpiece of breeding skill. He is keenly intelligent, high-spirited, and eager to follow his master's bidding. Some strains still carry on the "sharpness"—the hair-trigger readiness to attack Old Nick himself—that Herr Dobermann quite rightly felt would make for a superior watchdog, but most Dobermans are milder and less aggressive than this. They have been outstanding in police work, in war, and as guide dogs for the blind. ▪ They range from 24 to 28 inches at the shoulder and weigh from 45 to 75 pounds.

ROTTWEILER

The Rottweiler is one of the oldest working dogs in Europe. His history goes back to the first century A.D., when he helped drive the cattle that afforded fresh meat for the Roman legions invading Germany. As the herd diminished, the dogs were released—as was also true of the Bernese Mountain Dog. Because the Romans were stationed for some time in the township of Rottweil, on the Neckar River, southwest of Stuttgart, a great many of these sturdy dogs were turned loose here. ▪ Rottweil eventually became a large livestock trading center, and the Rottweiler now helped drive the cattle to market. When the owner received payment for his animals, he tied the bag of coins about the strong neck of his dog. Few men had the courage to try to take it away. In 1900, Germany passed a law prohibiting cattle driving with dogs. The practice had already been in decline, but the ban meant a gradual disappearance of the Rottweiler from the countryside. His capabilities had become known elsewhere, how-

ever, and when the German army decided to train dogs for use in World War I, the Rottweiler was one of the first breeds tried. He proved a success. He was strong, easy to train, and of a steady disposition. In Hamburg, where the police had always had trouble breaking up brawls along the *Reeperbahn*, the Rottweiler proved to be a great asset. He hurled himself into beer-hall melees, hitting the legs of the brawlers and knocking them down, and then standing guard until his patrolman-master took over. ▪ The Rottweiler has a strong streak of Mastiff in his background, but it took many generations of selective breeding before the present-day dog emerged. He is a principal ancestor of the Doberman Pinscher and bears some resemblance to him. The Rottweiler is a blockier dog, however, shorter than the Doberman and considerably heavier, weighing 100 pounds or more. His maximum height is 27 inches. His color is always black, with tan markings on muzzle, cheeks, chest, and legs.

KUVASZ

Third of the three great shepherd dogs of Hungary, the Kuvasz is related to the Komondor and, like him, has been known in his present form for 1,000 years. It is assumed that he, too, arrived in Europe with the Magyars and very likely traces back to the ancient and ubiquitous parent dog of Tibet. The two breeds are very large, strong bodied, and pure white in coat. Both have V-shaped drop ears and wide skulls. The Kuvasz, however, has a shorter and softer coat. ■ Unlike the Komondor, which is known principally in Hungary, the Kuvasz has been taken into many other countries, most notably Turkey, whence—it is thought—his name has derived. There he is called *Kawasz,* meaning "armed guard of the nobility," and there he was the dog that slept inside the door of the ruler's bedchamber to guard against assassins. He is said to have been even larger then than he is now, and more than a match for a man. In Hungary he rounded up livestock, although this work subsequently was taken over by smaller breeds. In modern times, the Kuvasz has been kept principally as a guard dog in the villages and towns; however, some of these dogs which were exported to the United States proved to be excellent sheep dogs in the Rockies. ■ King Matthias I of Hungary developed a pack of Kuvasz in the late fifteenth century for hunting big game. His kennels contained more than 1,000 dogs and were famous throughout Europe. The dogs he produced did much to consolidate the breed, and he conferred puppies on visiting nobles he felt to be worthy of such a valuable gift. ■ The Kuvasz is a large dog. The male is about 26 inches at the withers, the female about two inches less. Yet for all his size he moves with a lithe and easy gait. Long accustomed to his role as a guard of the home, he is friendly and affectionate with his family, particularly with small children, but standoffish with strangers. ■ The Kuvasz was introduced to the United States in the 1930's, a few years earlier than the Komondor, and has attracted some attention, but not enough to remove him from the rare-dog category. The Kuvasz multiplied becomes Kuvaszok.

WELSH CORGIS/CARDIGAN & PEMBROKE

Because they may be of identical size and color, the two Welsh Corgis often are confusing. Yet they are separate and distinct breeds. The Cardigan was brought to Wales in 1200 B.C. by Celtic tribes. The Pembroke came in 1107 A.D. with the Flemish weavers who emigrated to England when Henry I promised them homesteads. ▪ The two most obvious points of difference between the breeds are the ears and the tail. The Cardigan's ears are rounded, the Pembroke's erect and pointed at the tip. The Cardigan has a long tail, slightly feathered. The Pembroke's tail is short—docked short if not occurring naturally. (The fact that some Pembrokes are born with stump tails suggests a relationship with the Schipperke, another stumpy of Flemish origin.) ▪ Similarities and differences between the two Corgis—in Welsh, Cor-gi means dwarf-dog—have been studied for more than twenty years by W. Lloyd-Thomas of Cardiganshire. He has noted that the Cardigan's heavy leg bone and the angle at which his feet are turned suggests a common ancestry with the Basset Hound and the Dachshund. The Pembroke's bone is much lighter. The Cardigan's back also is longer than the Pembroke's. ▪ The size and weight of the two breeds are almost the same. The Cardigan runs from a minimum of 15 pounds for the female to a maximum of 25 pounds for the male. The Pembroke Standard specifies 18 to 24. The Cardigan is supposed to stand 12 inches at the shoulder; the Pembroke may range from 10 to 12. ▪ The breeds have somewhat similar coats. For the Cardigan the Standard says: "Short or medium, of hard texture." For the Pembroke: "Of medium length and dense, not wiry." Colors in the Cardigan may be anything but pure white. Usually they are the same as the Pembroke's: Fox-red, sable, fawn, black and tan. Cardigans occasionally are blue merles—a blue-gray with flecks of black—but Pembrokes never. Both breeds have white markings on chest, neck, and legs. ▪ Originally, both Corgis were cattle dogs. They were faster and more agile than their stubby legs might suggest. They hurried the cows along by nipping at their hocks, and avoided flying hooves by dropping flat on the ground when the cows kicked at them. ▪ In the United States, both breeds have been primarily show dogs or companions. Both have good dispositions.

ALASKAN MALAMUTE

The Malamute is the freight dog of the North. The motor-driven sled and airplanes of the modern era have reduced his importance to some degree, but he still can move heavier sledge loads faster and for longer periods of time than any other northern breed. He is a native Alaskan dog and qualifies thereby as one of the few authentic breeds developed on the North American continent. For all that, he is still not very numerous outside of Alaska, and is perhaps known better as a worker than as show dog or pet. ▪ The Malamute was the dog of the tribe of Innuit Indians known in the early days as Mahlemuts. They lived on the shores of Kotzebue Sound, in upper western Alaska, and were intelligent, industrious, and skillful. They permitted no crossing of their dog with other northern strains, and they treated him with kindness and respect. The brutality that turned so many dogs of other breeds sour and gave sled dogs as a whole a reputation for being vicious and unreliable was unknown among the Mahlemuts. As a result, the Malamute of today is a friendly and affectionate dog. He has his dignity, but he is a playful pup, enjoys a romp, and is utterly trustworthy with children. ▪ Like his close relatives, the Siberian Husky, the Samoyed, and the Eskimo Dog, the Malamute is of Wolf-Spitz stock. He has a double coat and a handsome ruff around his neck and shoulders. His undercoat may be as much as two inches thick, woolly in texture and oily to help him shed water. The outer hairs are long and coarse. His color may range from light gray to black, with white on the underbody and parts of the legs and feet. Two distinctive patterns are a black cap on the head and a solid, lighter colored face, or a black mask. He has dark, almond-shaped eyes and a plumed tail that waves over his back. The Malamute is a compact, heavy-boned, powerfully built dog that stands, on the average, about 25 inches at the shoulder and weighs about 85 pounds. (The female may be two inches shorter and some ten pounds lighter.) He has been used by explorers in both the Arctic and Antarctic regions.

SIBERIAN HUSKY

The Husky was the dog of the Chuchi tribe in northern Siberia for many centuries before he became known to the outside world. He was an all-purpose dog—working and playing with the tribesmen, and being admitted to the family dwelling at night to sleep. This friendly treatment engendered a friendly dog. The Husky has a gentle manner and an even temperament. ▪ Husky is a term generally applied to any northern sled dog; only the Siberian has it as part of his official name. He is somewhat smaller and lighter than the Alaskan Malamute and the Eskimo Dog, but pound for pound he is as rugged a draft dog as can be found. He stands 21 to 23½ inches tall at the shoulder and weighs 45 to 60 pounds. (Females: 20 to 22 inches and 35 to 50 pounds.) Like all dogs that must withstand a harsh climate he has a thick double coat, long and "full-furred" on the surface, dense and soft as down underneath. All colors and markings are allowed. Most frequently seen are wolf and silver grays, black with white points, and light sable. Siberian markings are widely varied and often quite bizarre. The cap, mask, and spectacle markings are quite common. His face is foxy, his eyes set slightly on a slant, though not as much as a Malamute's. Eye color is brown or China blue, and sometimes one of each—"odd-eyed," as it is called. His bushy tail is carried in a sickle curve over his back when he is running or standing at attention; otherwise it trails out behind. Like other Arctic breeds he has a "snowshoe foot," that is, somewhat webbed to help him pad through snow. He has great powers of endurance and keen ability to find a trail. He gives voice with a howl, rather than a bark. And he has no doggy odor. ▪ Americans in Alaska first heard of him shortly after the turn of the century and imported him in 1909 to compete in the All-Alaska Sweepstakes, the biggest dog-racing event in the territory. He finished third, and from then on was a fixture in most sled-dog races. It was teams of Siberian Huskies, working in relays, that carried antidiphtheria serum to the beleaguered Alaskan city of Nome during an epidemic in 1925.

7 TERRIERS

Terriers grow in Great Britain. Of the twenty breeds the class contains, sixteen were born and bred in England, Scotland, or Wales. One was developed in Australia by crossing a few of the others. Two come from neighboring Ireland. And only one is an outlander— the Miniature Schnauzer from Germany. These are dogs designed to go to ground for fox, badger, rabbit, or any other burrowing creature that has eluded the horseback hunter and his hounds. They must be willing to enter the lair and fight to the death, if necessary. For this kind of work, a dog needs a bristly coat for protection against harsh weather and a bright, bristly temperament for protection against harsh circumstances. Terriers have both. They are spirited, loyal, affectionate, and dead game. They make wonderful pets.

AIREDALE TERRIER

The Airedale is the acknowledged king of the Terriers. He is rather too large to follow his quarry to earth, but he has the classic terrier squareness and a full measure of the brisk terrier spirit. In the valley of the River Aire, in Yorkshire, he was an energetic hunter of the fox, the badger, the weasel, and the otter. ■ He is a dog of fairly recent vintage. He did not reach his present form until the nineteenth century and was first given classes at an English dog show in 1879. His principal forebear was the now-extinct Broken-haired, or Old English, Terrier, plus an infusion of Otterhound, from which he takes his size, some of his all-weather coat, and his hearty love of water. Airedales are exhibited in the show ring with their coats plucked close, like other Terriers, but anyone who has ever owned him knows that if his trimming is neglected he comes to look amazingly like an Otterhound. He also is said to have a touch of Irish, Welsh, and Fox Terrier in him. In the 1860's he was called variously the Working, Waterside, or Bingly Terrier (Bingly being a Yorkshire town), but so many were raised in the Airedale Valley that the Airedale he became. ■ He is regarded as one of the finest of all big-game hunters. Airedale teams have been used on mountain lion in the western United States and Canada, and on big cats in Africa and India. The dog has great courage, and many have been killed in their eagerness to bring their quarry to bay. He also has been used successfully as a police and military dog. ■ The Airedale stands from 21 to 23 inches at the shoulder and weighs 45 to 55 pounds. Over-sized specimens are used for hunting and will exceed these figures considerably. His coat is a double one—harsh and straight on the outside, but with short, soft hairs underneath. Traditionally, the body coat is blue black or silver black, and the head and legs a rich tan. ■ His hound inheritance has given the Airedale a sweet nature. He is a friendly and humorous dog, which makes him an attractive and playful member of the family. He is also a good watchdog.

IRISH TERRIER

The Irish Terrier's principal ancestor, and one he very likely shares with the Welsh and Scottish Terriers, is the Old English Terrier, the now-extinct, wire-haired, black-and-tan sporting dog known since the mid-eighteenth century. The evolution of the Irishman is uncertain, although he may be the Irish Sporting Terrier referred to in old manuscripts and probably came about after generations of selective breeding. Early in the game, of course, like most utility dogs, he was bred for function, not appearance, and ran to a wide range of sizes and colors (black and tan, gray and brindle, all wheaten shades). ▪ As a hunter he was superb. He was smart, enduring, and completely game. He was used on woodchuck, weasel, badger, rabbit, and other small game, and vermin, particularly the water rat. For this was a natural water dog. He could be trained to retrieve ducks in water and partridge on land. Many who saw him work felt him to be the equal of any spaniel. Like the Airedale, he has been used on big game from time to time. And his fanciers are especially proud of their

dog's record as sentinel and messenger in two world wars. ▪ The Irish Terrier Standard of Perfection was written in 1879, the year of the breed's first appearance in an English show ring, and it is an interesting point that almost from the start there was strong opposition to the age-old practice of ear cropping. There was resistance for a decade, but finally in 1889 cropping was effectively abolished by a ruling which forbade it for dogs born after a certain date. Ears now are small and V shaped, and drop forward to the cheek. ▪ The breed stands 18 inches at the shoulder and weighs between 25 and 27 pounds. The coat must be wiry, close lying, and so dense that the skin is hardly visible when the hairs are parted. It should have no silkiness or shagginess that disturbs the dog's outline. The Irish is a whole-colored dog. Red, red wheaten, and golden red are preferred; a patch of white on the chest is permitted. He is a good-tempered dog, affectionate, playful, and absolutely loyal. He is fine with children and a devoted guardian of the home.

KERRY BLUE TERRIER

This is an indigenous dog of Eire. He was developed in County Kerry's mountains, perhaps as early as 1780, perhaps even earlier, and for a hundred years or so was a locally cultivated, all-purpose working dog. He could herd sheep and cattle, kill rats in the barn, draw badgers for sport, hunt small game, and retrieve birds in water or on land. He was highly intelligent and had a gentle and lovable nature. What his ancestry was and where he got his unique blue coat, however, was not known. Some thought that perhaps he was related to the Irish Wolfhound. And Briard fanciers have noted that a Kerry Blue, whose coat has been allowed to grow long and shaggy, looks remarkably, though unaccountably, like a shepherd dog of Brie. This actually is not a hard comparison to make. In Ireland, the Kerry Blue is shown in a natural state, unclipped, unplucked, and unshorn. (The United States and England require him to be trimmed for show-ring appearances.) ▪ Once he had attracted attention, the Kerry Blue began to be introduced at shows, first in Dublin in 1913. Here he

caught the eye of English breeders, but World War I intervened and it was not until 1922 that he was shown in England. The same year, the first Kerry Blues in the United States were shown in the Miscellaneous class at the Westminster show. The breed was accepted by the A.K.C. in 1924 and a parent club was formed in 1926. ▪ The Kerry Blue stands between 17½ and 19½ inches at the shoulder. He weighs from 33 to 40 pounds. His coat is dense, soft, and wavy. The usual wiry or bristly terrier coat is a fault. Its color may be any shade of blue gray or gray blue, as long as it is uniform overall, except for the points which may be darker. The color is zealously protected by the Standard, which, however, recognizes that the breed goes through transitional stages before the adult color is fixed. The puppy's solid black, therefore, is acceptable up to twelve months, and intermediate and brown shades are permitted between twelve and eighteen months. After eighteen months, however, the traditional Kerry blue only is accepted.

WELSH TERRIER

Sometime in a confused and distant past, the Welsh Terrier may have been the original sire that started the Airedale and the Fox and Irish Terriers on their way into the realm of purebred dogs. This is no more than speculation, yet most authorities believe that one of the great parental breeds of the terrier family was the so-called Old English Wirehaired Black & Tan Terrier, and as far as anyone can tell that means the Welsh. Sporting prints and paintings of the nineteenth century show any number of rough-coated black-and-tans called Old English Wirehaired Black & Tan Terrier, much as the Welsh. And it is also interesting to note that as late as 1886 the Kennel Club of England was using the Welsh and Old English Terrier names interchangeably. All this being true, it should not be surprising that a fine Welsh Terrier type was produced in the 1880's by crossing an Airedale and a Fox Terrier.

■ The Welsh was another of the many implacable foes of the fox, the otter, and the badger. Today's Welsh has a slightly longer leg and a larger head than his forebear, but his color has not changed a jot in one hundred years. He is a spry and clever dog, game but not quarrelsome, well mannered, easy to handle, and with plenty of bone and substance. The Welsh head is broader than a Fox Terrier's, wider between the ears and with the eyes also set fairly wide. The eyes should be small, the stop not too well defined, the ears small, V shaped, and carried close to the cheek. The jaw should be powerful. Altogether these features should combine in an aspect of alertness and intelligence that is known as the "unmistakable Welsh expression." The dog should stand 15 inches at the shoulder and weigh 20 pounds, give or take one. His coat should be close and wiry. The usual colors are black and tan.

Three Welsh Terriers at left show obvious relationship to Airedale and Irish Terrier. Lakeland (below) is fox hunter from different sources.

LAKELAND TERRIER

Throughout the nineteenth century, England was over-run with locally bred terriers. Usually each took the name of the district where it was most numerous, or, as it persisted and became more generally known, went through a series of names before everyone agreed on one. Such was the experience of the Lakeland Terrier. He was born and bred in Cumberland, the lake district of England, a shire made famous too by the early nineteenth-century hunts of the almost-legendary John Peel. He was known locally as the Fell Terrier, after the district in which he flourished, and also as the Petterdale Terrier and the Colored Working Terrier. It was not until 1921, when a Standard finally was written, that the generic name Lakeland was adopted. ▪ Away back, it seems clear that the ancestors of the Lakeland were those that also produced the Border Terrier and the Bedlington. It is likely, too, that he was related to

the ubiquitous Old English Black & Tan Terrier. In the Border country, a dog's working ability was important, for hunting was a practical matter of protecting the sheepfolds from foxes, rather than a sport. The Lakelands hunted fox in company with hounds. Every pack needed a few terriers able and willing to go to ground if the fox should escape to a burrow or a rocky lair. The Lakeland had unbounded courage and was slender and agile enough to enter a fox's hideaway. The pups of the gamest of these terriers usually were distributed to friends and followers of the pack in order to perpetuate the quality. ▪ The Lakeland is a neat and attractive dog weighing about 17 pounds. (No height is specified in the Standard.) His tail is docked. His coat is hard, dense, and wiry. Colors are black, black and tan, blue, blue and tan, red, mustard, and wheaten grizzle. He is a quiet, well-mannered dog.

FOX TERRIER

There never has been much doubt about what a Fox Terrier should be. The original Standard of Perfection, written in 1876, enumerated the breed's qualities so precisely and so well that only one trifling change has ever been necessary—a lowering of the show-ring weight for males from 20 to 18 pounds. The Standard, except for coat, covers both the Wirehaired and Smoothhaired varieties, which, although starting from widely divergent points, are now to all intents and purposes the same dog. ∎ The Wirehaired is the elder of the two. He is a descendant of a rough-haired, black-and-tan working terrier known in Wales, Derby, and Durham. His type was already well-established by 1748, according to the evidence of a painting. ∎ The Smoothhaired Fox Terrier also was pegged by a portrait. This was a picture of Pitch, a dog belonging to a Colonel Thornton, which had achieved present-day perfection in 1790. The Smooth variety developed from several sources, at root probably from a smooth-coated Black & Tan Terrier. Known crosses have included the Bull Terrier, the Beagle, and the Greyhound. Although both dogs were used to hunt fox, the Smoothhaired was first to be called a Fox Terrier and the first to be classified for a dog show (1862). He had a remarkable nose, keen sight, and a hard-driving manner in the field. He was classified among the sporting dogs. ∎ The Wirehaired was first called the Rough-haired Terrier, then the Wirehaired Terrier, and finally Wirehaired Fox Terrier. In the early days, Smooth and Wire were interbred, mostly to improve the Wire's outline and increase the area of white in his coloration. His black-and-tan heritage had left him too reddish to hunt fox. Interbreeding has long since ceased, however. ∎ Today the Smoothhaired Fox Terrier is a gay and active dog standing 18 inches at the shoulder (and about 12 inches from shoulder to root of tail). His weight is a maximum of 15½ pounds. His coat is hard, flat, and dense, with white predominating. The Wirehaired has the same conformation and coloring, but a broken coat, the harder the better.

Smoothhaired Fox Terrier (above) and Wirehaired variety evolved from different sources, are now virtually the same dog, except for coat.

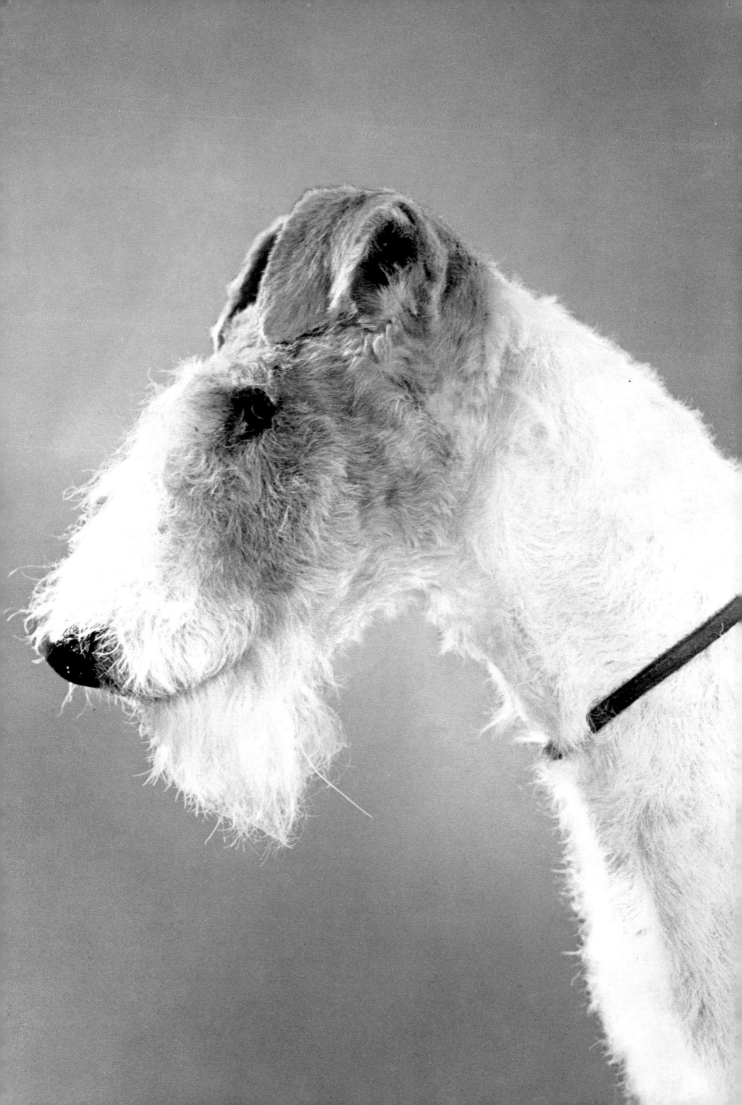

SCOTTISH TERRIER

The many partisans of the well-beloved Scottie would like to believe that he is the most ancient of Highland Terriers. Yet if, indeed, he is, the evidence is scant and must be read with a predilection for the breed weighing subtly in the balance. The Skye's claims to antiquity must generally be ignored, or put off on a dog that had not yet become the Skye. And various references in sixteenth-century documents must be accepted as descriptions of a dog not named until the nineteenth. If the task seems thankless, it is not too much for the Scottie's admirers, for he never has lacked for champions or a controversy. The Birmingham show of 1860 seems to have been the first which had a class for Scottish Terriers, but before long it was clear it was being used as a catchall for Skyes, Dandies, Cairns, and even Yorkshires. By 1877, Scottish protests were thundering in the pages of the provincial journals of animal husbandry, and the debate grew so hot the editors finally had to call a halt until someone should come up with a proper and accurate description of the Scottish Terrier breed. In 1880, a noted dog-show judge, J. B. Morrison, was induced to write a Standard, and it is this, with minor changes, that covers the breed today. ∎ The safest guess as to the origin of the breed would seem to be that the Scottie, like so many of his terrier relatives, sprang from the rough-haired Highland Terrier and emerged as a distinct type by 1879, if not before. Through much of the nineteenth century he also was called the Aberdeen Terrier because so many superior specimens of him were being bred there. The dog was imported to the United States in 1883, although a Standard was not drawn up until 1925. ∎ The amiable, playful, and thoroughly enjoyable Scottie stands about 10 inches at the shoulder and weighs 18 to 22 pounds. He has small, prick ears and an undocked, 7-inch tail. His coat is hard, wiry, and dense. His colors are steel or iron gray, grizzle or brindle, black, sandy, or wheaten. White marks are objectionable.

WEST HIGHLAND WHITE TERRIER

This is not simply a white Scottie. The Standard takes particular pains to point out that the West Highland White is a distinctly different breed, as comparison of various features will quickly demonstrate. Of course, there is no doubt that he is one of the Highland terriers, and doubtless somewhere in the past there is a common ancestor with the Scottie, the Cairn, and other breeds as well. There even was a brief period, before his present name was established, when he was called the White Scottish Terrier. ▪ His derivation seems to have been from all the unwanted white pups in litters of the principal Highland breeds. Usually whites were destroyed, but occasionally a promising one was kept and occasionally bred to another salvaged white. In time, the breeding was continued for color and type, until eventually a distinct variety evolved. Such was the West Highland White. He may be said to have originated at Poltalloch, on the estate of the Malcolm family, which apparently bred and maintained a pure strain

for more than one hundred years. Where the first crosses of the random whites took place is not clear; some suggest that James I's request that "earthdogges" be sent to him from Argyll referred to a forebear of the West Highland White. It's possible. Poltalloch is in Argyll and James I, having been James VI of Scotland, presumably would know where the best "earthdogges" could be got. In any event, Poltalloch Terriers, as they were called for a while in honor of the Malcolms (or Roseneaths, as they were called after the Duke of Argyll's kennels there), were the fully developed dog known today. ▪ The West Highland White is a sporty dog, a swift, intelligent hunter and a lighthearted companion. He stands 11 inches at the withers and weighs around 20 pounds. He has small, erect ears and a straight, 6-inch tail. His coat is double, furry underneath, hard and straight on top. It should be about 2 inches long. White is the only acceptable color. He is a pleasant, hardy dog. He is shown untrimmed.

CAIRN TERRIER

This one is very much like the Skye Terrier with a haircut. He is the smallest of the working terriers and could be the oldest, depending on how various sixteenth-century references are interpreted. It is not clear whether he comes directly from the Isle of Skye or from the Scottish mainland, but he was originally named the Shorthaired Skye Terrier and he currently represents a faithful preservation of the old Skye working terrier. He is a game, hardy, active dog with the courage and ability to rout the fox, the badger, and other vermin from their rockey lairs and to hunt the otter at the streamside. ▪ The Cairn today stands 9½ to 10 inches high at the withers and has an over-all length of 14½ to 15 inches, which means his height is about two thirds his body length. This makes him somewhat longer bodied than the Scottie and the West Highland White, but shorter than the Dandie Dinmont. He should weigh exactly one stone (14 pounds), females a pound less. His skull should be broad in proportion to its length and have a decided stop. The hair on the top of the head should be full. The ears are small, pointed, and erect, and set fairly wide apart. The tail is carried jauntily, but not curling over the back. The double coat should have a soft, furry underlayer and a harsh, weather-resistant outer jacket. Coat color may be anything but white. Points—ears, muzzle, tail tip—should be darker than the rest. The dog should be shown in a natural state. He needs no trimming beyond tidying up. "A winning Cairn," it has been said, "is the result of careful breeding, rather than careful barbering." ▪ The personality of the Cairn is a beguiling one. His alert interest in life makes him a gay and amusing companion. Like many breeds, he is somewhat aloof with strangers, but a welcoming friend to those he knows. He is a highly adaptable pet. Although primarily an outdoor dog and one that relishes exercise, he can get on without it and accommodate himself to apartment space. ▪ He was recognized by the Kennel Club (England) in 1910, was introduced to the United States in 1913, and registered by the A.K.C. in 1914.

AUSTRALIAN TERRIER

The Australian Terrier has a tangled and uncertain background, but there are many clues to his inheritance in his small, sturdy body. Like so many terriers, he stems first from the Broken-haired Terrier. His long back gives evidence of Skye Terrier, and there would seem to be Skye and/or Yorkshire in his blue-black and rich tan coloration. His weatherproof coat is Scottie. His small, erect ears are reminiscent of the Cairn. His light-colored topknot is Dandie Dinmont. It is not clear why so many crosses were introduced or exactly what qualities were being sought. The breeders who developed the Australian left no records explaining their procedures or intentions. ▪ Essentially he was a working terrier used by farmers in the Australian hinterlands for hunting small game and keeping the barns free of rats and mice. He must have begun to evolve toward his present form by the mid-nineteenth century, because fully developed specimens—then called Australian Roughs—were entered in a dog show at Melbourne in 1885. Interest in the dog outside of Australia was negligible. Specimens eventually were taken to England, but the breed did not achieve Kennel Club status there until 1933. In the United States, the Australian is of the most recent vintage. He was not listed by the A.K.C. until 1960, after a breeding cadre of several hundred specimens had been assembled. ▪ The Australian is a bright and courageous little dog. The Standard describes his personality as having the "aggressive spirit of the natural ratter and hedge hunter," yet friendly, affectionate, and "biddable" as well. He stands no more than 10 inches at the shoulder and never weighs more than 12 or 14 pounds. He has a harsh, straight-haired coat that grows to a length of two-and-a-half inches over the body. His colors are blue black, as mentioned, or silver black and with rich tan markings on head and legs. The hairs are blue at the roots with black tips, or alternately striped black and silver, with black tips. ▪ The Australian Terrier makes a most congenial companion and a watchdog that takes his job seriously.

BORDER TERRIER

The Border Terrier is a native of the Cheviot Hills, which are pasture land for the fleecy, barefaced Cheviot sheep and form a natural boundary between England and Scotland. He is a tough, rugged, dead-game little dog whose task always has been to hunt and kill the big hill foxes that prey on the farmer's livestock. He is among the oldest Terrier breeds in England, dating back at least to the late seventeenth century, and the only Terrier that is taller than he is long. Standing 10 to 12 inches at the withers, he generally will be an inch or an inch and a half shorter from stem to stern. This characteristic, although not typical of terriers, is a desirable one in the Border Terrier, who is bred for legs long enough to keep up with a hunting horse and a body small enough to follow the fox to ground. His dense, wiry, close-lying coat is ideal for the chill rains and heavy mists of the hills. And his driving spirit carries him over, under, around, and through any natural obstacle when on attack. ■ He seems to have developed from judicious breeding among a variety of hill terriers, although which ones and in what sequence are not known. It is believed that he is related to the Lakeland, the Bedlington, and the Dandie Dinmont through a common ancestor. The Border Terrier is notable for a head shaped like an otter's. The skull is broad and flat, with considerable width between the eyes and between the ears. The stop is slight, a broad curve rather than an indention. The hazel eyes are bright and interested. His tail is medium short, thick at the base and tapering toward the tip, and carried cheerfully. His coat has no curl or wave, and is colored red, grizzle and tan, blue and tan, or wheaten. Some white is permitted on the chest, but is not desirable. He ranges from 13 to 15½ pounds (11½ to 14 for females). ■ He still is quite scarce in the United States, being known mostly to hunters and show exhibitors, who find him a good-natured, obedient little fellow and a fine companion, although definitely an active, outdoor dog.

NORWICH TERRIER

The Norwich Terrier was created in the 1870's by British sportsmen who wanted a small, robust working dog that could hunt rabbits and would have the built-in terrier urge to destroy rats. As usual, the evolutionary steps are obscure. The principal parent was the Irish Terrier. Small specimens of Irish were crossed, very possibly with Border Terriers, to produce a game, all-weather hunter with a red coat. The first of the breed appeared at Norfolk and were named the Norwich Terrier. By the 1880's he was so popular at Cambridge University that it was strongly felt he should be called the Cantab Terrier, although the students called him the Trumpington Terrier after the nearby town where most of them acquired their dogs. ▪ Norwich Terriers arrived in the United States after World War I, and by then they were being called Jones Terriers after the breeder who had exported them. These dogs were sent to various hunt clubs, trained by Masters of Foxhounds, and proved to be a valuable asset when the quarry went to ground. Like several other breeds, they also appeared to have an affinity for horses and to enjoy being in their company. ▪ The Norwich stands a mere 10 inches at the shoulder and ranges in weight from 10 to 14 pounds; 11 is considered ideal. His wiry coat is harsh and close lying, straight haired, and nearly full enough to form a mane on the neck and shoulders. Trimming rarely is necessary and the Standard says the dog should be shown in as nearly a natural state as possible. Clipping and shaping the coat is to be heavily penalized. Red is the breed's basic color, but the coat may also be black, tan, or grizzle. White on the chest is acceptable, but not desirable. Ears may be either pointed and erect, or neat, small, and dropped. The tail is docked. ▪ Personally, says the Standard, the Norwich is "a perfect demon, yet not quarrelsome and of a lovable disposition, and a very hardy constitution." It adds: "Honorable scars from fair wear and tear shall not count against." He is a one-man dog.

SKYE TERRIER

The Skye is at least 400 years old. He is mentioned in Dr. Johannes Caius' famous sixteenth-century treatise, *Englisshe Dogges,* and was among the breeds listed in the first Kennel Club (England) studbook of 1874. He is named after the island to the northwest of Scotland where he originated and where the finest specimens are produced even today. For all his long coat, he is a working terrier capable of rooting his quarry from dens, burrows, boskets, and other Highland hiding places. Dr. Caius put it rather well. The Skye, he said, was "brought out of barbarous borders fro' the uttermost countryes northward...which, by reason of the length of heare, makes showe neither of face nor of body." This was written in 1570, in the reign of Elizabeth I. The dog was a fashionable favorite at court even then, and by the end of the nineteenth century was the most widely known and popular Terrier. Queen Victoria, who seems to have loved all dogs, was also partial to the little Skye. And Sir Edwin Landseer painted his portrait, which always was recognition of a breed's popularity and a guarantee that it immediately would become more so. In the United States the Skye was one of the important breeds at shows shortly before the turn of the century. But now, despite his distinguished past, the Skye is a bit in the shade and retains his prestige only in Scotland and England. ▪ The conformation of the Skye is mathematically precise. He is supposed to be two and a half times as long as his height at the shoulder. The length of his tail should equal his height, and his head should be a half inch less than his tail. Which means that a dog 9 inches at the shoulder would be 22½ inches over-all, have a 9-inch tail and an 8½-inch head. His double coat is profuse, obscures his sight, and should hang 5½ inches over the body. The long outer hairs should be hard and straight, and parted evenly from head to feathered tail. Any colors are permitted, including black, blue, gray, fawn, and cream. Muzzle, ears, and tail tip should be darker than the rest of the body. ▪ Personally, the Skye is good tempered, fearless, loyal, and canny.

SEALYHAM TERRIER

In his retirement, Captain John Edwardes became a somewhat eccentric old sportsman who spent some forty years developing a sporting terrier at his estate, called Sealyham, in Wales. The breeding sequence, for all the fact that it was accomplished by one man, has remained obscure, and the component dogs all have had to be induced from study of the finished Sealyham. Some think the Captain started about 1850 with a Corgi, a fair guess since he lived in Pembrokeshire. There is general agreement that the Sealyham's somewhat domed head, short leg, wide eye, and plucky nature suggest the Dandie Dinmont. There may be Bull Terrier in his jaw, and West Highland White and Bull Terrier in his coloration. But almost all of this is speculative and no one knows for sure. ▪ The dog that resulted—about 1891—was a substantial, smart looking, intelligent workman that went willingly to ground to battle the badger, fox, or otter, and was death on rats and rabbits. The Captain did not live to see his breed achieve Kennel Club recognition, but the breed had attracted attention locally, and there were a number of sportsmen who had hunted weasel with small Sealyham packs and knew just how good the dog was. They helped keep the strain pure. The dog first was entered in a show near the Captain's home in 1903. A Sealyham club was formed in 1908. Kennel Club (England) recognition came in 1911 and A.K.C. listing a little later in the same year, shortly after the first Sealyhams were imported to the United States. ▪ The Sealyham stands 10½ inches high at the shoulder and is the same length from shoulder to set on of tail. Factors of size are far more important in judging than weight, which runs about 21 pounds. The dog must have a sturdy, deep-chested look, yet be free of clumsiness. The ears are uncropped and fold forward. The tail is docked and held upright. The coat is the usual weather-resistant terrier combination of soft, dense undercoat and a hard, wiry outer one. Curls or silkiness are faults. Sealyham colors are all white, with lemon, tan, or badger markings on head and ears. He is a keen and alert dog.

Mop of hair obscures
sight of Skye Terrier, an
old breed known in
Elizabethan times. Sealyham
(below) was creation
of late 19th century, has
something of several
breeds in him.

DANDIE DINMONT TERRIER

In Sir Walter Scott's novel, *Guy Mannering*, Dandie Dinmont is a farmer living in the Cheviot Hills in the Border country between England and Scotland. He has six small hunting terriers—Auld, Young, and Little Pepper, and Auld, Young, and Little Mustard. He has trained them well. They are so bold "they fear naething that ever cam wi' a hairy skin on't." The dog had been known as a distinct breed for more than a hundred years when Scott's novel appeared in 1814, but he brought them new fame, and thenceforward they were called Dandie Dinmont's Terriers. ▪ The Dandie seems to have descended from selected specimens of the many rough Border hunting terriers and was well-established in the eighteenth century. A Gainsborough portrait of one of the Dukes of Buccleuch, done in 1770, shows a perfect present-day Dandie. The dog was notable as a hunter of badger and otter, although he long since has become a show dog and a pet. He is an extremely intelligent little fellow and serves both as a guardian and a companion. ▪ Unlike most terriers, the Dandie is a dog with no straight lines. Everything curves. He has a large, domed head which should be covered with soft, silky hair profuse enough to be brushed into a distinctive topknot for the show ring. The ears are pendulous and hang close to the cheek. The back curves downward, then rises at the hips. The tail is 8 to 10 inches long and has a scimitar curve. ▪ The Dandie's coat is a mixture of soft and hard hairs, and consequently has a crisp feel, but not the harshness of wire hair. He, too, is shown in a natural state, with little plucking or clipping. The pepper color ranges from blue gray to light silver, with light tan or silver points and a white or nearly white topknot. Mustard, the only other color, runs from reddish brown to pale fawn, with creamy white on head. Intermediate shades are preferred to extremes. The breed is 8 to 11 inches high and 15 to 16 inches long from shoulder to root of tail. The weight ranges from 18 to 24 pounds.

MINIATURE SCHNAUZER

Except for size and some variation in color, the Miniature Schnauzer is identical to his Working Group half brother, the Standard Schnauzer. The Miniature resulted from a cross of small Standard specimens with the Affenpinscher, and has been a distinct breed at least since 1899. The Schnauzer is German by origin and never has had a blood relationship with any of the English terrier breeds. But he is Terrier in group and temperament. He is sturdily built and nearly square. He has the harsh, wiry coat. And he is a great ratter. Terrier is only part of his background, however. The Standard Schnauzer emerged, perhaps as early as the fifteenth century, from crosses of black Poodle and the wolf-gray Spitz with old German pinscher (meaning "terrier") stock. This probably was a black-and-tan drover of the Württemberg type. The Schnauzer always has been a yard and stable dog, and a destroyer of vermin, although too large to go to ground like other terriers. Today's Miniature, although primarily a show dog or a pet, still is endowed with rat-catching ability.
■ The Miniature, or Zwergschnauzer, is a robust, active dog, with good bone and no trace of delicacy or "toyishness." He has a strong, rectangular head with the traditional abundance of whiskers that gives him his name (schnauze—beard). Ears are pointed if cropped; small, V shaped, and folding close to the skull if uncropped. The docked tail is set high and carried erect. The Schnauzer has a double coat, hard and wiry outside, softer underneath. His colors are salt and pepper, black and silver, or solid black. Tan shading is allowed. There is a somewhat wider range of grays and a somewhat softer black in the Miniature than the Standard.
■ Miniatures stand 12 to 14 inches high at the shoulder (13½ is ideal) and weigh about 12 to 15 pounds. They have been in the United States since 1925, and a parent club was formed in 1933. They have gained admirers rapidly. They are hardy, active, and of a gay disposition that makes them fine companions for children.

BEDLINGTON TERRIER

This is the neat little dog with the dainty walk that looks like a lamb and can fight like a demon. Today his nature is pleasant and tractable, and he makes a fine household pet. But he is a dog of the nineteenth century, bred to the savagery of the fighting pits, a racer, a rat killer, a drawer of badgers, and a favorite of the gentlemen gamesters who preferred death to surrender and let their dogs prove it for them. ■ His name comes from the Northumberland town where he was bred in about 1820, after some forty years of development. He seems to have sprung originally from a breed known as the Rothbury Terrier and to have been crossed along the way with the Dandie Dinmont, whence comes his long, flat ears and white topknot, and with the Whippet, which increased his speed, roached his back, and gave him the Greyhound's tucked-up loin. In Bedlington there were two principal industries: mining and nail-making. For generations there was great rivalry between the workers of the two crafts which often took the form of wagering on contests between favored animals. At first, the Bedlington was the nailers' dog, but his successes eventu-

Meek looking as a lamb,
the Bedlington has high courage,
gives ground to no one.

ally brought every man in the community over to his side. His local fame was such that wealthy landowners also began to take an interest in him. Through them he was exhibited at dog shows, and in 1877 a national breed club was formed. ■ The Bedlington is slightly larger than a Fox Terrier, standing 15 to 16 inches at the withers and weighing from 22 to 24 pounds. He has a distinctively narrow skull and a profuse, nearly white topknot; when properly trimmed the dog should have a "Roman nose," a gentle sweep, without a stop, from the occiput to the end of the nose. The long ears should hang flat against the cheek and should be virtually hairless, except for a silky, inch-long fringe at the tip. The tail is tapering, undocked, and, says the Standard, "scimitar shaped." The coat is unlike that of other terriers. It is thick and linty, must not be more than an inch long when in show condition, and should stand off from the body. It must be soft to the touch, cannot be harsh or wiry. Three colors are permitted: blue, which is currently most popular; liver, the dog's original color, and sandy. All of these colors may be mixed with tan.

BULL TERRIER

The Bull Terrier is a sweet-natured and affectionate dog. He is friendly with people and even tempered with other dogs. He provokes no fights. He is highly intelligent and easily trained, but is sensitive to criticism and must be encouraged rather than scolded. He is sociable, and even a humorist, within the family circle. ▪ Many people find this hard to believe. He appears to be something less than cuddly and is freely credited with all the fierce and fearsome qualities of his pit fighting ancestors. However undeserved, such a reputation dies hard. Actually, the Bull Terrier was bred for tractability rather than fighting skill, for pit fighting had been outlawed for a generation before he appeared. And so successful was the gentling process that the dog was dubbed "the white cavalier." ▪ The original cross was between a Bulldog and a White English Terrier, a breed now extinct. The result was called the Bull-and-Terrier, and with refinement he became the dog known as the Staffordshire today. The Bull-and-Terrier was a fighting

dog; he appeared about the time fighting and bullbaiting were being outlawed, but surreptitious contests went on for some time after that. ▪ About 1860, it was thought that an all-white dog might be attractive, and a breeder named James Hinks, of Birmingham, set about to produce him. He crossed the Staffordshire with the White English Terrier, and by selective breeding eventually achieved the Bull Terrier of today. At one stage the old Spanish Pointer was introduced for size. A touch of Dalmatian and Greyhound or Whippet may also have been added. ▪ The Bull Terrier is a powerful dog standing 15 to 17 inches at the shoulder and weighing, ideally, about 45 or 50 pounds. There is no stop at his brow; the profile curves gently from the top of the skull to the tip of the nose. The eyes are triangular in shape, the ears erect, the tail tapering. The skin is tight fitting; the coat short, flat, and glossy. ▪ Since 1936, a colored Bull Terrier, which may be anything but white, has also been recognized.

STAFFORDSHIRE TERRIER

This is what the ferocious fighting Bulldog of the early 1800's looked like. Not exactly, of course, for there have been crosses and refinements along the way. But the fellow known as the Bulldog today was a later development and would in any case have been too short-faced and bandy legged to survive the fighting pits. The Staffordshire was agile, muscular, and dead game, having a powerful body, straight legs, and pronounced cheek muscles on a strong jaw. ▪ Today, while still a dog of great strength for his size and with an air of no-nonsense authority, the Staffordshire is docile, tractable, and easy to train. Having finally achieved the show ring in 1935, he seems now to be content with the role of exhibition dog. ▪ The Staffordshire was the result of a cross between a Bulldog and a White English Terrier. He was a fighting dog, as some of his many early names suggest. He was first known as the Bull-and-Terrier Dog, then as Half and Half, Pit Dog, Pit Bullterrier, and Staffordshire Bull Terrier. In the United States, where

he was introduced in 1870, he was known not only as the Pit Dog and Pit Bullterrier, but also as the American Bull Terrier and Yankee Terrier. The A.K.C., accepting the breed for listing in 1935, recognized the name Staffordshire, which was an English mining town and a center of dog-fighting activity in the nineteenth century. ▪ The dog produced in the United States today is somewhat bigger and heavier than his English cousin. He stands 17 to 19 inches high and weighs 35 to 50 pounds (perhaps 10 pounds less in England). He is a stocky dog. His broad skull has a pronounced stop. Uncropped ears are preferred, although cropped are allowed. His tail is short, tapering, and not docked. The coat is short, stiff, and should have a gloss. Any color is permitted, and the body may be solid, parti-colored, or patched. Liver, black and tan, and more than eighty per cent white are not regarded with favor. ▪ The Staffordshire is not a widely popular dog, but he is intelligent, a good guardian, and a safe and affectionate pet.

Among the nine members of this catchall category are several of the more attractive and stylish breeds available today. Here is found the fabulously successful Poodle, far and away the world's most popular breed. Here is the taut, briskly animated Boston Terrier, the most favored of America's few original canine creations. Here are the beautifully ugly Bulldogs, the one from France, the other a gentled but still game version of the terror of England's fighting pits. And here is the uniquely spotted Dalmatian, the Coach Dog that trotted the king's highways under the axletrees of swaying carriages and stages. Four unusual dogs complete the roster: the Dutch Keeshond and Flemish Schipperke, faithful guards of the canal barges; the lordly Chow Chow of China, and the Lhasa Apso of Tibet.

POODLE

The Poodle is very chic these days. He always has been an intelligent and attractive dog, but recently he has been rediscovered and become the most popular pure-bred dog in the nation. His virtues are many. He has the beauty, brains, and unsurpassed style to be a desirable pet and an effective show dog. He is a star of obedience competition and, if need be, a rugged field dog, although his uses as a hunter have dwindled. He does not need much exercise and thus can adapt successfully to city living. His only drawback is his elaborate coat clip. Probably more money is spent on grooming the Poodle than on any other breed. Yet undeniably his bracelets and pom-poms and rosettes add greatly to his appeal. ▪ A dog that looks as modern as the latest Paris creation, the Poodle, nonetheless, traces far back into the past. Some profess to find evidence of him in the ancient world, but while there may have been a forebear in Egypt, Greece, or Rome, it is rather more likely that he began to approach his present form in western Europe. He often is referred to as the French Poodle, and

France has been pleased to accept him as her national dog, but the fact of the matter is that France has no stronger claim to him than any other country. ▪ Germany, which may in fact have been the place of origin, probably gave the breed its name—*Pudel*, meaning to splash in water. In France, he is called the *Caniche*, which derives from *Chien Canard*, or duck dog, a reference to his use in the field as a retriever. ▪ Most authorities agree that the Poodle belongs to the spaniel family and some suggest that he was the original Water Spaniel. Whether the spaniel ancestors actually came from Spain or whether they had already spread elsewhere by the time the Poodle began to evolve is not known. A link in the chain may well have been the Poodle-type breed called the Water Dog, which was known in England, Russia, and on the continent for centuries. He was being bred for retrieving game as late as the mid-nineteenth century. ▪ Whatever his derivation, the Poodle had achieved his present-day form at least by the fifteenth century, when he was

*Bevy of Poodles: Miniature
(opposite) and Standard (left).
Young dogs (below and
bottom) wear simple,
even Puppy clip.*

painted by both Dürer and Pinturicchio. ∎ More truly than of any other breed, it can be said of the Poodle that there is a size for every taste. There is the Standard Poodle, 15 inches or more at the shoulder; the Miniature, between 10 and 15, and the Toy, which is 10 inches or less. The Standard and Miniature varieties compete in the Non-Sporting Group at dog shows and the Toy, of course, in the Toy Group. In the United States and England, the Miniature Poodle is more widely accepted than the Standard. The Toy, identical except for size, has produced many remarkable specimens and won an army of admirers. ∎ The basic working Poodle was what would now be considered the Standard. When his usefulness as a hunter diminished, the Miniature was developed, perhaps as a lady's pet. Etchings and paintings indicate that good specimens of Miniature Poodles existed in the early 1800's. The Toy seems to have come a short while later. In the

United States, the dog has been known and shown since the 1880's, by which time he was no longer in use as a retriever, but solely as a companion and show dog. For about thirty years, between 1900 and 1929, the Poodle's popularity dwindled and a number of new breeds—the Collie, the German Shepherd, and a number of terriers—were found more interesting. In recent years, however, he has made a strong comeback. His wit, his intelligence, his elegance, and his convenient size have made him one of the very best apartment dwellers available. He is a squarely built dog, neat, well proportioned, with an alert stance and an expression of bright curiosity. He has a profuse and curly coat which looks most distinctive when neatly clipped in any of the stylish Poodle patterns (see page 219). Originally, the Poodle colors were solid white, black, or brown. Now, through a mingling of these basic hues, accomplished mostly by English breeders, Poodle coats of cream, cafe au lait, blue, silver, and apricot are permissible in the show ring.

DALMATIAN

He acquires his name from Dalmatia, today a province along the Adriatic coast of Yugoslavia. That much everyone agrees on. For the rest, no one is sure. He may well have been in existence before there was a Dalmatia. Early Egyptian art depicts spotted dogs following chariots that may have been Dalmatians, for wherever he began, he has come through the centuries unchanged. ▪ His nicknames are many: Fire-House Dog, English Coach Dog, Carriage Dog, Spotted Dick, and Plum-Pudding Dog. All bespeak his looks or several of his many functions. He is quite possibly the most utilitarian dog of all the purebreds. He has been used in war as a guard or sentry dog, he has been a draft dog and a shepherd. Sportsmen have found him entirely capable as a bird dog, a trail hound (although he is not a hound), and a retriever. He is both intelligent and trainable, and has, therefore, made a fine performing dog in circuses and vaudeville. But primarily he is the coach dog. Since the advent of wheeled vehicles, he seems to have been following them. He has been the cheerful companion of the road for countless grand lords and their equipages, and he has been the mascot of numberless fire companies. His position as coach dog never was fixed. At times he trotted ahead, at times behind. Often he stationed himself under the front or rear axle, and most spectacularly—with a coach-and-four—he ran along under the pole, between the lead pair and the wheel horses. ▪ His role demanded strength and endurance, both of which the well-muscled Dalmatian has always had. He is a clean-limbed dog standing 19 to 23 inches at the shoulder and weighing from 35 to 50 pounds. His spots are unique; the color and quality of the markings are the most important feature of the show dog. The ground color must be pure white, the spots either jet black or, in the liver-colored dog, deep brown. Spots should be as round as possible and range in size from a dime to a half dollar. They should not intermingle. Dalmatian pups are born pure white and their spots develop later. ▪ This dog has a happy and affectionate nature.

BULLDOG

No one ever has shown the Bulldog to be a product of any country but Britain, with the large, strong, broad-mouthed war dogs of the early Britons probably his earliest forebears. The name came from the cruel sport of bullbaiting, which required tenacity and extraordinary courage. There is a record of butchers' dogs fighting bulls in 1209. The equally barbaric sport of dog fighting was a natural outgrowth of bullbaiting, although the dogs used were quite different from the Bulldogs of today. They were higher in leg, lighter in bone, smaller in head, longer in muzzle, and not so wide in front. ▪ Dogfighting eventually was forbidden by law in 1835 and with it went the Bulldog's usefulness as a sporting dog. Extinction might have followed if efforts had not been made to preserve the breed's fine qualities while eliminating the old ferocity. Through breeding, the English Bulldog became one of the finest of physical specimens, with an appearance of immense strength and courage, but with an affectionate, docile nature. ▪ The breeding of Bulldogs is difficult. Their physical construction often makes Caesarean operations necessary. Sterility in bitches is commonplace. Physical beauty never has been an attribute of the breed, nor has beauty been desired. The breed Standard requires a dog of medium size and smooth coat with a heavy, thick-set, low-slung body, a massive, short-faced head, wide shoulders, and sturdy limbs. The gait should be loose-jointed and shuffling, with a characteristic roll, but free and vigorous. The chest should be broad, deep, and full, the legs short, straight, and strong. ▪ The first description of the breed in literature was by W. Wulcher, who referred to it as the Bondogge in 1500. Seventy years later there was a grouping that listed them as Mastine and Bondogge and Butchers Dogge, and it was not until 1630 that a reference was made to the Bulldog. Mastiff and Bulldog fanciers have argued for years which came first, with both sides claiming its breed to be the ancestor of the other. Both may have had a common ancestor in the Alaunt, a good bullbaiting dog believed to look like a Great Dane.

CHOW CHOW

There is a story which says that the Chow Chow's name derives from the pidgin English expression for bric-a-brac—the miscellaneous curios brought to Europe from the Orient. As early as the mid-eighteenth century these goods were called "chow chow"—much as we apply the term to "mixed pickles" today—and eventually it came to mean the dog, as well. The Chinese named him more sensibly. They call him Black Tongue or Blackmouthed Dog, which, unlike any other breed in the world, he is. ▪ The Chow Chow is a lordly dog, massive, powerfully built, and aloof in nature. His solidity is emphasized by his dense, woolly coat, particularly the great ruff around his neck. "Clothed in a shining, offstanding coat," proclaims the Standard, "the Chow is a masterpiece of beauty, dignity, and untouched naturalness." His coat often is red, but may be any solid color. ▪ The Chow Chow breed is at least 2,000 years old. Fanciers suggest that he may be one of the world's basic breeds, although if that is so he has unaccountably failed to pass on the prominent blue-black tongue. Another theory says he resulted from a cross between the old Tibetan Mastiff and the Samoyed. ▪ The first western description of the breed was written in England in 1780 by a minister, one of whose neighbors had brought a pair from Canton on an East India Company trading ship. If his observations were accurate, the breed has changed very little between then and now. For the next hundred years the dog was little more than a curiosity, but in the 1880's Queen Victoria herself took an interest in the Chow and his popularity began to spread. His first appearance in an American dog show was at Westminster in 1890. In the United States he has been primarily a show dog and to some extent a pet, but in China he is a distinguished guard and hunting dog. He has speed, stamina, a good nose, and he points staunchly, like a setter. ▪ Coolness toward strangers is characteristic of the Chow and he is likely to regard friendly advances with suspicion. He is an excellent watchdog as a result, and utterly devoted to his family.

Keeshond and Chow Chow are distantly related. Both are members of the Wolf-Spitz family, though trail that led one to the Netherlands and the other to China is not known.

KEESHOND

Toward the end of the eighteenth century, the Netherlands was split by internal political strife. On one side were the partisans of the Prince of Orange, on the other a people's party calling itself the Patriots. The leader of the Patriots was Cornelis de Gyselaer, and he had a pet dog that became the party mascot. Some say the dog's name was Kees, others that that simply was the Dutch nickname for Cornelis. In any event, the dog has become the Keeshond—pronounced "Case-hond," plural Keeshonden. Partnership with the Patriots almost proved fatal to the breed. When the Prince of Orange won out, it became a distinct embarrassment to have a Keeshond and a great many Patriots began disposing of their dogs. Only the most loyal admirers held on. (If the Patriots had won, the Pug would have had a hard time, for he was the symbol of the House of Orange in this affair.) ▪ The story is a good one as far as it goes, but does not account for the dog's being called a Keeshond for many of the several hundred years' of its existence prior to these events. ▪ The Kees-

hond is an alert, compact dog with a dense, harsh, silver-gray coat, tipped with black. He has been likened to an overweight Pomeranian, and there is little doubt that he is of the same Spitz-type dog that produced the Pom, the Samoyed, Elkhound, Chow Chow, and the rest. He also has been called the Foxdog—because of a foxy face, most likely, for he has never been a hunter. And those of a facetious turn of mind have called him the Cheesehound. His function as guardian of the barges on Holland's canals led to his being called the Dutch Barge Dog, but he also lived on farms and was a truckman's pet. His bushy coat forms a lionlike mane around the neck and shoulders and gives him feathers on the trailing edge of his front legs and "pants" on the rear ones. The tail should lie close to the body and should seem to be part of its owner's outline, rather than an appendage. It once was the fashion in Holland to clip him in the manner of a Poodle. ▪ The Keeshond stands 17 to 18 inches, and is a pleasant and tractable dog, who serves well as guard or companion.

FRENCH BULLDOG

The *Boule-Dogue Français* dates from 1860, when small specimens of the English Bulldog were sent to France and bred with several unidentified breeds there. Some say that the English export was a Toy Bulldog, a type never highly favored in Britain, but all that is certain is that the dog emerging from these crosses was small. In conformation, he resembles his heavier and more cumbersome English relative, but with two major points of difference: the skull and ear. The Frenchie's skull is flat between the ears and slightly rounded at the forehead. The English Bull's has no curved or domed appearance; the planes are flatter. And the French Bulldog has prominent bat ears, rather than the rose ears—small, drop ears—of the Englishman. The bat ears are broad at the base, elongated, and well rounded at the top. They are spread fairly wide apart and carried erect. When the breed first became popular in France, both rose and bat ears were permitted. Insistence on the bat ear as a distinctive feature of the breed came from American breeders late in the last century, as the dog began to make his mark in the United States. They felt that the rose ear robbed him of his individuality and made him appear to be no more than a miniature of the English Bulldog. A French Bulldog Club of America was organized and the bat ear adopted in the Standard. Any other kind constitutes a disqualifying fault at shows today. The club gave its specialty a tremendous promotional boost by holding a French Bulldog show in the Grand Ballroom of the Waldorf-Astoria Hotel in 1898. The event was a sensation and most of society began clamoring for the dog. ■ As a personality, the Frenchie is affectionate and sweet-natured. He barks very little. He is an intelligent and reliable watchdog. His short coat is easy to keep clean and well groomed. Permissible colors include: all brindle, fawn, white, brindle and white. Definitely excluded are: black, liver, black and tan, or black and white. There are two weight divisions. Lightweight is under 22 pounds. Heavyweight over 22, but not over 28. The breed is something of a rarity today.

BOSTON TERRIER

The bright, energetic, and tautly strung Boston Terrier has always stood high in popular favor in the United States. He generally has been among the first ten in the annual American Kennel Club registrations, and well he might be. He is one of America's few native breeds. He was developed in and about Boston from English and French bulldog stock crossed with terriers. As in the case of many older breeds, dates have a way of blurring, but an important one is 1865, when Robert C. Hooper of Boston imported an English crossbred named Judge that was mostly Bulldog and part terrier. He became the foundation sire. Another recorded date is 1889, when there was a sufficient number of fanciers to form the American Bull Terrier Club and show the breed as Round Heads or Bull Terriers. In 1891 the breed was renamed the Boston Terrier, and two years later the dog was accepted by the A.K.C. ▪ The breed has undergone many changes in size and structure. Line breeding and inbreeding have reduced the size, encouraged compactness, and brought refinements. Lit-

tle dogs from Europe, notably a 6-pound runt named the Perry Dog, helped. Attention also was paid to markings. The terrier eye was given up in favor of the large, full eye. The ideal dog now weighs no more than 25 pounds, is smooth coated, compact, and well balanced in body, and has a square, wrinkle-free head and a short, wide muzzle. The Boston Terrier is a clean-cut dog with snow-white markings on a brindle frame. ▪ He has come through many controversies over what should constitute the correct type, and although fighting dogs are in his background, he is not a fighting dog. A merry, gentle disposition has won him the name "American Gentleman" and an honored place in the home. During a period in the late 1920's and early 1930's, he was the most popular breed of all and he never has fallen far from that position. The type now is firmly entrenched not only in the United States, but in many countries throughout the world. Few dogs can equal his style and elegance. Intelligence and alertness have been bred into him as fully as physical appearance.

SCHIPPERKE

This is a Flemish dog found on the canal barges of Belgium. The name is pronounced "Skeep-er-ker," with the final "r" almost silent, and means "little Captain." That he is. Bargemen, shoemakers, artisans, craftsmen, and the Queen herself, Marie Henriette, all have liked and admired the active little dog with the keen curiosity and the sharp bark. ■ The Standard of the Schipperke Club of America goes to unusual lengths in praising its breed's qualities. The Schip's virtues include excellence as a guard dog, kindness to children, and a coat that needs little attention to keep it looking well. He is not primarily a sporting dog, but he has been used successfully to hunt rabbits, moles, and vermin. Unaccountably, he is fond of horses and likes to be in their company. He is suspicious of strangers. ■ The breed is believed to be a descendant of a rather large, 40-pound sheep dog called the Leauvenaar. This also was a forebear of the Groenendael. From it the Groenendael gradually was bred larger and the Schipperke smaller. The Schip is at least 300 years old. Guild workmen in the Grand Palace of Brussels had an exhibition of them, for reasons unknown, as far back as 1690. At that time the dog was called Spits, or Spitske. Schipperke was made the official designation in 1888, after a parent club was formed. Some say the name was chosen to honor the owner of a Brussels-Antwerp barge company who had many "little Captains" on his boats and was also instrumental in promoting the breed. ■ The dog made his first appearance in the United States in 1888, and was first admitted to A.K.C. registration in 1904. ■ The Schipperke's appearance is distinctive. He resembles no other breed. The body is short and thickset, the head foxy, the expression keen —almost mischievous. He is a cobby dog whose chestiness is accentuated by a thick, neck-and-shoulder ruff. He also has a long culotte—the hair on the back of the thighs. He often is born tailless, but if not, must be docked to no more than a 1-inch length. His coat is harsh. Solid black is his only color. He should not weigh more than 18 pounds.

LHASA APSO

In Tibet, this small, long-haired, hard-coated dog is called Abso Seng Kye, or "Bark Lion Sentinel Dog." He is a guardian of the house and has a warning bark at the approach of strangers. This is not actually very leonine, but in China the name Lion Dog is commonly used to describe any small dog with a heavy coat. The Pekingese, for instance, which sometimes is declared to be an offshoot or descendant of the Lhasa, is also known as a Lion Dog. ▪ Tibetan dogs may well have a common ancestor, for the three other major breeds—the Tibetan Terrier, Spaniel, and Mastiff—all have the Lhasa's dense coat and his habit of carrying his tail curled over his back. The most notable feature of the Lhasa Apso is the profuse hair of the head that falls heavily over the eyes, as with the Old English Sheepdog. The hair is straight and of good length, and has a hard texture, not a woolly or silky one. As befits a Lion Dog, the preferred colors are gold, sand, honey. But acceptable colors include: slate, smoke, dark grizzle, black, white, brown, and parti-colored. ▪ The breed is believed to have existed in Tibet for 800 years or more, but for much of this time it was rarely seen by outsiders. From the beginning of the Manchu Dynasty in 1583, until its fall at the turn of the twentieth century, it was the custom of the Dalai Lama to present Lhasa Apsos to members of the Chinese Imperial families. The gift was considered an honor and a good luck token. ▪ In the United States, the name and the breed were established about 1934, when a parent association was formed. Even so, the breed was so imperfectly understood that it was accepted into the A.K.C. studbook under the wrong name. It was thought to be the Lhasa Terrier. The error was compounded when the dog was classified as a Terrier. The name finally was corrected in 1943, the transfer to the Non-Sporting group some time later. ▪ The Lhasa stands only 10 to 11 inches at the shoulder, but is a responsive companion and devoted to his owner. His generations of training as a watchdog have given him a strong instinct for defending his family.

Originally, Toy dogs were playthings of the leisure class. They were ladies' dogs, lap dogs, boudoir dogs. In China and Japan, they were called "sleeve dogs" because they were small enough to be carried in the capacious sleeves of silken Oriental gowns. They never have been utilitarian dogs. They never have pulled a cart, corralled a sheep, or retrieved a bird. They were the favorites of courtiers—elegant, decorative, the perfect accent for a portrait by Fragonard. Yet for all their ribbons, Toys always have been bold and jaunty dogs. Their association with luxury has never made them slack. Indolence has never made them lazy. They are smart, spirited, and brave. They are easily trained, well mannered, and score impressively in obedience trials. They are ideal apartment dwellers and ideal pets.

CHIHUAHUA

The Chihuahua is the smallest dog in the world. He may weigh as little as a single pound, and the ideal show-ring weight for the smooth-coated variety is from 2 to 4 pounds, with a top limit of 6. (Long-coated Chihuahuas may range from 2 to 8.) In judging the breed the smaller of two dogs is always preferred if they are otherwise equal in type. ■ The Chihuahua has been the favorite Toy breed in the United States for many years and one of the most popular of all pure-bred dogs. With none of the physical attributes that make other dogs useful as guards or for sport, the Chihuahua owes his lofty position entirely to his appeal as a pet. He is not even much of a show dog. In proportion to the Chihuahua population, the number entered in competition is small. And when a Chihuahua wins a variety group or Best-in-Show, it is an event. The explanation for their few bench appearances lies first in the fact that they are delicate travelers, and secondly in their owners' unwillingness to subject pet dogs to the rigors of shows. The only area outside the home

where the breed often excels is obedience training. Properly trained, the bright little Chihuahua takes a back seat to none. ■ Besides intelligence and diminutive size, the breed has appeal because of its variety of coats and colors. The smooth-coated are more numerous in the United States, but the long coat is making progress. The smooth coat is soft textured, close lying, and glossy. The long coat has the same qualities but may be slightly curly and have an undercoat. The dog should have a large neck ruff, feathering, and a plumed tail. As for colors, anything goes, from snow white to jet black and solid, marked, or splashed. Solid colors usually are preferred in the United States. ■ The Chihuahua is a compact little dog, with the energy, speed, and darting grace of a terrier. The Standards for the two varieties, except in coat, are almost identical. Two prominent features are the ears, which are large and flare out at a forty-five-degree angle when in repose, and the tail, which is moderately long and may be carried in a loop over the back. ■ The Chihuahua's back-

*Tiny Chihuahua is an
extremely bright dog. Opposite
is good specimen of
standard smooth-hair. Pair
below are attractive
long-hairs. Apple-round
Chihuahua skull can be seen in
pups whose ears have not yet
grown to adult size.*

ground is hopelessly confused. There is not even any agreement that he is a Mexican breed, despite his name. Some authorities are certain he is the oldest North American breed and that he traces back 1,000 years to the Toltec civilization of ancient Mexico. This opinion is based largely on stone carvings depicting a dog that closely resembles the modern breed, and on a theory which says the Chihuahua resulted from a cross between a Toltec dog, the Techichi, and a dwarf, hairless dog that crossed to North America from Asia via the Bering Strait. Others say the Techichi was a prairie dog, a rodent rather than a canine, and that there were no dogs at all in Mexico until Cortez arrived in 1519. One distinguished paleontologist states firmly that no dog fossils have ever been discovered in the country,

thus leading to the conclusion that the dog came at a later period and very possibly from abroad. Interestingly enough, Chihuahuas of the present type do not seem to have been numerous or popular in Mexico until about 1895, and even today breed standards and development are maintained far more strenuously in the United States than in Mexico. Interest in the breed was aroused when Americans discovered that Chihuahuas could thrive as house dogs even in the colder areas of the United States. The Chihuahua Club of America was formed in 1923 and has been a strong influence in promoting the breed ever since. ■ The Chihuahua has a pleasant and engaging personality with people and other Chihuahuas, but is somewhat clannish and does not like other breeds of dog.

SILKY TERRIER

The Silky Terrier, the result of a cross between the Australian and Yorkshire Terriers, is the newest addition to the A.K.C.'s official family of purebred dogs. He was admitted to the studbook in 1959. He is not, in fact, a brand new dog, having been known in his home territory of Australia since the nineteenth century, and having been shown there for the first time in 1907. A Standard was written in 1909, and thereafter the dog spread to India, to England, and finally to the United States. ▪ Even though he is of relatively recent origin, the Silky leaves a number of questions unanswered. Did the first Australian breeders deliberately set out to produce a different dog than the Australian Terrier, or was the Silky a by-product of another breeding experiment, or a sport? No one knows. There may also be a trace of Skye Terrier in him to contribute to his silkiness, but at what point this might have happened, or whether it might not merely have come out of his Australian Terrier inheritance again is not known. In any event, the effort—random or not—has ultimately produced a fine little dog. ▪ The Silky has pronounced terrier characteristics and spirit. He has the flat terrier skull, and small, dark, piercingly keen eyes. Erect ears add to the impression of alertness. The feet are small, the tail docked. He stands 9 to 10 inches at the withers and weighs 8 to 10 pounds. His coat is, indeed, silky. It is blue and tan, and on the body, from behind the ears to the seton of the tail, it measures 5 to 6 inches long. It is worn in a part from nose to tail. The hair on the head is profuse enough to create a topknot; it should be fawn or silver. The blue, which may be pigeon, slate, or silver blue, covers most of the body. The deep, rich tan is an accent: muzzle, cheeks, a spot over each eye, at the base of the ears, on part of the legs. At home he has been known as Sydney Silky, after the city of his origin, and as the Australian Silky Terrier. He is a friendly, lively dog, responsive and curious. And despite some terrierlike devastation among the rats and snakes, he should be classified as an engaging household pet.

YORKSHIRE TERRIER

The Yorkshire Terrier was a creation of the late nineteenth century. His principal forebear seems to have been the Skye Terrier, which accompanied the Scots weavers who migrated to England around 1850. These Scots settled in the textile-manufacturing centers of Lancashire and Yorkshire, and their dogs bred with the various Toy and Terrier breeds already known there. The exact progression that resulted in the Yorkshire is not on record, but one of the major crosses was between a Skye and a black-and-tan Manchester Terrier in 1850. It also is believed that Maltese and Dandie Dinmont crosses were made along the way. The type had evolved far enough to be shown at Leeds in 1861, although at that time it was grouped with Scotch Terriers. (Scotch was a very loose category. It was even used to cover Skyes.) ■ The original Yorkshire—which was not called Yorkshire until the breed was recognized by the Kennel Club of England in 1886—ran 12 to 14 pounds and was far too large to be judged with the Toys. There were small dogs in his heritage, but the reduction in size most likely was the result of selective breeding. Curiously enough, the dog was very nearly down to his present size in the first twenty years of his existence—an amazingly fast bit of work by the breeders. Today neither size nor weight is specified by the Standard, but an average Yorkshire stands about 7 inches at the shoulder and weighs about 4 pounds. ■ His most remarkable feature is his long, silky coat. It must hang straight and evenly on either side of a top-to-tail part. Some breeders let the hair grow all the way to the ground, and some Yorkshires must wear boots or stockings to keep from ruining their coats when they scratch. Because the coat is so silky it used to be said, as a jibe at the Scots, that they wove it on their looms. Keeping the coat in show condition requires constant care and considerable dedication. Coat colors are dark steel blue from top to tail, golden tan on the head, and a bright tan on the chest. Pups are born black, perhaps a reminder of their Manchester inheritance. The breed currently is extremely popular.

MALTESE

The tiny, silky, white-coated Maltese is something of a mystery. His name obviously refers to the island, but whether the breed did in fact originate there, no one really knows. Edward C. Ash, a noted dog historian, set himself the task of examining every work on Malta in the British Museum and found no mention of the Maltese dog in any of them. Other writers are equally skeptical of claims that the Maltese was the lap dog of the aristocratic ladies of Greece and Rome, saying that the ancient dog was more likely a Pomeranian type. His place and time of origin, then, are unknown, but it seems possible that he was in existence in Queen Elizabeth's time—for from that time forward there are references to dogs the size of ferrets or of squirrels, of dogs small enough to be carried in a lady's sleeve, all of which could fit the Maltese. Sir Joshua Reynolds portrayed an unmistakable Maltese in 1763, and by 1800, the breed was popular in England and on the continent. Various names were applied to it, including Shock Dog, which probably referred to the breed's

great shock of hair, for there is otherwise nothing shocking about the tiny Maltese. His first appearance in a show was at London's Agricultural Hall in 1862. He became increasingly popular for twenty years or so, but then leveled off, and has been dwindling since World War I. In the United States, the Maltese has held a firm, respected place for many years. ▪ He is a delightful pet, as well as a striking, sharp little show dog, and can be an excellent obedience competitor when trained to his highest potential. His distinctive feature, of course, is the long, straight, incredibly white and silky coat, which is parted from nose to tail and hangs down evenly on each side of the body. The head is slightly round and rather broad between the ears. The eyes are very dark and the expression gentle but alert. The tail is carried gracefully, the end resting on the hindquarters and to one side. Despite his minute size, the Maltese has a well-proportioned body. Show dogs may not exceed 7 pounds and the Standard declares specimens under 3 to be ideal.

ENGLISH TOY SPANIEL

In the United States the name English Toy Spaniel covers four varieties of dog: the King Charles Spaniel, a black and tan; the Prince Charles, a black, white, and tan tricolor; the Ruby, a chestnut red, and the Blenheim, a white and red. Except for color, all are the same dog, a compact, short-nosed breed with a long, soft, wavy coat, which seems to have originated in Japan. It is not at all clear how the dog made his way west, but it is not true that he first reached England in the reign of King Charles II (1660-1685). The King favored the dog and lent his name to it—only the black and tan variety existed then—but it had been known in the country at least a hundred years earlier. Queen Elizabeth knew of the Toy Spaniel, and Mary Queen of Scots is said to have brought them into Scotland from France. ■ The Blenheim variety is credited to John Churchill, the Duke of Marlborough, who acquired Blenheim Palace with his dukedom in 1702, after service to the crown as soldier and diplomat. His dogs were used to hunt woodcock and thus were called Cockers or Cocking Spaniels; some said they were the best, as well as the smallest, in England. Even today, when 12 pounds is the outside weight limit and some little fellows weigh no more than 6, the Toy Spaniel has not entirely lost his natural hunting instinct. ■ The King Charles and Blenheim varieties had the field to themselves until late in the nineteenth century, when breeding for color was better understood and the Prince Charles and Ruby types were established. These two were given separate registration in 1892. ■ The short muzzle was also introduced in the nineteenth century, beginning about 1835. By the 1880's the Toy Spaniel had achieved his present conformation. Specimens shown in photographs of the period could hardly be improved on today. The breed has been known in the United States for perhaps 150 years and has been registered by the A.K.C. since 1902, but has never been particularly popular. (In England, since 1923, all four varieties have been listed as King Charles Spaniels. The American designation is not used at all.)

PAPILLON

The Papillon is a variety of spaniel with a French name that refers to the way his large, fringed ears sit on his head like a butterfly's wings. He is a lively, graceful little dog and the delicacy of his appearance hides a bold nature and a sturdy constitution. In times past he was a good ratter. These days he is a show dog and pet that has proved adaptable to city or country living. ▪The Papillon is a descendant of a breed known in the sixteenth century as the Dwarf Spaniel. He was a favorite of many great ladies and appears with them in the portraits they commissioned from such masters as Watteau, Fragonard, and Rubens. Madame de Pompadour had a pair of Papillons. Marie Antoinette is supposed to have had one named Thisbe that sat faithfully outside her prison. ▪ The breed is believed to be quite old, and Spain the country of origin. Giovanni Filipponi, an Italian dealer, is credited with introducing it to France, where the pick of the lot went to Louis XIV. At this time the breed's ears were drooping, but in the course of its development the erect, "butterfly" ear appeared and with it came the change of name. Today both the erect and the drooping ear are permitted in the show ring and may even appear in the same litter. If the ear hangs, however, it must hang completely. A partial droop is a fault. ▪ Originally, almost all Papillons were a solid color, but the predominant pattern today is a white ground with patches or ticking of other colors. The coat is short and smooth on the head, muzzle, and parts of the legs, flat on the back and sides, and abundant around the neck and shoulders. The tail is richly plumed, set fairly high, and carried like a squirrel's. The Standard specifies a height at the withers of 11 inches or under and a weight "in proportion." ▪ Papillons were recognized in England in 1923. In the United States, although they had been shown for many years, a parent club was not established for the breed until 1935. The dog is still something of a rarity, although his owners find him hardy and attractive.

JAPANESE SPANIEL

The Japanese Spaniel is a dainty dog with a perky spirit and a stylish leg action when under way. His build is square, his chest wide, and his plumed tail carried proudly over his back. His coat is profuse, the hairs long and straight. He comes in two colors only: black and white, and red and white, although red includes lemon, orange, sable, and brindle shades. ■ It is not at all certain that the dog originated in Japan. Most authorities agree that the Pekingese, the Pug, and the Japanese Spaniel, or Japanese Chin, as he is also called, are ancient Oriental types, but that purebred dogs probably were not native to Japan. It is also true that pictures of dogs closely resembling the Japanese Spaniel are rather frequently found in China—in temples, on ceramics, in embroidery. Since dogs often were presented or exchanged as royal gifts in ancient times, it may be that the Spaniel reached Japan through the generosity of one emperor to another. In Japan the Spaniel was a possession of the nobility and was awarded to foreigners only in gratitude for assistance rendered to the nation. When Commodore Matthew C. Perry opened Japan to the West in 1853-1854, "four small dogs of a rare breed were sent to the President (Fillmore) as part of the Emperor's gift." These seem to have been Spaniels, or Chin. Perry later gave a pair to Queen Victoria. Once introduced abroad, the breed took hold. It was well-established in the United States by 1882. ■ The Japanese Spaniel comes in several sizes, although it is the small ones that best meet show standards. Over and under 7 pounds are the two weight classes. There is a saying that "As a Japanese Spaniel looks when he is exactly six weeks of age, so he finishes." Like most sayings, it is rooted somewhere in wisdom, but difficult to prove. ■ The breed has an extremely sensitive nature. Dogs have been known to sulk for days at a time because of an imaginary affront. Normally, however, the Spaniel's temperament is friendly enough and he makes a fine pet.

Brave and beautiful Peke was known in 8th-century China, has been a western favorite since 19th. Classic Pekingese is at right. Specimen at left wears newly developed white coat.

PEKINGESE

The Standard of Perfection for the Pekingese says that the dog must suggest his Chinese origin by the "quaintness and individuality" of his expression; his resemblance to the lion by his "directness and independence," and over-all "should imply courage, boldness, self-esteem and combativeness rather than prettiness, daintiness or delicacy." The Standard is notably correct. The Peke is no lap dog, but one with an extra measure of audacity coupled with stamina not generally credited to the Toy breeds. He has a remarkable independence of spirit; there is no servility in him. He has a reputation for being somewhat self-willed, stubborn, and even disobedient. Yet he is a faithful and devoted pet in the home, with instinctive good manners and neat habits. ■ No breed has a more fascinating history than the centuries-old "Lion Dog" of Imperial China. He has been traced back at least as far as the Tang Dynasty of the eighth century and survives in a number of beautifully carved figures of ivory, bronze, and wood. He was, in fact, a sacred possession of the Imperial family. To steal a Pekingese was a crime punishable by death. ■ War and invasion brought him to the notice of the west. When the British looted the Imperial palace at Peking in 1860, five dogs were found in the rooms of the Emperor's aunt and taken to England. One, a gift to Queen Victoria, received the appropriate name of Looty. ■ Toward the end of the nineteenth century, the Dowager Manchu Empress, T'su Hsi, showed her favor to Americans by making gifts of some of her dogs. Few, however, were bred in the United States. The best American breeding stock, then as now, came from Britain. ■ For all his small size, the Peke is a strongly built dog. Like the lion, he has a massive chest and mane and narrow hindquarters. The Standard puts a maximum of 14 pounds on him. The smallest Pekes—what in China would once have been called "sleeve dogs" because they could be carried in the sleeve of a robe—are 6 pounds or under when full grown. All colors are allowable. Red, fawn, black, sable are common.

BRUSSELS GRIFFON

The Brussels Griffon generally seen in the United States is a sturdy, bewhiskered dog with a short, thick-set body, and a dense, wiry coat. He is no beauty by ordinary standards and his background is neither ancient nor distinguished, but those who know him are captivated by his animated personality and his endearing expression of quizzical intelligence. ▪ He is of Belgian origin, as his name suggests, and gained wide popularity in that country between 1870 and 1880, partly because of the patronage of Queens Henrietta Maria and Astrid. The Griffon is believed to have sprung from the Belgian street dog of the seventeenth century. These peasant dogs evidently conformed to a type which was nearly as large as the present-day Fox Terrier, but with a thicker body. They were quite unattractive in appearance—with rough, shaggy coats, the color of mud. They were called *Griffons d'Ecurie,* or stable Griffons, and were extremely capable ratters. The development of the contemporary Griffon is not known for sure, but seems to have involved the street dog and the Affenpinscher, with further infusions of Pug and English Toy Spaniel. The breed reached its present stage by 1880, was imported to England in the 1890's, and to the United States about 1900. ▪ The Brussels Griffon's rough coat may be reddish brown, reddish brown mixed with black, black with uniform reddish-brown markings, and solid black. A smooth-coated Griffon variety, known as the Brabancon, has no trace of wire and does not come in solid black. Griffons are divided into two weight classes for show purposes: not over 7 pounds for smaller dogs and up to 12 pounds for others. ▪ Never a pampered dog, the Brussels Griffon makes a delightful pet. He is intelligent, alert, and active, and has unusual strength and endurance for his size. He is a companionable dog and reportedly enjoys hikes and swimming. He is ordinarily an obedient fellow, but sometimes quite difficult to break to a leash. It is urged that this training begin at an early age. The Griffon is still an uncommon dog in the United States, although seen occasionally at shows.

AFFENPINSCHER

Simply because this little fellow has bushy eyebrows, bristly whiskers, a small goatee, and shaggy hair that grows every which way from his head and face, he often is called the "Monkey Dog." Most unfair. The Affenpinscher is a hardy, intelligent dog with a quiet manner, but of a fiery temperament when aroused. "He carries himself with comical seriousness," says the Standard, but acknowledges that he can get "vehemently" excited when attacked. ■ The ideal Affenpinscher stands no more than 10¼ inches at the shoulder and weighs a mere 7 or 8 pounds. The coat is an important feature, particularly in the show ring. It should be stiff and wiry in texture—short and dense on the body, long and shaggy on head, neck, and legs. The mustaches and tuft of hair on the chin should be prominent. The usual color is black, although black with tan, red, or gray are permissible. The eyes are dark and the eyelids rimmed in black. Many specimens wear a black mask. The ears are cropped and the tail is docked. The general impression should be one of sturdiness, with no hint of delicacy, despite the small size. He has the terrier characteristic of spunkiness. ■ The origins of the Affenpinscher are not clear. He has been said to trace back to seventeenth-century Germany, but proof is lacking. His coat undoubtedly resulted from crosses with other German wire-haired breeds, although it is not clear just which ones. It has been suggested that there is a streak of Miniature Pinscher in him, and it is known that he himself contributed to the development of the Brussels Griffon. The most that can be said for sure is that he had reached his present conformation by 1900. He also is a parent of the Miniature Schnauzer. ■ He made his first appearance in the United States in the 1930's and began to attract attention at dog shows after 1936, when the first outstanding specimen of the breed was imported. Affenpinschers have continued to be shown, but never in large numbers, nor does any year produce many A.K.C. registrations. The Affenpinscher is a devoted little dog and makes a bright and lively family pet.

PUG

The Pug is currently among the most popular breeds in the United States. This is his second climb to favor. He was well regarded in the last half of the nineteenth century, and then virtually ignored as new breeds, such as the Pomeranian, came to the fore. Between 1901 and 1906, only twenty-four Pugs were registered with the A.K.C. Today registrations are rising toward 7,000. ▪ Although he is often called the "Dutch Pug," there is no evidence to suggest that the dog originated in Holland. It is rather more likely that he had his beginnings in China, the traditional home of short-faced, large-headed breeds with curly tails. Traders of the Dutch East India Company, who did a lively business in China, seem to have been the first to bring the dog to Europe. He gained wide and early popularity in the Netherlands, and then in England, where he made his first appearance at a show in 1866. The first Standard was written in 1883. And by 1889 he was established in the United States. ▪ The Pug's name is something of a mystery. It is possible that it derived from "pugilist," for good specimens do, indeed, have something of the air of a well-conditioned prize fighter whose face has suffered a bit from the warfare of the ring. The Pug is a cobby dog—square, compact, and firmly muscled. The Standard does not specify a limit on height, but the dog must be well knit and well proportioned, and somewhere between 14 and 18 pounds in weight. The coat is short, smooth, soft, and glossy; this is one Toy breed that is easily groomed. The accepted colors are silver fawn, apricot fawn, and black. The Pug's markings are important and should be clearly defined and as black as possible. These include the markings on the muzzle or mask, the ears, and the trace—a line that runs from the top of the skull to the tail. Two other distinctive Pug features are a tightly curled tail ("The double curl is perfection," the Standard exults) and button ears, which have a flap folding forward. The Pug is an alert, tractable, and companionable dog.

POMERANIAN

At the beginning of the nineteenth century, the Pomeranian was a 30-pound dog capable of herding sheep. Runts usually were destroyed, although as time went on, they occasionally were brought to maturity and found to lose nothing either as to conformation or coat. These smaller dogs weighed perhaps 16 pounds, or even as little as 12. They were exported to other countries where eventually they found such favor that the larger variety was allowed to dwindle and die out. Today the Toy size—3 to 7 pounds—is supreme. ▪ The Pom is one of the many descendants of the Spitz-type dog. The American Pomeranian Club says that the forebears were large white Spitz, bred down from sled dogs of Iceland and Lapland. Other theories place the essential dog as far back as ancient Rome. But whatever the time and place, the Spitz derivation surely seems indicated by the foxy face, erect and pointed ears, and the mane around the neck and shoulders. The breed name comes from the German duchy of Pomerania, although this was not the point of origin, but, perhaps, one of the centers where the breeding down to small size took place. ▪ The most important single feature in judging the Pom is the coat, which is allotted 25 points out of a possible one hundred in the Standard scale. Breeders have made great improvements in the coat in this century in lustre, luxuriousness, and color. The best coats are soft and fluffy underneath and have a long, straight, glistening outer coat that covers the entire body. The ruff should be particularly abundant. The tail should be covered profusely with long, spreading hair, and should be carried flat over the back. A dozen colors are permitted in the show ring: black, brown, chocolate, red, orange, cream, beaver (a dark beige), blue, white, orange sable (light tan undercoat, orange guard coat, steel gray hairs with black tips), and parti-colored (white with orange or black in even patches on the body). ▪ As a personality, the Pomeranian is alert, bold, and vivacious.

ITALIAN GREYHOUND

This handsome little dog has absolutely no use at all, except as a charming and elegant pet. "The small Italian Greyhound is not above half the size (of the Greyhound)," wrote Thomas Bewick, the artist, in 1790, "but perfectly similar in form. In shape it is exquisitely beautiful and delicate. It is not common to this country (England), the climate being too rigorous for the extreme delicacy of its constitution." He was right and wrong. Right about the dog's stylishness and wrong about his hardihood. Although frail-looking, he is as strong and weather resistant as any other household dog, and has thrived wherever he has been introduced, including England, Scotland, Canada, and the United States. ▪ How old this miniature Greyhound really is, or when he first appeared in Italy, is a matter for speculation. There is some evidence that he has existed in his present form for more than 2,000 years, and that he was a favorite of the indolent aristocrats of Greece and Rome. He is known to have been established as a breed by Renaissance times and to have been introduced to England in the reign of Charles I (1625-1649). Frederick the Great of Prussia had one, admired it much, and at its death buried it with his own hands on the grounds of his Berlin palace. The breed reached its height of popularity in England in the Victorian era. It was fairly popular in the United States between 1875 and 1900. As a matter of fact, it was American stock that helped revive the breed in England after World War I. ▪ The Italian Greyhound is a dwarfed version of the Standard Greyhound. It undoubtedly was achieved by inbreeding; there are records of specimens as small as 5 pounds. With refinement, the Miniature has become somewhat more slender than the Greyhound, proportionately. The skull is long, narrow, and flat, the neck long and arched, the back curved downward to the hindquarters. The skin is supple, the coat thin and glossy as satin. Colors include fawn, red, mouse, blue, cream, and white.

MINIATURE PINSCHER

The pert and peppy Min Pin looks exactly like a small Doberman Pinscher. The Miniature Pinscher Club of America, however, does not acknowledge a relationship between the two dogs, but holds that the miniature breed has been in existence for several centuries. That certainly is long enough to establish him as an independent breed, for Louis Dobermann's breeding program did not produce the Doberman until about 1890. ▪ At the same time, the parent club's Standard of Perfection for the breed adds something to the confusion by emphasizing the similarity of one dog to the other: "A miniature of the Doberman Pinscher, having on a modified scale most of its physical qualifications and specifications." At the least, it must be noted that the development of the Toy type was not pursued until the formation of Germany's Pinscher Klub in 1895, when the Doberman was emerging. It appears likely that two patterns of breeding were working toward common objectives, but different sizes. What can be said is that the dog originated in Germany, where he was also called the Reh Pinscher after the small, delicate, and animated Reh deer. ▪ The Min Pin has a quite bold nature that suggests a much larger dog, a quality that contributes to his usefulness as an alert, though hardly dangerous, watchdog. He has good intelligence, he is lively and attentive. In conformation he is slim, symmetrical, with well-distributed muscle and a perky carriage. In the show ring he moves with a high knee action, like a little Hackney horse, that always draws a buzz of admiration from the crowd. ▪ His coat is slick and smooth and sheds hardly at all, which makes him a desirable pet for apartment living. Favored colors are a so-called "stag" red, black and tan, or brown with rust or yellow markings. In size he is ideally 11 to 11½ inches high at the withers. In weight he runs from 6 to 10 pounds. ▪ In the United States, his popularity has risen steadily since the formation of the parent club in 1929. He is a lively and affectionate pet.

MANCHESTER TERRIER

There are two varieties of Manchester Terrier. The Standard type, a dog weighing from 12 to 22 pounds, is grouped with the Terriers by the A.K.C. The miniature, essentially the same dog except for size, is grouped with the Toys. Until 1959, the two were considered separate breeds, although close enough in type that interbreeding was permitted. Since then they have been one breed with two varieties. The Toy is rather more popular in the United States. ▪ Both stem from an early black-and-tan English terrier universally admired as an accomplished rat killer. This Black & Tan Terrier, as he was called, was a coarser dog than his descendants. His coloration was weak and he lacked the elegance of the contemporary Manchester's dotted brows and penciled toes. Nonetheless, he was a dog with possibilities. ▪ In Manchester in the middle of the nineteenth century there were two notable "poor men's sports"—rat killing and rabbit coursing. Seeking a dog that could be skillful at both games, a man named John Hulme bred

a Whippet bitch to a crossbred dark brown terrier with a good reputation as a rat killer. The issue proved sound, other breeders followed suit, and a new breed became established. It was designated the Manchester Terrier in 1860, but as the dog actually became known in many parts of England, the name later was dropped as too restrictive. He then was called the Black & Tan Terrier until 1923, when the Manchester Terrier Club of America was formed and declared a preference to the original name. ▪ The breed developed in the United States about the same time it was spreading through England. The dogs were in demand as ratters in the stables of the rich and also were favored house pets just before the turn of the century. Passage of a law prohibiting the cropping of ears caused a drop in the dog's popularity in England in the early 1900's. Many of the old breeders quit raising the breed when discouraged in their efforts to produce an attractive Manchester with the small button ear that was now the Stand-

ard. In the United States, too, interest in the breed waned after its initial success. A foundation for today's fine dog was being laid, nevertheless, and with the formation of the parent club the breed soon regained its popularity. ▪ The Manchester now is a trim, long-headed, smooth-coated fellow. He is definitely a terrier type. The Whippet has long since been bred out of him. (It showed primarily in a curved "roachback.") His short, glossy coat is jet black and rich mahogany tan. His tail is a whip. Only in the ears are the features of the two Manchester varieties distinctly different. The Standard dog has erect or button ears set as closely as possible on top of the head. The Toy dog's ears are naturally erect and with pointed tips. The Toy weighs under 12 pounds; for the show ring there are two weight divisions: over and under 7 pounds. Both varieties have a keen, wide-awake expression and an alert and energetic appearance, which are part of the terrier personality. They are clean dogs and easy to groom.

SPECIAL BREEDS

The 115 varieties of dog discussed in the preceding pages probably represent about half of the pure breeds existing in the world today. Virtually every country has a hunting dog, a shepherd, a terrier, a hound, or a toy that is locally known and admired, and may have bred true for centuries. They are not seen in the United States, however, because no one has yet become interested enough in them to bring them here and breed them and register them.

It may be that some of them are, indeed, uninteresting dogs, or too similar to a breed already flourishing, or to one out of favor, or subject to export restrictions, or simply too large a risk. It is important for purebred dogs to be admitted to the studbook of a registering organization, preferably the A.K.C., but certain standards and qualifications must be met. It must be proved that the dog breeds true to type. A well-established American club of fans and fanciers must be prepared to sponsor it. And there must be enough dogs and breeders around to make all the effort worth-while. The American breeder who spots a Mediterranean fisherman's dog during his summer cruise of the Greek islands will think twice before he invests heavily in attempting to promote the breed.

TIBETAN MASTIFFS

Nonetheless, from time to time this is exactly what happens. New York's well-beloved governor, the late Herbert H. Lehman, was instrumental in popularizing the Boxer. Edith Wharton had much to do with exciting interest in the Yorkshire Terrier. As noted at several points in the text, the Marquis de Lafayette sent several varieties of European dog to American friends.

Not all catch on. Relatively new and still extremely scarce, with only a very few new registrations each year, are such dogs as the Belgian Malinois, the Komondor, the Kuvasz, and the Field and Sussex Spaniels. If interest flags too much, one or another of these dogs could be dropped.

And one or another of those which follow might be added. This is merely a sampling of the many purebred dogs that might be among the show-ring champions and warmly regarded pets of the United States at some time in the future.

TIBETAN MASTIFF:

Most of the larger purebreds have a trace of this dog in them. For he is the modern version of the great parental dog whose characteristics have been carried across continents and centuries and are perpetuated today in Great Danes, Boxers, St.

Bernards, Newfoundlands, and many others. He has been shown for some years at English dog shows, but otherwise is not very well known outside of India and Tibet. He is a big dog, measuring 28 to 30 inches at the withers and weighing 130 to 150 pounds. He has a medium-length coat of black or black and tan, and a plumed tail which is carried over the back.

TIBETAN SPANIEL:

A real rarity outside of Tibet or India, this little dog somewhat resembles the Toy Japanese Spaniel, but has a foxier, more pointed muzzle. He stands 10 inches at the shoulder and comes in red, red and fawn, or biscuit.

LURCHER:

This dog has found its way into many canine history books, but so many conflicting statements have been made about its origin that its absence from the studbooks of every recognized registry is quite understandable. One reason for confusion about him is his centuries-old association with the wandering gypsies of England and the continent. One writer claims the Lurcher was used by English poachers in the time of Charles I to take game from the royal forests. Yet he also claims that the dog is a cross between the Whippet and the Collie. Since Whippets were not known before the early nineteenth century and the Collie before the eighteenth, the case for their having produced the poacher's dog of a century before is rather weakened. Another writer says the Lurcher's ancestors are the Irish Terrier and the Greyhound, and still another says Greyhound and Bedlington. Greyhound perhaps, but the others again were creations of a later period. A swift and hardy dog, the Lurcher has a resemblance to the Greyhound, although rough-haired. He stands 24 inches at the withers and weighs some 50 pounds. His colors are grizzle, black, or black and tan.

BORDER COLLIE:

Many authorities consider the Border Collie to be the greatest working sheep dog in the world. He has been known in the southern part of Scotland since the middle of the sixteenth century and was first imported to the United States shortly after World War I. Although a small dog weighing only 30 to 50 pounds, he can maneuver sheep several times his size. Since working ability is his foremost quality not too much emphasis has ever been placed on his appearance. Some Border Collies may be as short as 13 inches at the shoulder. Most are closer to 18. The colors generally are black with white markings. Coats may be smooth or long. A variation on the long-haired dog is the Bearded Collie, which has abundant whiskers about the head and muzzle.

AUSTRALIAN KELPIE:

As sheep and cattle raising became increasingly important industries in Australia, it was recognized that the terrain and the conditions of the country called for something different in working

BORDER COLLIES AT WORK.

dogs. Shepherd dogs imported from the British Isles always fell a little short of what was expected of them. Various crosses were tried and, finally, between 1870 and 1880, the sheepherders developed the breed now known as the Kelpie. His basic inheritance is from Scotland's smooth Collie and the native wild dog, the Dingo. Today there are four color varieties: black and tan, blue speckled (somewhat different than the blue merle found in the Collie), red (tracing back to a presumed crossing with a fox), and the barb, which is all black.

AUSTRALIAN BLUE CATTLE DOG:

Cattlemen also created a work dog, using either the same Collie-Dingo cross, or a blue-merle Collie and a Kelpie. The dog is a good worker, stands 17 to 22 inches high, weighs between 32 and 35 pounds, and comes in the color patterns of its parental breeds: blue mottled and red speckled.

SOFT-COATED WHEATEN TERRIER:

This is a native of Ireland whose distinctive feature is his coat. It is the color of wheat and, although its owner is a terrier, it lacks all the terrier's wiry harshness. In size he is a little smaller than the Kerry Blue, standing 17 inches at the withers and weighing 45 pounds. In Ireland he is a farm dog, able to bring cows in from pasture, exterminate rats in the stable, and go out with the hunters and scare up game.

ITALIAN SPINONE:

American soldiers of World War II first brought this dog to the United States. They had found him to be not only an excellent, all-around hunting dog, but a pet with a friendly and even temperament. He resembles the Pointer, but has a rough-haired coat suitable for all types of cover. He is of medium size. His colors are white, or white with red or blue markings. At present he is shown in the Miscellaneous class.

SPITZ:

In the United States, a small, white, long-coated dog of uncertain ancestry has long been known as a Spitz, or a "Miniature Samoyed." These dogs do not breed true, however, and are not related to the ancient Wolf-Spitz family. The so-called Finnish

ITALIAN SPINONE

AUSTRALIAN KELPIE

SOFT-COATED WHEATEN TERRIER

Spitz is a legitimate member of it, although not currently standardized or recognized by the A.K.C. This dog stands 16 to 19 inches at the shoulder, and has a fox-red double coat.

SHIH TZU:

This Chinese dog is a somewhat smaller version of its cousin, the Lhasa Apso. Characteristics are a heavy though silky coat, thickly plumed tail, and hair falling over the eyes. The Shih Tzu is primarily a house companion, but occasionally is exhibited in the Miscellaneous class at shows.

AKITA:

This dog is named after the Prefecture of Akita, one of the northern islands of Japan. His known history goes back about 300 years and one of his ancestors is the Chow Chow. At one time he was used largely as a hunting dog; the Japanese claim that two Akitas, weighing some 130 pounds apiece, could pull down an 800-pound bear. Akitas also have been used on wild boar, deer, other big game —and duck. They have served as war and police dogs. The Akita stands 25½ to 27½ inches at the shoulder—about the size of the Airedale or the Giant Schnauzer. His double coat is of moderate length. His bushy tail is set high and carried over the back. In the United States he usually is seen in the Miscellaneous class, which is reserved for breeds lacking the numbers or distribution to qualify for A.K.C. registration.

ESKIMO DOG:

This is another member of the Wolf-Spitz family and a resident of the eternally snowy areas above

SPITZ

SHIH TZU

AKITA

ESKIMO DOG

MEXICAN HAIRLESS

the Arctic Circle. He is found in the far north of Greenland, Baffin Land, and eastern Siberia. He is a capable sled dog, a fine hunter, and an excellent tracker and trailer. He stands 20 to 25 inches high and weighs 50 to 85 pounds. He once was recognized by the A.K.C., but interest in him declined and he was dropped from registration.

PORTUGUESE WATER DOG:

Virtually unknown in the United States, the Portuguese Water Dog is an excellent swimmer and retriever. In Portugal he is the companion of the fishing fleet and relied upon to retrieve any gear that falls into the water. Sportsmen have found that he is equally proficient in bringing back duck. He somewhat resembles the Poodle, and it is customary to clip him to facilitate his swimming and keep him from getting waterlogged. He stands about 20 inches.

PORTUGUESE POINTER:

This is a short-coated, fawn-colored dog with red ears. He stands about 25 inches high and has a heavy build suggesting a link with the Spanish Pointer or another dog with a hound inheritance.

MEXICAN HAIRLESS:

Hairlessness is not a factor that is well understood, but several denuded breeds are known in several parts of the world. There is one in Turkey, two in Africa, and one in China, as well as the Mexican Hairless. Actually, there is a strong likelihood that the so-called Mexican Hairless is not Mexican at all, but that he originally was brought to Mexico from China in trading ships some 300 or 400 years ago. One oddity is that the Mexicans themselves have always called him the Chinese Dog. The breed was once registered by the A.K.C., but after a long period in which no new entries were recorded it was dropped. It is believed that there are no longer any Mexican Hairless dogs to be found in the United States. It is Toy sized and bare except for a tuft of hair on the top of the skull.

CHINESE CRESTED:

Similar in appearance to the Mexican Hairless and probably related, if speculation about the Mexican's Oriental origin is correct. The breed has been exhibited in the Miscellaneous class at A.K.C. shows in recent years.

PORTUGUESE WATER DOG

CHINESE CRESTED DOG

THE FAMILY PET

Parents may do their child no favor by allowing him to choose the kind of puppy he wants.

An instance of this came one day in a telephone call from a distraught father. His little girl had seen a Collie puppy being walked on a lead and had fallen in love with it. The father and mother had seen it, too, but felt that a full-grown Collie would be much too large for their small apartment. But the little girl's ears were closed to argument or reason, and with tears and stubbornness she was holding out for the puppy of her choice.

A few questions asked over the phone revealed that the parents did not know many breeds of dog. They were advised to bring the little girl to A.K.C. headquarters where she could see pictures of the many appealing breeds raised in America. The father agreed and the family came. At first the little girl was balky. Gradually, however, her attitude softened. Some very attractive pictures of puppies of other breeds were shown to her, and finally one moved her to say, "That's like the one I wanted." It was of a Shetland Sheepdog—very much like her first choice, but considerably smaller in size. The parents were then given a list of nearby kennels. A few days later the father called to say that a Sheltie had been purchased.

The right way to go about selecting a puppy for a child is to do the preliminary work before the youngster realizes he is to have the privilege of helping to pick a pet. The child's part of the selection should be limited to the final group of puppies already checked out as eligible candidates. This should be a happy task for the child. His only consideration should be the particular puppy personality that has the most appeal—or which puppy decides to choose the child. But this part comes at the end of what should be a pleasant quest, not an agonizing problem.

Anyone deciding on a dog should consider size first. What dog will fit the family's living space? There are five size categories. Smallest are the Toys—the Peke and Chihuahua, for example. Then small—the Beagle, the Cairn, the Sealyham, and other little terriers. Medium would include the Springer Spaniel, Poodle, and Dalmatian. Large gets into the Boxer, German Shepherd, and Collie groups. Giants are the St. Bernard and Great Dane. For the small apartment either the Toy or the small dog would be the first recommendations. Many medium-sized dogs do live happily in small apartments, but they manage best under such conditions with people who are accustomed to dogs.

The large and giant sizes should not be considered by city dwellers under any circumstances. Whatever the owner may be willing to put up with, the living conditions cannot help but be deleterious to these large-muscled dogs. Wolfhounds, Danes, big Schnauzers, and the like are suitable only for country estates or farms where they can run at will, without danger from traffic, and where constant exercise will help keep them in condition. Few sights are more pathetic than a big-bodied dog with legs so weak he cannot walk or run properly.

Of course, being dogs and liking people, the giants have put up with confinement as willingly as smaller breeds. Many a St. Bernard has lived in a trailer. Yet in fairness to the dog, some provision should be made to give him the benefits of outdoor living for as much of the year as possible.

The family living in a detached house in the city or the suburbs will not be inconvenienced by any dog from Toy through medium size. Usually there is a back yard, which simplifies the task of giving the dog his daily exercise. No dog should be left in a yard all day, however. The lonely, nothing-to-do hours can be so boring that he becomes a barker. A nuisance dog irritates everyone. There may be complaints to the police that he is disturbing the peace or to the humane society that he is being neglected. He may stir up the dog haters, and he certainly will invite teasing by youngsters.

This raises serious questions every would-be

Cy deuise du chenil ou les chiens doiuent demourer & comment

Valuable dogs were well cared for in 1400's.

dog owner must consider: Why do you want a dog? Whose dog is he going to be?

Many people unfortunately do not think beyond the first appealing notion that it might be fun to have a pup around the house. But there is a vast difference between liking dogs, which is not hard to do, and respecting them enough to care properly for them. Caring properly, furthermore, does not simply mean feeding, watering, and walking the dog. It means paying attention to him, playing with him, talking to him. It means enjoying him in a way that communicates itself, so that the dog feels his master's affection and esteem. To the extent that he does, he will be a livelier, happier, more companionable dog.

Proper care also means a willingness to take the time to teach a dog rudimentary good manners. In our evermore crowded community life it does a dog no favor to allow him to run unchecked. Yet there are thousands of undisciplined family pets

217

who go through life without sense enough to answer to their names. The conscientious dog owner who has his pet's best interests at heart will undertake to train him in at least the basic forms of obedience. It is a chore, but also a pleasure. Dogs, by and large, are intelligent, as dog owners are the first to say. Obedience training is a way to channel it, usefully and constructively. (See Chapter Twelve for a more complete discussion of "Teaching and Learning.")

If this investment of time and effort, if this degree of involvement with your dog seems more than you can, or wish to, spend, then the question of whether to get a dog may have to be answered in the negative.

Secondly, whose dog will it be? This is corollary to the first question. For while it is the nature of dogs to join the family and to like everyone in it, they are likely to fasten on one person as *the* person. This usually is the master, sometimes the mistress, and very often *not* the youngster for whom

Well-chosen pup will delight everyone.

the pet has been acquired. Unless the chosen person is happy to take the responsibility, the dog may be a confused and unhappy fellow. This is likely to be particularly true of the Toy dogs, which are rather more dependent on their masters for affection than most other breeds. The owner has to be willing to spend time with them.

If, on the other hand, the son or daughter of the family is making an earnest effort to gain the dog's friendship and allegiance, it is important for other family members to respect the youngster's authority over the dog and not interfere with or countermand directions the dog has been given.

Having one's intentions and aims as an owner in mind will help in the dog-selection process. It is also important to understand that some breeds are more adaptable than others. A hunting dog loves to hunt, a retriever to swim, a terrier to dig, a sight hound to unlimber his long legs in the chase. But modern living offers comparatively few opportunities for dogs to utilize their traditional skills, and those seeking a dog may do well to choose a breed known for its ability to enjoy itself in a modern setting. Among the most adaptable of dogs has been the Poodle. Once an excellent duck dog, he also has been trained as a circus clown and a vaudeville performer. Although of German origin, he long ago so impressed the French that they adopted him as their national dog. English hairdressers made his dandified coat pattern famous. Americans took him to their hearts because he could amuse his human friends one moment and whip the neighborhood's canine bully the next.

Even so, the Poodle very likely would not be so popular today if he did not come in three sizes. Although the Standard Poodle measures between 15 and 20 inches at the withers—hardly a large dog—it is the Toys and Miniatures, wrapping all the good qualities of the breed in capsule form, that have brought the Poodle his international renown.

When the Poodle first started to gain popularity

Undistinguished lineage is no bar if dog is sound.

in the United States in the early 1930's, his greatest handicap was his coat, which needs to be clipped by a specialist if the dog is to look his best. There are many styles of clipping, but for the show ring only three are accepted: the Continental (without English saddle, or "pants," but with rosettes on hindquarters), the English Saddle, and the Puppy (an even, over-all trim, without bracelets or rosettes).

Today almost any large community has one or more shops making a specialty of clipping Poodles. However, for the man or woman with a do-it-yourself inclination, charts explaining how to achieve the various effects are available from the electric-clipper manufacturers.

How much care a dog's coat will require is always a prime factor in selecting a pet. It is suggested that a novice owner refrain from choosing one of the breeds whose attractive appearance depends on constant trimming, plucking, and clipping. Please note, however, that it is more difficult to pluck and trim many of the terriers than it is to clip a Poodle. Plucking is a matter of removing dead hairs from the coat. Trimming is the tidying up that must be done after the old coat has been thinned out. Breeds that need such tonsorial attention to look their best are the Airedale Terrier, the

Bedlington (which, unlike most other terriers, has a soft coat), the wire-haired Fox Terrier, the Irish, Kerry Blue, and Lakeland Terriers, the Miniature and Standard Schnauzer, and the Scottish, Sealyham, and Welsh Terriers.

It should be said that these are breeds whose *everyday* appearance would change materially by being untrimmed, for there are many show dogs that must, of course, be trimmed or tidied up for competition. Much of the trimming that dog owners insist on is unnecessary, and the national breed clubs try to discourage it.

Practically all dogs have heavier coats in the winter than in summer. Spring is the season for shedding. Breeds that have really long coats, such as the Old English Sheepdog, the Collie, and the Chow Chow, lose a considerable amount of hair. The best, if not the only satisfactory answer, is to brush the dog daily with a stiff-bristled brush. Shedding, of course, is not limited to the long-coated breeds, so it is important for all dogs to have daily grooming.

For many housewives, an important considera-

Biscuit is better for young teeth than bones.

Highland dogs were bred to their tasks.

tion is "doggy odor." The source of this is body oil on the dog's skin. It is normal and natural, particularly for the water breeds. It is oil that enables these fellows to withstand very cold water temperatures. The presence of dog odor does not necessarily mean an unclean dog, but for those people who find it unpleasant the best advice is to avoid breeds that have it to a pronounced degree. No amount of bathing or brushing is going to remove it sufficiently to satisfy a really sensitive human nose. Get a Basenji or an Italian Greyhound.

If the pet is to be a companion for children the age factor should be considered. It can be taken for granted that the younger the children, the less consideration they will give to the feelings of a pup. Young children sometimes hurt puppies without realizing it, and although most pups are forgiving, they occasionally snap back.

The Toy breeds are not recommended for households where there are young children. These dogs are too fragile to withstand rough treatment. Even a loving squeeze might do serious harm to a Miniature, and particularly to a Miniature puppy. Also, the little fellows might defend themselves with their teeth. Older dogs—and the bigger breeds—usually understand that children mean no harm. They take a great deal of punishment without retaliating, and when the situation becomes intolerable, they simply walk away. Parents should make it a point to teach children to respect their puppy

pets. When a child has reached seven years, he is old enough to begin to take some responsibility for his pet. Perhaps he can keep the dog's water dish filled or help with the daily brushing. Dogs relish attention and will feel warmly toward the person who gives it. Very often a dog likes a parent better than the child whose pet he is supposed to be simply because the adult gives the care and attention a dog must have to get on in the human world.

While individuals vary even in litters from the same sire and dam, it is generally agreed that a greater number of well-adjusted temperaments are found among gun dogs, hounds, and the larger of the working breeds. Anyone choosing a puppy, however, can form a better idea of what his adult dog will be by visiting a kennel and noting the way the dogs react to the owner and his kennel helpers. If any of them cringes on the approach of people, it is an indication of mistreatment. Try another kennel, for there is nothing more unpredictable and unreliable than a shy dog.

The majority of new pet owners selects male puppies because of a belief that the female will burden them with countless unwanted litters. This should not cause concern. The female dog is receptive only twice a year. The reproductive cycle begins between the sixth and the eighth month, and thereafter takes place every six months. The period usually lasts twenty-one days, and of this time there are only about nine days when she can be-

St. Bernard is great—if you have the room and someone who can handle him.

come pregnant. For this period the female should not be allowed to run free.

Spaying—a quick and relatively simple operation to remove the ovaries—is, of course, the solution for pet owners who have females, but do not wish to raise puppies.

Many veteran dog owners greatly prefer female dogs because they seem to have a more understanding nature than the male. Females are slightly restless only twice a year. Most of the time they are entirely content within the family circle. Whichever way a person inclines, his choice should be made before visiting a kennel to make his selection.

A kennel is the best place to select a purebred puppy. There are several reasons for advising this. First, the conditions under which the puppies have been raised can be inspected. Secondly, the people who have been shaping the personality of the dogs can be talked to. Third, there is an opportunity to get firsthand information on the procedures to follow so that the puppy develops into a sound and well-humored dog. Furthermore, many fine dog breeders will not sell a puppy unless they meet the people who are buying him. They want to ask questions about the conditions under which the pup will live.

Of course, anyone can get a puppy from a mail-order house, and probably at a lower price. The difference is that such a puppy, very likely, will have been raised at a so-called "puppy mill" where females are bred every time they come in season and where there is little time or inclination to give pups a sense of what it means to live with caring human friends, or to encourage his impulse to be a good little family dog. Commercial breeders such as these often sell entire litters to the mail-order houses for about the same amount of money that a sportsmen breeder charges for a single puppy. The eventual owner of this kind of pup may pay less initially, but very often he has bought a never-ending succession of medical problems—and worst of all, his dog often proves to be an unsatisfactory pet. Remember, there are no bargains in dogs. You get exactly what you pay for.

The average breeder-exhibitor raises and shows dogs because he loves dogs. Chances are that he got into the sport because of one pet that had a special appeal. That particular dog may have departed long since, but there usually is a lingering memory of him. A breeder with such feelings sells dogs only because it is not possible for him to keep all the dogs he produces. His kennel, like most kennels, is not a highly profitable proposition. The only time a kennel really makes money is when it is fortunate enough to have a champion male that every other breeder wants to introduce into the pedigrees of his pups. Stud fees then bring in a considerable amount of cash. There are breeders, however, who restrict the number of times a stud is used rather than jeopardize his welfare.

It is well to consider the dog's viewpoint about people. He accepts many of them because they are thrust upon him, but if he can make a free choice he will be a much happier dog. When the choice of a puppy finally has narrowed down to a few likely candidates, it is suggested that the person most interested in getting a pet be left alone with the "possibles." Chances are that when a human being steps into their pen all of the puppies will immediately crowd around. But after their curiosity has been satisfied, most of them will turn to some new interest, such as a low-flying butterfly or a noise from another pen. If one remains, however, that is the one to purchase. A puppy that is interested in a person from the beginning will quite possibly have an even closer affinity for him in the future.

Before a pup is carried off, the purchaser should verify its age. As noted earlier, the ideal time to change a pup's environment is between the sev-

enth and twelfth weeks. The purchaser also should receive from the breeder a paper signed by a veterinarian showing that the puppy has been wormed and has received inoculations for distemper and hepatitis. Proof of this sort of care makes a detailed inspection of the pup unnecessary. Otherwise: a mucous discharge from eyes or nose, or teeth with a yellowish tinge, are signs that the pup probably has a serious sickness, such as distemper. Teeth, of course, should be white, gums pink and firm. There should be no runny nose or eyes. The insides of the ears should be smooth and pink. (Ears are tender. The breeder will not thank you for probing farther than you can see.) A distended tummy, particularly around the navel, could indicate a hernia. A puppy's coat should be clean and smooth, with no scaly patches. If the coat does show patches, it could well be that he has picked up a skin disease; the three most common troubles are ringworm, mange, and eczema. (If the kennel

Chihuahua and Dachshund are at the peak of popularity.

222

itself is clean and the older dogs appear to be in good shape, it is very unlikely that such conditions will exist.) Puppies of most breeds should have straight, sturdy legs. They should be able to move without obvious effort and their joints should show no enlargement. If the joints are at all enlarged, someone has been neglecting to supplement the diet with cod-liver oil, which contains the Vitamin D necessary to prevent rickets. (Exceptions: Basset Hound and Dachshund pups. The forelegs of the former are normally bent to support the deep brisket, and the latter has feet that turn outward to facilitate his digging for badgers and other underground quarry.) The final test should be for congenital deafness, which can occur in any breed, but is found more often in all-white specimens. To find out if the pup can hear, stand in back of him and make some noise. If the noise does not catch his attention, you can be fairly certain he is deaf.

A buyer whose puppy passes all the tests can be reasonably sure that he has a pet to be proud of. Eagerness to examine and analyze the dog, of course, should not be so obvious as to incur the antipathy of the breeder. It is important to keep on friendly terms with him, for there may be times in the ensuing weeks and months when there will be questions about further care. Usually, however, a sincere and reputable breeder of worth-while dogs is happy to see a puppy go to people who know what they are looking for. The breeder knows that the care taken in selecting a puppy indicates the kind of care he will get in the future.

Before the new owner leaves the breeder's kennel, it is important that he receive not only a list of all the foods and supplements that are to be given the puppy, but a definite time schedule of feedings. These things may change from kennel to kennel, so that a perfectly good schedule taken from a guidebook might be an unwelcome change from what the puppy has been receiving. Such a change can be very upsetting to a puppy, especially

A properly fed dog is a happy dog.

at a time when he is being called upon to make a big adjustment in his style of living.

Some breeders give new buyers a food packet sufficient for several days, until additional supplies of the same brands can be purchased. This assures that there will be no upsetting change in the dog's diet.

Some stores will co-operate by ordering supplies of the food you will be buying regularly. Chainstore managers are generally not able to choose the dog foods they stock, so you may have to seek your puppy's supplies in neighborhoods some distance from your home.

Once your pup has arrived home with you, the selection process has ended. All that remains is to give him a good start toward being a proper dog, and thus avoid doubts and second thoughts about the wisdom of your choice. He is small, uninformed, and a stranger in the house. He has much to learn. But if he is like most puppies, he is the soul of good humor, and eager to please. He is full of possibilities. He can be just about anything you want him to be. But you must lead the way. And why not? He is your dog. You chose him.

Injured dogs were carefully tended after strenuous 15th-century hunt.

Dogs are subject to as many ailments as their masters and from as many causes. Diseases of the skin, eyes, ears, or organs, all affect the pet pup, and he can be harassed by colds, catch pneumonia, and even suffer from rheumatism, arthritis, or, when his time comes, the infirmities of old age. There is hardly a disease known to man that "man's best friend" cannot contract, plus a few more.

Since the dog owner knows what is normal and abnormal in his pet's daily routine, the signs of an oncoming illness will generally be obvious. For instance, the pup that is usually bouncy and has a healthy appetite is probably coming down with something when he begins to act listless or refuses his food. Or the signals of illness may be more dramatic: frequent coughing or gagging, vomiting, high fever, or bloody discharges in the dog's stool. What the dog owner will not know—and should never rely on his own ability to determine—is the reason for his pup's discomfort. The first rule of dog care is to leave diagnosis to the expert. That is the best advice, this, or any, book can give the pet owner.

True enough, there is a wealth of literature on the subject of doggy diseases, but much of it has been written by veterinarians for veterinarians, or for students of veterinary medicine, and the material is highly technical. Books of a more general nature, written in terms the layman can easily comprehend, also exist, but certainly none of the better ones pretends to be a guide to home diagnosis. They are designed merely to provide the owner with an understanding of what illnesses his pet is likely to contract and how to avoid them.

One of the surest ways for the layman to multiply his dog's problems is to experiment with home treatments while the dog lies ill. The possibility of an unschooled and inexperienced owner correctly guessing his pet's ailment and successfully providing a remedial treatment are about 1,000,000 to one. Worst of all, while the owner experiments, the dog's condition can become graver through use of improper medication, and it may even be rendered beyond help through loss of time. At best, the animal will be forced to suffer for an unnecessarily prolonged period, and the owner will probably find treatment costs higher than usual because the illness is in a late or more serious stage.

In his book, *The Complete Book of Dog Care*, a volume consulted by both layman and professional, Dr. Leon F. Whitney explains that the average dog owner needs a great deal more information than he thinks to understand and treat a sick pup, but more than that he needs experience, which no book can provide. However, Dr. Whitney does note that if the owner observes his pet closely and works with him constantly, he may, in time, develop many of the skills required. It would be well to keep in mind, on the other hand, that in this case the learning period described by Dr. Whitney will necessarily be long and require concentrated effort such as few owners can afford.

One of the major difficulties with trying to be your own doctor is that the same symptoms frequently point to more than one disease, and the layman has no sure method for determining what disease the symptoms are pointing toward. A dog that shakes his head continually or cocks his head so that one ear is lower than the other may have an earache; unusual licking of a toe or paw or any part of the body may indicate injury or infection, and continual squinting or avoidance of light may be a sign of a painful eye condition. Yet such symptoms may also indicate a score of other doggy problems. Distemper, the scourge of dogdom, cannot be identified merely by runny eyes and nose, fever-

ishness and a reluctance to eat. These same irregularities may mean any number of other ailments.

In addition, *Canine Medicine,* a journal published by American Veterinary Publications, points out that behavior normal in one instance may be abnormal in another:

"For example, a tendency for the dog to seek a cold spot on which to lie on a hot day will be normal—to seek such a spot in cool weather may indicate fever or abdominal pain. Although sitting is a natural position, too much sitting, or sitting to eat or drink, may indicate locomotor pain or weakness. Sore feet, spondylitis and arthritis are some of the conditions which may cause too much sitting. Severe arthritis or weakness result in protracted recumbency."

Only an experienced veterinarian can properly evaluate a sick animal's condition and prescribe the necessary treatment. Even if the practitioner cannot read the symptoms accurately every time, he is better equipped to read them accurately more frequently than anyone else. And if he warrants his client's trust, he will be quick to admit it when he is baffled.

But the veterinarian's role is not simply one of curer. The competent vet today, unlike the "horse doctor" of a century ago, also is able to practice a good deal of preventative medicine. Modern vaccines and periodic checkups have provided him with satisfactory means for curtailing the spread of a number of canine disorders.

Certainly, where the checkup is not too much of a financial burden to the owner, he should not hesitate to take advantage of it for the good of his pet. The procedure, followed every six or twelve months, is fairly basic, but it allows the veterinarian to keep a record of each patient and makes it easier for him to spot an irregularity when it arises. The doctor simply will take the dog's temperature with a rectal thermometer (normal dog temperature is 101 degrees Fahrenheit), check his teeth, eyes, ears, and skin for abnormalities, keep a close watch for worms or external parasites, and, finally, take corrective measures if they are needed.

Dog owners who pay attention during these checkups can learn a great deal about what constitutes the healthy dog. Without trying to become a diagnostician, or do the veterinarian's job for him, the owner can cultivate a sharp eye for illness simply by having a clear picture of health.

Another way in which the dog owner can be forehanded and forewarned is to have a plainly marked first-aid kit for his pet. It is simple enough and safer hygiene to have the dog's swabs, applicators, eye droppers, and surface ointments and antiseptics separate from the family's and always in one place. The veterinarian can prescribe the elements it should contain and the circumstances under which they can be used.

Under normal conditions, a dog owner can expect to be sensible enough to treat a minor cut, splinter, a scratch, a minor sprain, even a minor burn. People often overlook the fact that their dogs are patient and good-natured creatures that place a great deal of trust in a well-loved master. The removal of a splinter, the cleaning and dressing of a cut foot pad are ministrations an owner can easily manage and a dog will willingly submit to.

Owners should be sure that the regimen they establish for their dogs is a reasonable one. Many owners, for instance, bathe their dogs far too frequently under the mistaken impression that cleanliness is next to healthiness. It is, but not through soap and water. Most dogs are best kept clean through daily combing and brushing, plus a rubdown with a damp washcloth if necessary. Puppies definitely should not be bathed until past the age of three months. The adult dog needs a bath only when he has rolled in the mud or has otherwise become really dirty.

If a bath is called for, keep the water mildly warm. And under no circumstances let soapy water get into the dog's eyes or ears. Dog ears are extremely delicate and sensitive. The less handling

they get from owners, the better off the dog will be.

A most important rule for owners, which should not need saying, but does, is to follow a veterinarian's instructions carefully and thoroughly. After the doctor has given expert attention to the dog's problem and outlined the recuperative treatment, do not second guess him. If pills or liquid medicine must be administered, learn how to do it properly and don't shirk the task. Again, the patient dog will try to do what you seem to think is good for him, but medicines are strange, and if he is excited or afraid, he will balk or spit them out. This is the time to show him what a good doctor you can be.

Like people, recuperating dogs need a chance to get well. Observe the canine patient regularly and closely, so that any after effects—infection, or what not—can be noted before they become serious. Otherwise, let him rest, keep him quiet. See that he is clean, has fresh water, and friendly encouragement. This said, leave major treatment of all kinds to the veterinarian.

Worms are a particular hazard to dog and master, and sooner or later one with which almost every dog owner becomes familiar. Part of the seriousness of the ailment comes from the fact that there are so many patent worm medicines on the market and worming procedures have become so familiar, particularly in the case of puppies, that most owners feel they are equipped to handle treatment at home. They are not.

To begin with, worms that prey upon dogs are not one type, but many. Most owners are unaware of the number of varieties that exists and the degree of danger each presents. Secondly, only when an infested stool is examined under a microscope by an experienced eye is it possible to determine exactly which variety of worm has attacked the individual dog. The four most common types are the roundworm, tapeworm, hookworm, and whipworm. But dogs also are susceptible to a type of pinworm that, though fairly rare, is difficult to eradicate. Beyond these, there is the heartworm, an extremely dangerous parasite which, as its name implies, directly affects the heart, and the lungworm which strikes the dog's bronchial tubes. The lungworm, however, is seldom found in city dogs.

Young dogs are most frequently plagued by roundworms. Puppies pick them up from the nipples of the nursing dam. They are whitish, round, and pointed at each end, and generally range from two to five inches in length. All things considered, they are easy to identify and combat. The tapeworm, on the other hand, usually is limited to older dogs. Many scientists believe the appearance of this long, flat, ribbonlike worm in an animal is directly related to an earlier infestation with fleas or some other external parasite. Whatever the cause, an owner who believes his dog has a tapeworm should waste no time in having the animal examined by a physician. Hookworms can be found in dogs of any age, and should be looked on as equally serious, inasmuch as they gravitate to the intestines and feed on the dog's blood, causing anemia. Hooks protruding from their mouths (hence their name) make them easy for a professional to identify. This is not true of the whipworm. Of the four major varieties, whipworms are the least common and the most difficult to detect. But these inch-long pests, no thicker than thread, can cause serious illness unless discovered and treated quickly. In all cases, the checkup is the best armor science has yet been able to provide for dogdom in combating the discomforts and possibility of death due to internal parasites.

Interestingly enough, the disease which strikes the greatest chill in the dog lover is the disease the dog is least likely to get—rabies. It is estimated that the total number of dogs afflicted in the United States runs to under 1,000 per year, a relatively small number in a nation with a canine population of many millions. In the fiftieth state, Hawaii, where there is rigid enforcement of a six-month quarantine law, the disease is virtually unknown, but elsewhere success in curbing rabies is more the result of the discovery and availability of an effective vaccine.

In many communities, immunization programs are carried out at no expense to the dog owner. On specific days in spring, inoculations are provided for free to those who wish to take advantage of the offer. Some states, and Canada, have taken even more stringent measures and require that any dog traveling in or through their boundaries be vaccinated. Of course, the prudent owner will see to it that his dog is vaccinated each year as a matter of routine, no matter what the community provides or the state demands. Particular care must be taken by those owners who live in an area where their pets are likely to encounter foxes or vermin, notorious carriers of the disease.

Since the only way that rabies can be passed from one animal to another is by bite, local ordinances which force licensing of pets and restrict dogs from running free on city streets have also proved helpful in preventing the spread of the illness. Stray or ownerless dogs—always a menace because their exposure to the disease is so much greater—are now caught and billeted in a local pound until a proper home can be provided for them. Once bitten by a rabid animal, a healthy dog becomes infected, his actions no longer sensible. When either dog or man is bitten by a wild creature, whether or not the attacker is believed to be infected, the wound should be checked and treated by a physician immediately.

Of all the illnesses to which dogs are susceptible, distemper is the Number One enemy, and the mortality rate from it is high. While much progress has been made in determining its causes, and studies such as those currently being carried on at the Cornell Research Laboratory for Disease of Dogs continue, the riddle remains unsolved. Some scientists believe distemper is not a single virus, but a complex of virus disorders. But to date, the best available means for warding off the disease or at least minimizing its effects once it has been contracted is inoculation.

One source of distemper for the purebred is the dog show. For this reason, most major kennels maintain isolation quarters separated from breeding stock for dogs returning from competition. At shows, where spectators are constantly passing from bench to bench and petting the competing dogs, and where judges must touch the mouths of many dogs in succession while examining each competitor's teeth, infections are easily spread. More and more it is becoming the practice for judges to let the handler open his own dog's mouth, and thus reduce the possibility of passing on another dog's disease.

Other more direct measures to limit the spread of canine diseases through shows have been taken by the American Kennel Club, which requires that one or more veterinarians be present at all times while a show is in progress. The doctor's position is defined as follows by John C. Neff, executive vice-president of the A.K.C.:

"He (the doctor) differs from all other officials in that he is not licensed by the A.K.C. He is not directly obligated to the A.K.C., which recognizes that his first obligation is to the ethical standards of his profession. He does, however, have stated responsibilities and authorities. In his work at a dog show he sometimes answers to nobody. Sometimes he provides the authority on which others automatically act and, finally, he sometimes provides the expert opinion upon which others base their official decisions."

The responsibility for a veterinarian's presence rests with the show committee and show superintendent, and the A.K.C. sees to it that its ruling is strictly enforced. Despite their rigid requirement that a vet be present at each show given under its auspices, the A.K.C. exercises no control over fees or other arrangements made between club and doctor. It does, however, frown upon clubs that attempt to use their position in the dog-owning community to force local professionals to do service for unrealistic rates.

Until a few years ago, one of the veterinarian's major responsibilities at shows was to examine each dog as he entered the premises, but the system was not practical and in many places was abandoned. Now the show-giving club has the option of conducting an "examined" event or not—and relatively few clubs do.

If the dogs are to be examined at the gate, the premium list must record the fact and the exhibitors are expected to accept without complaint the delays that necessarily occur. Similarly, those who enter dogs in shows where no health examination is provided should understand the risk involved for their dogs.

Nevertheless, at all shows, whether or not examinations are required, each exhibitor has the right to request the examination of any dog on the premises which, in his opinion, may be suffering from a communicable disease and, therefore, endangering the health of the others. It was hoped that this would discourage the showing of unhealthy dogs. And so far it seems to have been successful. Certainly since the practice was instituted, A.K.C. records show no increase in the spread of doggy diseases and infections at events under its jurisdiction.

When the time comes for a dog owner to select a veterinarian the question is inevitably the same —which veterinarian is the competent veterinarian? The best way to answer for oneself is simply to apply approximately the same standards in choosing your dog's doctor that you would use in choosing a physician for your family.

Is his manner with animals good? Has he been properly educated? Does he carry out his duties well? How does he maintain his office and/or hospital? And, of course, does he keep abreast of happenings in his profession or has his interest in the world of veterinary medicine ended with his formal education?

Almost without a doubt, the undesirable practitioner will reveal himself on the first or second visit. An ill-kept waiting room or office is the first tip-off that this man is not for you. Such practices as seeking payment before treatment is rendered, advertising in a tasteless manner, and guaranteeing cures through mysterious powers, all of which, of course, are condemned by the American Veterinary Medical Association, will also serve as warnings. The man who violates any or all of these is not a good doctor.

An ethical veterinarian does not exaggerate illnesses or charge exorbitant fees for unnecessary injections, for among other things, sky-high fees tend to discourage ownership of pets. It is hard for a housewife to consider spending what she thinks is a lot of money on the family pup when Junior needs his teeth straightened or Mary needs new glasses. And, unfortunately, too few people are aware of the fact that most fees are quite reasonable. Usually an office visit for an examination, including shots for rabies or distemper, will cost no more than $5. If the owner has some fear concerning a particular doctor's rates, however, the safest procedure is to ask him what his fees are before engaging him. Some veterinarians, if they operate on a standard-fee basis, may even have cards for would-be clients itemizing treatments and costs.

The pet owner expects a lot of the veterinarian he chooses, and for the most part, he has a right to. Sometimes, though, he expects more than can possibly be delivered and too often he is mystified by a veterinarian's explanations of illnesses and treatments. Mail received by the Gaines Dog Research Center in New York attests to this and indicates, too, that many dog owners are afraid of discussion with their dog's doctor or seem reluctant to impose on his time. "The vet didn't seem to know," or "He mumbled something," or "He didn't say much," are ever recurring phrases in most of the center's letters.

Some of this bafflement must be eradicated by the veterinarian, but some can also be cleared away by the owner. As client, the owner has a right to know in terms that he can understand exactly for what illness and in what manner his pup is being treated. It is not enough for a bill to list "shots." If the dog must be taken to another doctor at some later date, the owner should have a record of what type of shots his dog has received and approximately at what intervals. If the veterinarian doesn't offer the information, it is the owner's duty to question him.

Of course, the professional's first responsibility is to his patient—the animal owned by his client. This is the way Dr. J.O. Knowles of Miami, Florida, president of the American Veterinary Medical Association, put it in an article in the *Canadian Veterinary Journal*:

"When the client says, 'I have confidence in him,' he speaks about a successful veterinarian. There are all manner of ways of engendering this confidence, but to be really successful every practitioner has to possess the confidence of a significant number of animal lovers.... Good personal relations with our clients and competent service to our patients are the vital ingredients of a successful veterinarian-client relationship. The third necessary ingredient is what I would like to call an alert social conscience. You must become imbued with a feeling of your responsibility to society and, particularly, to the community in which you live. ...A veterinarian is not a professional man if he cannot appreciate his place and his responsibility as a man living among men. If he is culturally sterile and intellectually stagnant, he is not a doctor in the fullest meaning of the word."

The veterinarian who meets the ideal of service to the community, his fellow men, and his patients, and who ethically maintains the standards of his profession may be difficult to find, but such men do exist, and the dog owner who is a dog lover will take the time to find him.

12 TEACHING AND LEARNING

Everyone says dogs are intelligent animals, and so they are—only some are more intelligent than others. It is worth remembering this throughout these pages, which will deal mostly with training.

No dog springs to man's service without being taught to do so. He ordinarily is quite capable of learning. He is a creature of evolution, and the millions of domesticated dogs who have gone before him have sharpened his faculties for comprehending man's ways and accustomed him to many essentially unnatural features in his environment. One has only to observe the ease with which dogs accept, or adapt to, automobiles, elevators, cement sidewalks, and other aspects of modern living to understand what it means when it is said that the dog is man's greatest conquest!

Even so, to do his master's bidding, the dog must understand what is expected of him. He must associate it with simple words of command. And he must learn in a friendly atmosphere with constant encouragement and without fear.

For the trainer this means the gentle hand and quiet voice that bespeak bottomless patience. It also means persistence—steadfastly, resolutely sticking with the task until it is done. And it means awareness—awareness of the student's capabilities, his temperament, and his responsiveness. If these qualities cannot be provided, a professional trainer had best be hired.

This is not at all unusual at the higher levels of canine education, but should not be necessary for the puppy of kindergarten age whose only future lies in the home. The simple tricks that will make him a mannerly dog can and should be taught by some member of the family. One of the follies of human association with dogs is that all too often the fat, bright little pup is allowed to remain uneducated and undisciplined merely because no one is willing to give him the proper attention, and follow through. Almost before you know it, little Bootsie is overturning garbage cans, tearing up lawns, barking like mad, jumping up on visitors, and chasing automobiles.

The results of this kind of carrying on are predictable, if not almost inevitable. The head of the house recognizes that the family has a nuisance dog that is an embarrassment in the neighborhood and gets rid of him. Or sooner or later a passing car smacks Bootsie into the Great Beyond.

The late Clarence Harbison, who became a canine psychologist after a long career in other parts of the dog world, always said that there were no bad dogs, only bad dog owners. He frequently proved his point by taking an obstreperous, scatterbrained castoff into his Connecticut home and turning him into a gentle, well-mannered pet.

The first rule of training, he would say, was to catch and hold the dog's attention: "If you want *real* attention, don't shout—whisper."

He may have exaggerated slightly for effect, but there is no doubt that a firm, even tone of voice carries more authority with a dog than yelling and bullying, which frighten the student and paralyze his ability to act.

The first point of training for any family with a new puppy is housebreaking. And the key to success is to establish a regular, unvarying pattern of activity. Take the dog outdoors as soon as possible in the morning and after each meal, which will be four times a day for a puppy. Also take him out in the evening just before bedtime to be on the safe side. After he is six months old, this schedule can be reduced to four times a day. By the time he is a year old, morning, afternoon, and evening outings will be sufficient.

A corner also should be provided indoors where the puppy can relieve himself in emergencies or in case the outdoor schedule cannot be held to. Any of the new absorbent litter products are a vast improvement over torn newspaper, but whatever is used, make sure the dog understands its purpose. Only when he does, will it be fair or reasonable to punish him for wetting elsewhere in the house. Try to deal with infractions promptly. A firm scolding and a noisy whack on the rear with folded newspaper are standard and acceptable treatment—but not two hours later or the pup will not know what he is being punished for. A light poke on the muzzle will offend the dog's dignity and get the message across as well. A hand slap hurts and should not be used. Nor should rubbing a dog's nose in his accidental mess. It is an unpleasant sort of corrective measure and doesn't seem to do much good, anyway.

Do not end the lesson with a punishment. Having made it clear what is *verboten*, put the pup outside or in his pen to demonstrate what is permissible. And give him his due. When he has performed properly, praise him. Much of his satisfaction in learning comes from pleasing you, so let him know that his efforts are worth-while.

Depending on the age and intelligence of your pup, housebreaking will take four to eight weeks. The more consistent his program, the faster his learning is likely to be. A dog learns by repetition, not by reasoning.

All dogs should know their names. Even a pup of three or four months will learn who he is fairly quickly. Pick one name and stay with it. Do not call him Poopsie one minute, Here, Boy, the next, and Hargreaves Wonder of Tarantula later.

Every dog must also learn the meaning of "No." Don't bother with "Bad dog," or "Stop it, Harry," or "You are being an ill-mannered beast." "No" is a nice, clear word when used emphatically, and it is certainly short enough for the cloudiest little intellect to grasp.

Training is a matter of implanting good habits. Bad ones can form just as readily and once established are difficult to break.

The careful housewife, for instance, never allows a dog to acquire the habit of resting on chairs, sofas, and beds. The comfort of this furniture is a delight to the dog and he will never go anywhere else if his impulse is not curbed immediately. The

A 17th-century Dutchman playing with his Mastiff.

remedy is simple enough. Shove him off the first time he jumps onto forbidden furniture and keep shoving him off thereafter. He will get the idea.

Dogs are sometimes astonishingly perceptive. A certain house dog known to the authors never, never gets on the furniture at home unless invited —and she is never invited. At a country home, however, where the furniture is older and the rules more lax, she's on the sofa all the time. Although her people are the same in both places, she evidently senses that the atmosphere is different.

Barking is a tiresome and annoying habit, and one that will not improve the owner's standing in the neighborhood. And if it is to be controlled, it should be controlled quickly.

Almost any puppy will howl the first few times he is locked up alone in a room away from the rest of the household. One cure is to let him howl and cry until he gets over it. He will, usually in a few nights. This is hard on the nerves, however, and all too many owners cave in and take the whimpering culprit into the bedroom.

A pup usually barks because he is lonesome and afraid of strange surroundings, sometimes because he is hungry, thirsty, or uncomfortable. See that his basic needs are attended to before retiring for the night. His bed should be comfortable and out

When training a dog, it is important to be clear, firm, and patient. Most dogs are eager to learn, but must understand what is being asked. Springer (below) is getting good, strong instruction. Make lessons short. Do not expect too much.

HEEL   COME   SIT

of drafts. Leave a light on. Sometimes an old sock or shirt or other piece of clothing belonging to the owner is comforting for the pup to have with him. A ticking clock works wonders. Very soothing. The nights also will be easier if the pup can be accustomed to being alone for an hour or so during the day. Putting him in his pen or in a separate room need not be a penalty. Most dogs get to like it, even as human beings like occasional privacy.

Every adult dog, excepting the Basenji, will bark once in a while. It is in the nature of the beast, and often it may be a welcome warning of an intruder. The dog who barks nervously and senselessly at everyone, however, can be a serious problem. Half the battle is in dealing with the barking before it gets out of hand. Beyond that point there is nothing to do but treat each incident with the severity it deserves. If the dog is otherwise obedient, it may be that he will respond to a firm voice and a whack with a newspaper, repeated consistently until the lesson is learned. In some kennels, a sudden dousing with a pail of cold water is salutary. The householder cannot do this in the living room, but he might keep a pail handy in the garage for weekend incidents with the mailman and delivery boys.

The overfriendly dog can be as much of a pest as the excessive barker, in particular the jumper who dances around on his hind feet while pawing at people's clothes. If simple scolding fails, try raising your knee just as he comes toward you. It will catch him in the chest and throw him off balance. He should not be kicked, of course, just jolted by coming up against the sudden, unyielding knee. Some trainers prefer to hold the front paws, as the dog comes dancing toward them, and step lightly and carefully on a hind foot. Again, the idea is not to injure the dog, but to demonstrate that a certain action is followed immediately by discomfort. Over a period of time, most dogs will desist.

No dog learns his lesson the first time, or the first dozen times. So get used to teaching him in short sessions, by easy stages. The younger the dog the shorter his attention span. Too much instruction can make him frustrated and sulky. Furthermore, do not be disconcerted if he relapses into disobedience after presumably becoming letter perfect. Your dog is fallible. Treat him just as you have all along: patiently, persistently, understandingly. Correct him gently. Be generous with praise for good performance.

If professional guidance seems advisable or welcome, apply to one of the hundreds of obedience schools and obedience instructors now available in and around most large cities. The point of these schools is to teach the owner, who is expected to

practice with his dog at home between classes. Sessions usually last forty-five minutes to an hour. Courses run eight to ten weeks. A diligent owner should have a pretty well-behaved pet in that length of time. The training is rigorous, however, and no dog under six months old should be subjected to it. Some instructors will not take a dog under a year old.

Most of the commercial schools and any classes conducted by breed clubs go beyond elementary instruction, for a number of owners are interested in advancing into obedience competition. This is a sport that was first introduced here from England in 1934 and is now booming at most dog shows and as an independent event throughout the United States.

Whether interested in competition or simply in getting Rover to behave himself, an owner can gain a great deal from a visit to a training school.

The basics of obedience training have been pretty well established and include lead training, walking at heel, coming on call, sitting, and lying down on command. Advanced instruction includes leaping over obstacles, retrieving objects, scent discrimination, and such exercises as the "long sit," in which the dog is ordered to remain stationary while the owner moves off out of sight for an extended period of time.

The lead—or leash, as nondog people call it—is the means of controlling the dog in training regardless of the ultimate objective. The dog must be taught to walk at the end of the lead without straining or pulling. Obedience adherents call this "heeling."

HEELING: The dog is always held at the left side of the handler. Once he is in position, start walking, at the same time saying, "Heel," sharply and emphatically to impress it on his mind. If he pulls away or holds back, give the lead a light tug. An unruly dog may be tapped on the nose with a newspaper to remind him to stick to business.

Remember to use the word "Heel" at the beginning of every walk and to enforce it, but do not let the lesson become an ordeal. Fifteen minutes is long enough for a young dog, half an hour for an older one. Hold the lessons regularly. If complete non-co-operation is encountered, postpone instruction until the next day.

COMING ON CALL: "Come" is one of the simple words every dog should have in his vocabulary, and there are two methods for getting him to respond to it. One is to entice him by calling the command from twenty or thirty feet away, meanwhile coaxing him by patting the ground. Reward compliance with both praise and a small tidbit.

If he should need restraint, tie a thirty-foot check line to his collar. Give the command to "Come" and urge him along with a gentle tug on the rope. If it is necessary to reel him in the whole way, do so, but pat him, praise him, and slip him a small treat when he has covered the distance. There is one problem with the rope trick. The dog may get the impression that he should comply only under compulsion. No rope, no response. This can be countered by firmness, by never allowing the dog to think he is the boss. Once an order is given, be sure it is obeyed.

SIT: The dog should be placed in front of the handler or at his left side. Take a short grip on the lead with the right hand and push firmly on the dog's rump with the left. The word "Sit" should always accompany the hand pressure. When the dog is in a sitting position, praise him. Then repeat the procedure. Eventually, the dog will sit on the verbal order alone. At first he may lie down instead of sitting. Do not settle for this. Haul him up and set him in the correct position.

DOWN: When the dog has learned what "Sit" means, he can begin practicing "Down." The two obviously are quite similar and should not be taught at the same time. The order "Down" should be accompanied by a downward-sweeping motion of the right hand. The lead should then be stepped on, so that the dog is pulled to a lying position. When command and motion sink in, step a few feet away from the student and repeat the command. He may want to "Come," but keep him away until he knows he is to lie where he is. When he can do this, try him without the lead. Use only the hand motion and vocal command. A bright dog will soon respond to either hand or voice.

German Shepherd has responded nicely to command–"Sit"–which was accompanied by hand signal or pressure on leash.

The dog that has mastered these elementary exercises has put down a foundation upon which an owner can build in several directions. The owner may be content simply to have a mannerly companion. Or he may be preparing the dog for show, for field trials, or for work in civilian or military occupations. All of these, of course, require special training procedures, but these may be accelerated if the trainee has a head start in canine education.

Obedience competition is the usual first step beyond basic training. This is a highly formal kind of sport played according to a small bookful of rules issued by the American Kennel Club. All of the contestants must be purebred. Judging is not at all concerned with physical standards but with performance alone. It demands little of the dog's owner besides an ability to walk. The dog does the rest—and usually with such fascinating, almost military precision that many visitors to shows automatically gravitate to the obedience ring to watch the dogs as they are put through their paces.

The dogs are not separated by breeds, but by classes—Novice, Open, and Utility. Each has a prescribed set of exercises, each exercise has a specific point value, and the total of points establishes the winner. A perfect score is 200, and it is not uncommon for the better dogs to achieve it.

As the dogs progress in proficiency, they earn degrees—C.D. for Companion Dog, C.D.X. for Companion Dog Excellent, U.D. for Utility Dog, the highest possible rating. Degrees are attached to a dog's name the way a college degree is attached to a man's. Some dogs have records of achievement in both bench and obedience circles. They will carry the prefix "Ch." for bench champion and the suffix "C.D.X.," or whatever, signifying their rank in obedience competition.

Some rare graduates of obedience trials go on to an extra special form of field sport called "tracking." This rewards the highly developed scenting talent. A stranger's glove or other object is placed at the end of a course not more than 500 yards long. It is up to the dog to find it over a trail that is not less than thirty minutes or more than two hours old. The dog that passes gets the T.D. (Tracking Dog) degree. Not many pass in any given year, but those that do include a surprising variety of breeds, not just the predictable Bloodhound.

Among the most rugged of the organized canine sports are field trials. These test a dog's hunting skills under a formal procedure that reproduces the conditions he might encounter in the field. There are events for the pointing breeds, the retrievers, the spaniels, and—the largest division of all—the Beagles. The dogs are categorized by age and ability. The progression is Puppy, Derby (up to thirty months of age), and All-Age. Beagles are further divided according to size—those 13 inches and under, and those more than 13 inches but not exceeding 15 inches.

Trials for the pointing breeds originated in 1874 with an event held by the Tennessee State Sportsmen's Association at Memphis. The Beagle trials came next—in 1890 under the auspices of the National Beagle Club in Salem, New Hampshire. Spaniel trials came from England and were introduced in America in 1924 with two events, one at Fishers Island, New York, and one at Verbank, New York. Last to get started were the retriever trials, which were inaugurated by the Labrador Retriever Club in 1931.

Trials vary according to the functions of the dogs involved. Following is a brief outline of the principal kinds of trials.

POINTING BREEDS: These dogs are required to cover a great deal of ground at top speed in what are called "races." At the end of the course is a special area, usually in view of the spectators, which is called the bird field and in which pheasant or quail are planted. The manner and expediency with which the dogs find and point the birds, as well as cover the course, form the basis for judging. The judges, who follow the dogs on horseback, look for style, pace, drive, nose, bird sense,

Boy and Dog: 19th-century painting of traditional pair.

and the manner of handling game. In the bird field the dogs are expected to hunt naturally and at a fair pace, using the wind to find the birds by body scent. Dogs that linger over ground scent, go from bush to bush at an unnaturally slow pace, or hunt in any other unauthorized manner are said to be "pottering" and are penalized. Style is best described as "joy in hunting," which is a characteristic of all great hunting dogs. It shows itself in the dog's verve and dash, in briskness, eagerness, in a merry spirit.

As in other trials, the dogs hunt in braces, but they do not necessarily compete only against their bracemates. The performance of each dog is recorded by the judges, and when all have finished their trials, the judges determine how the leaders will be placed.

The most difficult and distinguished trial in the country is the National Bird Dog Championship at the Grand Junction, Tennessee, plantation of the late Hobart Ames, for many years president of the N.B.D.C. Association. Here the heats last three hours—a severe test of the nation's outstanding bird dogs—and the winner gains lasting fame.

Most of the pointing breeds that participate in field trials are registered by the *American Field,* a Chicago publication considered to be the gun-dog enthusiast's bible.

RETRIEVERS: Here, too, the dogs work in pairs, but they do not work together or at the same time.

One of them must sit quietly by his handler's side while the other handler sends his dog. Retrieving before ordered is a disqualifying fault. The A.K.C., which registers most of the dogs and draws the rules, has this to say: "The function of the retriever is to seek and retrieve fallen game when ordered to do so. He should sit quietly in line or in the blind, walk at heel, or assume any station designated by his handler until sent to retrieve. When ordered, a dog should retrieve quickly and briskly, without unduly disturbing too much ground, and should deliver tenderly to hand. Retrievers which bark, give tongue or whine in line, in the blind, on a drive, or while retrieving should be penalized."

The dogs are judged on intelligence, attention, control, courage, perseverance, and style. "Hard mouth," which means holding the bird in any but a tender manner, is a disqualifying fault. The usual trial consists of a specific number of land tests and a similar number in water.

SPANIELS: Like the pointing breeds, these dogs are expected to find game and, like the retrievers, bring it to hand. They are judged on game-finding ability, including scenting, and on their manner of covering ground (they move in a zigzag pattern, like tacking sailboats), briskness, perseverance, steadiness to flush and shot, and aptitude in marking the fall of a bird. As with retrievers, a hard mouth is a serious fault.

In spaniel trials the emphasis is on the land work rather than the water work. A water series usually is held, but more to test the dog's willingness to enter the water than anything else.

Spaniels flush game and work close to the gun, usually within its range of about thirty yards. Handlers, judges, and gallery follow on foot—carefully, for there is no bird field and game may be found anywhere along the course. The handlers use whistle, voice, and hand signals to direct the dogs.

English Springer Spaniels and the Cocker Spaniels run under the same rules, but do not compete against each other.

BEAGLES: The rabbit is this nation's most numerous and popular game animal and the Beagle is a superb rabbit dog. He is essentially a hunting hound, and his objective is to find game and then drive it "in an energetic and decisive manner and to show an animated desire to overtake it," according to the A.K.C. rules. The quality of a dog's work counts more in his score than the amount of game he finds. The judges look for intelligence, the method of working the ground, and the ambition and industry displayed whether game is found or not. Accuracy in trailing, voice, endurance, starting ability, style—"joy in hunting," again—and obedience to the handler also are factors weighing heavily in a judge's estimate of a dog.

Beagles compete both in packs and braces, depending on whether the game is hare (the pack) or rabbit (the brace).

Beagle trials have grown enormously in popularity, in large part because they are relatively inexpensive to run and because the dog is small enough to be kept by almost anyone. The man who buys one for a pet often finds his dog leading him

into a sport that is good fun, without requiring the expertness in handling or the intensive training routines that other field-trial breeds must have.

All trials are interesting to watch and are held in many parts of the country during much of the year. The dog owner who thinks he might like to become a participant will do well to observe a few trials and ask a few questions. Like most specialties, its adherents are generally willing to encourage and inform the newcomer.

It was just this simply that Prince Tom III got his start. He was a little Cocker owned by a midwestern jukebox serviceman named Tom Clute, and he was no different than 10,000 other pet Cockers. What proved to be important was the fact that from the time he was given to Tom Clute as a young pup, he spent virtually every minute with the big, likable, openhearted man. They got up together early in the morning, shared breakfast, and then drove on Tom's rounds, fixing the machines that needed attention. Big Tom talked to the dog as they rolled along the highways. When they stopped, the little dog went along, taking an interest in his master's work.

In time, the little dog picked up a dozen tricks. He put out the match after Tom lit his cigarette. At home he would fetch articles of clothing his man wanted. Tom took pride in the dog and was pleased to show him off. One day an interested onlooker suggested that a dog as bright as that could probably do well in obedience competition.

Clute got a book on the subject and began to instruct his dog during their lunch hours. Once he was ready Prince Tom earned his three principal degrees—C.D., C.D.X., and U.D.—in an impressive minimum of time.

Hearing of Prince Tom's accomplishments, someone suggested jokingly that Clute now should enter him in the National Cocker Spaniel Field Trial Championship, the highest possible peak of achievement for his breed. Tom knew the suggestion was an idle one, but the idea intrigued him and his confidence in his dog's ability by now was unbounded. Again he got a book. Again he coached the dog himself in their spare time together.

This in itself was quite remarkable, since most dogs that aim for field-trial honors come from kennels where they have been schooled since puppyhood, and approach a big event like a National Championship only after intensive tutelage by a professional handler. Tom Clute was not a hunting man. In fact, he had neither hunted nor seen a field trial before he competed in one.

But he handled Prince Tom adroitly and the little dog did his job to perfection. First crack out of the box, Prince Tom III won the big one.

The story of the two Toms says all there is to say about teaching and learning.

STANDARD SCHNAUZER

SAMOYEDE

ROTTWEILER

PULI

OLD ENGLISH SHEEPDOG

WORKING GROUP

OUVIER FLANDRE

B MA

13 THE WORLD OF DOG SHOWS

The showing of dogs probably reflects life itself about as well as any sporting activity can. The dogs are the central figures and around them swirl their owners or handlers, whose individual anxieties and hopes concerning the outcome of the contest charge the air with tension. It seems a lot to say for what is after all a prosaic pastime, but fully as much as the dogs themselves, a dog show is people. The participants—men, women, and children—from the richest to the poorest—are all energized with the same one wish: to have their dog judged better than another and, if possible, better than any other. And many an owner's psyche is more deeply disturbed by his dog's misfortunes than by his own.

There is no physical contact, as in the more robust sports, other than the probing of a judge's hands as he tests for condition and soundness. But just watch at ringside for even a little while and you will see from the expressions of those inside that tension, hope, and fear are rampant. Even otherwise impassive professional handlers with thousands of ring contests behind them perspire and fret when one person's opinion, good or bad, means success or failure in some such glamour event as the Westminster Show in New York's Madison Square Garden. This show brings out the best of American dogdom, and each dog has at least one rooter to whom a ribbon is of vital importance. The professionals hate the show because they must work harder against fiercer opposition for no more money, but none can afford to stay away. For them, too, a Westminster victory is prized beyond all others.

There are persons who love dogs, but love dog shows better. For them the competitions are a social outlet, a chance to meet others with like interests and perhaps to have a part in the picture by serving as stewards for the judges. There are persons who derive all or part of their living directly from the shows, such as paid superintendents with their staffs of runners, roustabouts, supervisory assistants, truck drivers, catalogue printers, and ribbonmakers. Also present are paid American Kennel Club field representatives, professional judges, those who make or sell dog food and accessories, canine artists and photographers, in addition to editors and writers of dog-world publications. These are the regulars, whose gains are more or less assured, as opposed to the exhibitors, who may or may not profit through sales, stud fees, and the breeding of puppies.

Approximately 900 shows, including small ones limited to a single breed and called "specialties," are held under the American Kennel Club's auspices each year. The smallest shows for which all 115 breeds registered by the A.K.C. are eligible may have 300 or 400 dogs competing. The giants, like Westminster, the International Kennel Club event in Chicago, and the Harbor Cities Kennel Club Show in California, may have close to 3,000 entries. Big and small, the shows are held in all parts of the United States, almost always on weekends, and form the biggest organized segment of canine competition.

Prosperous exhibitors able to bear the expense will show their dogs week after week throughout the year, wherever a worth-while victory may be gained. For such enthusiasts the pursuit of championship and the acquisition of Best-in-Show honors are more important than a mere breed ribbon, and while it is doubtful that many of these people break even financially, material rewards are possible, particularly if a dog can earn the coveted prefix "Ch." This means accumulating fifteen championship points under a complex scale that is different for every breed and locality, and need not be dealt with here; the point scales usually are printed in show catalogues. But it is obvious that a champion is worth more at stud or as a brood bitch than a dog who has no title. Every major victory adds to a winner's value. It is not unusual for a finished show dog to cost as much as $5,000, and the truly great dogs often cannot be bought for any price.

While the out-and-out show dogs, meticulously groomed by paid attendants and campaigned with suave skill by men and women who make a business of showing dogs, are likely to take most of any show's top honors, the dog-show world is not made up entirely of such aristocrats. Good roads and easy transportation have made shows a game for everyone. Where thirty years ago gentry with elaborate kennels containing fifty or sixty dogs dominated an esoteric sport, today we have a preponderance of one- and two-dog owners. A cabdriver or mechanic or small businessman or a tavern owner has a good dog, visits a show or two, then enters the dog. Maybe he gets a ribbon. In any event, he is hooked. It has been said that the average exhibitor's enthusiasm lasts about five years. Then he becomes discouraged and tired of it all. Or he simply has nothing worth showing and drifts away. The really hard-bitten exhibitor and breeder hangs on forever, and when his campaigning is finished, he becomes a judge.

What is a dog show? To the first-time visitor it is organized confusion spread over a large armory, hall, or open field, in which spectators, exhibitors, handlers, and dogs all participate. Incessant barking, jammed aisles, and a good deal of apparently aimless running about as people lead dogs here and there surround the islands of quiet that are the show rings. Despite this impression of chaos, however, a dog show is among the most orderly of sports enterprises. Everything is governed by rule. Every dog has an assigned role in his own particular class and the progression of judging moves inexorably from the smallest Puppy class to the grand title, Best-in-Show. The steps are the same for all shows, great and small.

First there is competition within each breed. Then the breed winners become eligible for further judging in what is known as a variety group. These are six groups described and portrayed between pages 50 and 203 of this book.

The judges award four places in each group. The dog awarded a first advances to the next stage of the elimination. From the six group winners one is chosen as best of all. He presumably is better than any other in the show. That's the theory anyway; although dogs as good or better may have fallen along the way. A really great dog, like a great race horse, however, will find his level even though beset by occasional defeats.

Now let us assume that you have a dog you think is good enough to compete successfully against a number of other dogs. You have an urge to enter him in competition. How do you go about it?

The first step is a scouting expedition to several shows. Go without your dog and study the operation not as a spectator but as a prospective exhibitor. If you like what you see, subscribe to *Pure-Bred Dogs, The American Kennel Gazette,* a monthly magazine published by the American Kennel Club, 51 Madison Avenue, New York City. It contains a calendar of all the country's licensed shows for several months in advance. Included is the name of the superintendent handling the show, as well as the names and addresses of a club officer or two. Write to the superintendent of the show nearest your home for a premium list that includes an entry blank and excerpts from the rules. Fill out and return your entry blank and pay the entry fee, and that's that. You're now an exhibitor.

The rules should be read carefully, particularly those dealing with the closing date for entries, the time you must arrive at the show, and the time you may remove a dog from the premises. Some shows are "benched," meaning that dogs must remain for a specified period of time. Otherwise, of course, those who have paid admission will have nothing to look at except the judging of the dogs. At "unbenched" shows the dogs may be removed any time after they are judged. The latter are, of course, fine for exhibitors but not for spectators.

When entering a show, be sure you have placed

your dog in the proper class. The regular classes for both sexes are: Puppy, Novice, American-bred, Bred-by-Exhibitor, and Open. Puppy classes are for dogs aged six months to a year. Novice classes are for dogs over six months that never have won a first prize at a championship show. Bred-by-Exhibitor classes are for those owned by the breeder and shown by him or a member of his immediate family. The American-bred class is for dogs whelped in the United States from an American mating. The Open class is one in which any dog six months or older, including champions, may be entered. Foreign-bred dogs that have not gained championship status must go into it, with the exception of Canadian-bred puppies, which are eligible for the regular Puppy class. The competition in the Open class is usually stiff, though less so than in the "Specials Only" class, which is for champions of record of both sexes. While champions can compete in the open classes, most exhibitors refrain from entering them because what would be a comparatively meaningless win for them would deprive younger dogs of important championship points.

No dog that is not of pure breeding that can be proved may be entered in an approved show. Exhibitors and breeders have a high stake in the integrity of A.K.C. pedigrees, and if they hear of irregularities, they are quick to blow the whistle. There was a case of a woman whose dog died. She got another dog at a pound and used the dead dog's papers to sell the castoff's pups. The A.K.C. heard about it from a neighbor and barred the lady from the purebred business by denying her registration privileges for life. Mostly, however, the system is based on a presumption of honesty on the part of applicants.

There's more to showing a dog than just parading him in and out of a ring and bearing your disappointments or rewards, as circumstances dictate. Show dogs are judged on their soundness and adherence to the breed standard, but they must have style, too. Ring manners are important and to acquire them the dog must be trained to submit constantly to the handler's control. He must stand perfectly still when posed, must walk or trot at the handler's side without breaking stride or pulling, and he must yield to the close examination and touch of a stranger—the judge. He should not be distracted by crowds or the presence of other dogs.

In posing, the dog must remain motionless, his legs set so that the weight is borne evenly by all four. Once your dog is standing correctly, get a friend to touch him, look at his teeth, and push him down at the rump—all of which are part of the judging procedure. He must not sit down under the hand's pressure, as an obedience-trained dog does. A sitting dog makes a bad impression at a show, and many professional handlers never allow their charges to relax for an instant in the ring.

In action, the dog must move at the handler's side in a straight line. Any departures from an even gait must be checked immediately with a tug on the leash until he gets the idea that he must follow naturally at whatever pace the handler selects. There must be no jumping or pulling or loafing. Obedience must become instinctive.

Dog shows mean crowds, so accustom your dog to them. Take him into the streets to get used to passing strangers. A weekly training class, aside from hastening the disciplinary process, will help him to become used to other dogs and people. Some clubs conduct periodic "match" shows for novice dogs and handlers. These are run like point events, but the competition is less intense, and the practice in showing is valuable experience. Other exhibitors present usually are willing to help with advice and instruction.

In the long run, the dog himself must supply the soundness and conformation that make a polished campaigner, but the training, conditioning, and care is up to you. His physical condition will develop from exercise. Even chasing a ball helps. Tend to his coat by brushing, cleaning, and clipping. Check his teeth and nails. And study the breed standard to learn what a judge will look for.

If all this sounds like a lot of work, it is. Professional handlers licensed by the American Kennel Club will take the burden from you for a fee. The amount depends on the handler. There is no set price, but most will charge from $25 up for taking a dog into the ring and giving him limited preliminary attention. On the other hand, the holder of a license is required to operate a substantial kennel, so you are not likely to encounter fly-by-nights. Competence varies, of course, but handlers often train young dogs in ring manners, groom them, and sometimes board them. Some owners just turn their dogs over to a handler, who thereafter guides all the candidate's ring destinies, even to the extent of picking which shows to enter and which to bypass. The owner pays the board and the entry fees, and gets the ribbons and trophies. The handler gets any prize money earned, as well as his fee. An excellent and experienced handler, the late Walter Foster of Old Westbury, New York, once said of his job: "When showing a dog, a novice may allow him to slouch or lie down if he thinks the judge is not looking. The professional keeps the dog showing all the time because he knows the judge is always looking. Besides, another judge before whom the dog may some day appear could very well be watching from ringside. He'll be forming an opinion, too, and it might as well be a good one."

Pros like Walter Foster know dogs better than any other group in the dog field. They must to survive. An amateur may not know what is good or bad about his dog, or may be subject to an ailment known as "kennel-blindness." The professional will have no such illusions. He will recognize an exceptionally good front, for example, and keep it before the judge. If there is a fault, he will do his best to minimize it. Getting a dog ready for the ring can take fifteen minutes or, in difficult cases, up to a year. A smooth-haired dog, like a Boxer, may require only the clipping of nails and the trimming of stray hairs. But a long-haired dog, like a Skye Terrier, that needs fussy work just before ring time may cause his handler to spend an hour or more brushing and combing the meticulous part down the back.

"I've had Lakeland terriers from England that have needed six months of conditioning," Foster recalled. "The change from England's cooler, damper climate to the hot, dry weather here sometimes causes them to lose coat. You have to take the coat right down to the skin, then let it come in a little at a time. Poodles in poor coat might take a year, starting from scratch."

The top handlers help their clients choose the best dogs from litters. They see more dogs in their travels than most exhibitors and can recommend good prospects.

As masters of make-up they also have been responsible for some of the rules by which the A.K.C. governs purebred dogdom. Several years ago a leading professional artificially blackened the flesh-colored, or "butterfly," nose of a Bull Terrier, which is a disqualifying fault in the breed. The incident touched off a furor over faking. Henry D. Bixby, then executive vice-president of the A.K.C., asked whether "we are awarding prizes for the best dogs or the best make-up jobs" and added, "We ought to show dogs as God made 'em, not as a beauty parlor fixed 'em."

The upshot was a strengthened rule forbidding make-up and coloring powder in the ring. Judges who failed to disqualify when they uncovered chicanery in the ring became subject to disciplinary action. Only the greenest recruits to competition try subterfuge through make-up nowadays, and usually they are caught and "suspended from privileges," which means their dogs cannot be shown or registered until the suspension is lifted.

The beauty-parlor excitement was mild compared to pre-American Kennel Club high jinks. In the bad old days, pedigree mills were commonplace. Ringers were routine. Judges often were bribed, and the rules of competition were sketchy where they existed at all. Not that everybody now is as pure as Arctic snow, but the severity of A.K.C. discipline, which can deprive a guilty handler or official of his livelihood is a powerful influence toward virtue.

The A.K.C., of course, is the strongest single factor in organized dog activity in the United States. Its functions include the registration of dogs, the keeping of a studbook, and the formulation of rules for shows and some field trials, notably those for Beagles and retrievers. Similar, although smaller organizations are the American Field in Chicago, which keeps the Field Dog Stud Book and is concerned mainly with gun-dog trials, and the United Kennel Club of Kalamazoo, Michigan, which recognizes some breeds the A.K.C. does not.

Born in 1884 to curb man's inclination toward skulduggery, the A.K.C. today goes about its business with the efficiency and the trappings of a General Motors, but without profit as an objective. Nobody "belongs" to the A.K.C. It is an organization of clubs, not of individuals. Its New York state charter of objectives says the A.K.C. strives "To adopt and enforce uniform rules...to regulate the conduct of persons interested in exhibiting, running, breeding, registering, purchasing and selling dogs...to detect, prevent and punish frauds...."

The rules have grown with the years. They are frequently overhauled and always enforced to the letter. An Illinois woman once took a dog under her care for a friend entering military service with the understanding that she was to own any puppies that were born to the animal. The serviceman went overseas. The woman bred the dog. The puppies could not be registered because the A.K.C. insists that the registration application be signed by the owner of the dog—in this case the serviceman. Unfortunately, he could not be found and the woman's customers yelled in vain for papers.

John C. Neff, executive vice-president of the A.K.C., has recommended: "If registration is important to you, never breed a dog, or to a dog, on which papers have not been granted." He pointed out that if you did not sell the puppies, they would eat their heads off at your expense, and if you did sell them, the original problem would multiply through the unregistered dog's pups. Buyers would be on your neck forever for documents that you could not supply.

Although the A.K.C. makes the show rules, it does not sponsor shows. There has been only one exception. In 1926, it put on a show in connection with the Philadelphia Sesquicentennial Exposition. The number of dogs benched was 1,767—a medium-large event. Pinegrade Perfection, a sparkling Sealyham of the era, became the only dog ever to win an event conducted under the auspices of the A.K.C.

The club does not influence breed preferences either, although its annual registration figures are considered the nation's mirror of purebred-dog popularity. The figures have been kept by breeds only since 1926 and the fluctuations in popularity have been wide. However, only five breeds—the German Shepherd, Boston Terrier, Cocker Spaniel, Beagle, and Poodle—have held first place.

George F. Foley, whose Foley Dog Show Organization in Philadelphia has made him the country's leader as a superintendent, used the rage for Boston Terriers to start himself on an illustrious career. While in his teens he had an idea that if he could place a dog in a home for a short while, he could make a sale. He tested his idea by advertising in rural newspapers (most purebred dogs were sold at shows at the turn of the century) and guaranteed money back if the buyer was not satisfied. The only stipulation was that the dog be kept a week. Human nature being what it is, he made money. The mail-order puppy almost always won over the family within the week, even if he was not top grade.

Eye appeal, size, and outstanding qualities as pet and show dogs helped Cocker Spaniels hold the lead as the most popular purebred longer than any other breed. The Cockers were No. 1 for an unprecedented seventeen years, from 1936 through 1952. Before them came the Boston Terriers from 1929 to 1935, and the German Shepherds from 1926 to 1928. Beagles finally succeeded the Cockers in 1953, and for a very special reason —the rabbit. Rabbits are this country's chief game animal, Beagles the foremost rabbit dogs, and Beagle field trials on rabbits are a fast-growing and popular sporting event. The A.K.C. registers all the field-trial dogs, hence their high place in the standing. Still in 1960, the Beagles were forced to step aside for the Poodles, and the three varieties of Poodle—Toy, Miniature, and Standard—have ruled the roost for the last few years. At least some of the Poodles' popularity can probably be charged off to their role as a status symbol, but certainly they have also risen to this position of prominence because they are flashy, intelligent, and hardy dogs.

The reasons for the rise and fall of breed registrations are many and not necessarily related to show successes and failures. When the Cocker Spaniel, Ch. Carmor's Rise and Shine, took Best-in-Show at Westminster in 1954, registrations in his breed kept right on sagging. The same title at the same prestige-laden show two years running (1952 and 1953) won by the Doberman Pinscher, Ch. Rancho Dobe's Storm, caused hardly a registration ripple.

A show dog that did produce some effect, though, was the Cocker Spaniel, Ch. My Own Brucie, who won at Westminster in 1940 and again in 1941. Most owners of the breed remember him to this day, and take particular pride if there is a trace of Brucie in their own dog's bloodlines. Brucie caught the public's imagination so thoroughly that when he died the New York Sun put his obituary on page 1. But Brucie didn't "make" Cocker Spaniels. Inherent beauty, small size, a joyous nature, and adaptability to life afield or in the city are the qualities most responsible for the breed's success. Over-production by breeders interested only in sales and the inevitable outcropping of character flaws started its decline, a decline that now appears to have been checked through the vigorous efforts of the American Spaniel Club.

Cocker Spaniels never fell as far as German Shepherds, however. From 21,596 registrations in 1926—then a very high figure—the shepherds dropped to 792 in 1934. Mass production, the dumping of misfits by Germans on the American market, and movies that depicted shepherds as "wolf dogs" almost destroyed the breed. Later dedicated backers helped to rehabilitate both the dog and his reputation. In 1963, the German Shepherd was second on the list, behind the Poodle and just ahead of the Beagle and Dachshund.

Although shows have little influence on registrations, they have a lot to do with breed styles. The A.K.C. approves the Standards of Perfection that are drawn up by the parent breed clubs, and the clubs are influenced in the physical outlines of their breeds by the products of the leading breeders. The latter, in turn, try for the kind of dogs that win at shows.

Percy Roberts of Noroton, Connecticut, one of the country's foremost professional judges, put it this way: "The good judge is the architect and the breeder the builder. The dogs that win are the ones the breeders try to build to."

What he meant was that respected judges are heavyweights when it comes to creating dog fashions. For example, if they consistently give ribbons to terriers with long, narrow heads, judges with less knowledge and less experience are likely to follow suit. Once a trend emerges, breeders try to satisfy it by producing the kinds of dogs judges prefer. Eventually a style of conformation is established.

The heads of terriers have, in truth, been drawn out to exaggerated lengths over the past decade or two. Collie heads have been made leaner and longer, too. Scottish Terriers have been bred shorter in body and lower to the ground. Boston Terriers have been reduced in size. The Boston Terrier, the product of a controversial Bulldog-terrier cross in the 1860's, used to weigh about 35 pounds. Now the breed's top limit is 25 pounds. The American variety of Cocker Spaniel has been made smaller than its forebear, the English Cocker. For a time great emphasis was placed on richness of coat, although now an overabundant coat is frowned upon. Bulldogs have been bred to be stockier, stubbier in the legs, and shorter in the face.

Who are these people who exert such influence? They are men and women from all walks of life who have proved to the A.K.C.'s satisfaction that they are competent to pass on the breeds for which they are licensed. Some, called "all-arounders," are licensed to judge every breed, but most of them are expert in only a few breeds or simply in one.

Their abilities, their methods of judging, their interpretations of the breed standards, and their opinions of the dogs brought before them may vary widely and keep exhibitors and handlers in a stew of uncertainty and controversy. But for all their idiosyncrasies, they are thoroughly honest. The dishonest judge is a rarity if for no other reason than that sooner or later he will be discovered and expelled from the fraternity.

The best ones have what is called "an eye for a dog." Alva Rosenberg, one of the most respected of the all-arounders, once told the writer that the good judge had his mind made up almost as soon as the dogs were led into the ring. Subsequent close examination sometimes disclosed faults in detail, but the first impression almost always was the right one. The person who did not have the "eye" could never be a first-class judge, he said.

Dogs are judged according to the Standard of Perfection for the breed, and against each other. In addition to desirable physical qualities, those that are undesirable and some that may lead to out-right disqualification are listed. Some standards also carry a scale of points totaling one hundred to serve as a judging guide. For example, in Cocker Spaniels the maximum points for neck and shoulders are fifteen, for body fifteen, for action twelve, for skull eight, and so on.

The usual procedure is for the judge to have all the dogs circle him for a quick comparison of gaits. The dogs are then lined up in a row while the judge goes over each in detail, checking teeth, eyes, and coat. If a dog is limping, it is mandatory that the judge call in a veterinarian to establish whether the condition is temporary or permanent. If permanent, or if the cause cannot be found without X-ray examination, the dog must be disqualified.

After the initial testing, each dog is gaited separately. The dog is led away from the judge at a brisk pace, then toward him, and then in such a manner that a side or profile view can be studied. The dog's action will tell the judge a great deal about how the dog is put together, whether he is suited for the work for which he is bred, whether there are deficiencies in soundness. For example, in the Great Dane, a working dog, the gait counts as many points (ten) as general appearance.

After the gaiting the judge may call back several dogs to repeat the process and eliminate other candidates entirely. He may recheck the dogs' bodies, eyes, and heads, then mark his book according to his selections. Four places are awarded in each class and in each variety group, but in the selection of Best-in-Show there is only one. The judge may or may not indicate a second choice afterwards, but if he does, it carries no official weight.

One thing about dog shows that is not common to other sports events is that most spectators have left before the climactic choice is made. Perhaps it is because the spectators are interested in dogs in general, not in dogs in detail, and don't much care which one wins. So they go about their business while the final judging is held in relative privacy.

This is not likely to be true, however, in major shows, such as Westminster, where the Best-in-Show award carries national distinction. With 10,000 people watching from the seats and uncounted thousands tuning in on television, the final becomes an event of high drama. Every move of each contestant is closely watched and the judge is studied for indications of the direction in which he is leaning. The suspense that builds as he passes the dogs a second or third time becomes almost unbearable as he wheels away from them, marks his book, and finally points to the dog of his choice.

The losers drift away. The crowd applauds, relaxes, and heads for the exits as the dog of the year is engulfed by photographers zeroing in to record one of the sports world's big moments.

SOURCES OF PRINTS AND PAINTINGS

2-3   Metropolitan Museum of Art.

10-11   Metropolitan Museum of Art, The Cloisters Collection, Gift of John D. Rockefeller, 1937.

15   (1) Musée du Louvre, Paris.
(2) Edward, Duke of York, *The Master of Game*, W. A. Baillie-Grohman, ed., London, 1904.
(3) Metropolitan Museum of Art, Gift of J. Pierpont Morgan, 1905.
(4) Chicago Natural History Museum.
(5) Musée du Louvre, Paris.
(6) Museo Della Città Del Vaticana, Rome.
(7) Metropolitan Museum of Art, Rogers Fund, 1940.

16-17   (1) Courtesy of Provost and Fellows of King's College, Cambridge University, England.
(2) Courtesy of Museum of Fine Arts, Boston.
(3) New York Public Library.
(4) Kennedy Galleries, New York.
(5) Metropolitan Museum of Art, Dick Fund, 1926.

18   (1) Metropolitan Museum of Art, Bequest of Mrs. H. O. Havemeyer, 1929.
(2) Metropolitan Museum of Art, Kennedy Fund, 1910.
(3) Metropolitan Museum of Art, The Jules Bache Collection, 1949.
(4) Metropolitan Museum of Art, Rogers Fund, 1937.
(5) Metropolitan Museum of Art, Fletcher Fund, 1937.

20-21   (both) New York Public Library.

23   (top left and bottom) Reproduced by courtesy of the Trustees of the Tate Gallery, London.
(top right) New York Public Library.

24   (all) New York Public Library.

26-27   Library of Congress.

30   John James Audubon, *The Viviparous Quadrupeds of North America*, Volume 3, New York, 1845.

31   (top) Culver Pictures, New York.
(bottom) New York Public Library.

32   New York Public Library.

34   New York Public Library.

35   Philadelphia Museum of Art.

40-41   Kennedy Galleries, New York.

42-43   (1) Metropolitan Museum of Art, Gift of Cornelius Vanderbilt, 1880.
(2) British Museum, London.

42-43   (3) Reproduced by courtesy of the Trustees of the Tate Gallery, London.
(4) Metropolitan Museum of Art, Bequest of Frederick Townsend Martin, 1914.

44   (bottom right) Metropolitan Museum of Art, Gift of James C. McGuire, 1926.

48   Reproduced by courtesy of the Trustees of the Tate Gallery, London.

217 & 226   Edward, Duke of York, *The Master of Game*, W. A. Baillie-Grohman, ed., London, 1904.

220 & 235   New York Public Library.

239   Metropolitan Museum of Art, Bequest of Collis P. Huntington, 1925.

240   (top left) New York Public Library.

PHOTOGRAPHY SOURCES

All photographs by Walter Chandoha, except the following:

ASPCA Photograph: page 218.

C. M. Cooke & Son, London: pages 56, 59 (both), 205, 208, 210, 213 (top).

Erwitt, Elliott, Magnum Photos: pages 38-39.

Frederick Lewis Photographs: pages 125, 148, 148-49, 150, (right), 203, 212 (left).

Gramachree Wheatens, Brooklyn, New York. Homenocks Gramachree courtesy of Mrs. A. C. O'Connor: page 209 (bottom).

Haas, Ernst, Magnum Photos: pages 242-43.

Kerryall Kennels, San Francisco, California. Ch. Tithebarn Limelight courtesy of Mr. and Mrs. Robert L. Weil: page 149.

Lacey, Peter: pages 54-55 (Ch. Angelica), 224-25.

Mincheff, Dr. and Mrs. Thomas V., Croton-on-Hudson, New York: page 81 (top left: Siegfried; top right and bottom: Hilka).

Monkmeyer Press Photo Service: pages 131 (bottom), 194.

Myrack Collie Kennels, Bayshore, New York. Ch. Myrack Smooth Black Satin courtesy of Myrtle Ackerman: page 110.

Seeing Eye Dogs: page 238.

Shaefer, Evelyn, for Sakura Kennels, Upper Marlboro, Maryland: page 211 (bottom).

Si-Kiangs Kennel, Middletown, Pennsylvania. Fr. Ch. Jungfalets Jung-Wu courtesy of Ingrid Colwell: page 211 (top).

United Press International: pages 204, 212 (right).

Vujs, Joseph and Charlotte, Newington, Connecticut. Suzie Wong: page 213 (bottom).

Wide World Photos: pages 36 (top right), 131 (top), 163.